Sydney Pollack

Sydney Pollack

A Critical Filmography

Janet L. Meyer

McFarland & Company, Inc., Publishers
Jefferson, North Carolina and London

The present work is a reprint of the library bound edition of
Sydney Pollack: A Critical Filmography, first published in
1998 by McFarland.

Frontispiece: Sydney Pollack, 1991

LIBRARY OF CONGRESS CATALOGUING-IN-PUBLICATION DATA

Meyer, Janet L.
    Sydney Pollack : a critical filmography / Janet L. Meyer.
        p.   cm.
    Filmography: p.
    Includes bibliographical references and index.

    ISBN 978-0-7864-3752-8
    softcover : 50# alkaline paper ∞

    1. Pollack, Sydney, 1934–   — Criticism and interpretation.
    I. Title.
    PN1998.3.P655M48   2008
    791.43'0233'092 — dc21   98-25890

British Library cataloguing data are available

On the cover: Director Sydney Pollack on the set of the 1985 film
Out of Africa (Universal Pictures/Photofest)

Manufactured in the United States of America

McFarland & Company, Inc., Publishers
    Box 611, Jefferson, North Carolina 28640
        www.mcfarlandpub.com

To the memory of my mother
November 17, 1921–December 14, 1996

Acknowledgments

IT WOULD BE impossible to acknowledge every individual who contributed to this reference book. I was continually amazed by the interest that others displayed in my project, and how far some were willing to extend themselves to acquire details concerning Mr. Pollack's film, television and theater credits. I am very grateful for their hours of research, kind words and good wishes.

Most deserving of my thanks is Sydney Pollack, whose cooperation made this project possible. He offered his time and his personal reflections, and he placed his staff and resources (including his personal print of *Castle Keep*) at my disposal.

I would also like to extend my thanks to the Mirage Enterprises employees, including Donna Ostroff, Mr. Pollack's capable assistant, who made the endeavor of acquiring film credits and photographs a pleasure; and Todd Malta, Marcelo Layera and Janet Jeffries for always extending a warm welcome. To projectionist Bill Suhr at Paramount Pictures, I offer my thanks for facilitating the screening of *Castle Keep*.

I owe a great debt to my family and friends who supported my efforts in writing this book: my mother, Mildred Cecaci, who was in every way my greatest ally and to whom this book is dedicated; my daughters, Mandy and Christie, whose love and support are unconditional, and who showed it by helping to type and proofread the filmography; Ona Rieder, who graciously assisted with the proofreading; and Mark Lager of California Lutheran University in Thousand Oaks, California, whose friendship, research expertise and good will were indispensable.

Among the sources of information for this volume were the database of the Museum of Television and Radio, New York and Los Angeles; the film files of the Academy of Motion Picture Arts and Sciences Margaret Herrick Library in Los Angeles; the Theater Department of the New York City Public Library (Lincoln Center); the Music Department of the Library of Congress (Washington, D.C.); books, periodicals and databases of the research libraries at UCLA, the University of California at Santa Barbara, California Lutheran University and Thousand Oaks Library; Mirage Enterprises production files, scripts and interview tapes; *Baseline* film databases; *Cinemania* '95 on CD-Rom; and film reviews via the Internet. Thirty-five millimeter prints, videorecordings and laserdiscs were used for the purpose of film analysis as well as published film reviews and criticism.

Television credits from the 1950s and 1960s were challenging to acquire. In an effort to provide the most accurate information possible, I relied on the distributors and producers who had access to episode synopses, which appear to be the most reliable source of information available in print. Sources stating that Mr. Pollack directed episodes of the TV series *Naked City* and *The Doctors and the Nurses (The Nurses)* were found to be inaccurate.

Television credits could not have been gathered without the resources and the cooperation of Mary Mandebach, Wally Chan and Rich Orosco of Paramount Television; Steve Anderson of MCA Universal Television Distribution; Andrea Kaplan of Worldvision Enterprises, Inc.; Judy Jeffers of Bing Crosby Productions; Brinda Kempton of Warner Bros. Residuals Department; Erin Schack of the Directors Guild of America, Los Angeles; Sally Salerno of BRAVO Cable Network; Robert McDonald of KCET, Los Angeles; Melinda Priddy of Cinemax, New York; the programming staffs at PBS, KCET-LA, HBO, the Arts and Entertainment Network, Showtime, AMC, Fox Television, CBS and NBC; the staff at the audience information department of ABC; Ellen Krass Productions; and Alison Bossert of Columbia Tri-Star Television Distribution Marketing Department.

Larry Gianakos' *Television Drama Series Programming: A Comprehensive Chronicle 1959–1975* was extremely helpful in providing basic information on television programs, episodes and air dates. Other reference books and periodicals used extensively in my research included *The Encyclopedia of Television: Series, Plots and Specials 1937–1973*; *Contemporary Theatre, Film and Television*; *Universal Television: The Studio and Its Programs, 1950–1980*; *The Television Encyclopedia: Variety*; *Variety Film Reviews*; *New York Times Theatrical Reviews*; *New York Times Film Reviews*; and *TV Guide*. *BIB Television Programming Source Books* were invaluable in cross-referencing television series with production companies and distributors. Books on specific television series such as *Alfred Hitchcock Presents*, *The Fugitive* and *The Twilight Zone* were also useful in providing complete cast and credits and verifying the accuracy of information obtained elsewhere.

I wish to thank the staff at The Video Project for information relating to the environmental documentary *The Forest Through the Trees*; Birgitta Bond at the Michener Art Museum in Doylestown, Pennsylvania; and Geraldine Duclow of the theater department of the Philadelphia Free Library, whose dedicated research on behalf of Mr. Pollack's theatrical role in *Stalag 17* (1954) far exceeded my expectations.

Finally, permission to reprint stills from the motion pictures discussed herein was graciously granted by Viacom/Paramount Pictures, MGM/United Artists, MCA Universal, Sony/Columbia Pictures and ABC Films. Margarita Medina (Columbia Pictures), Sheila Clarke (Paramount Pictures), Jeremy Laws

(MGM/UA), Christiane Townsend (Universal Studios) and Michael Dragotto (ABC Films) provided outstanding service during the still licensing process.

Additional consent to use stills was obtained from Ray Stark of Rastar Productions for *The Way We Were, This Property Is Condemned* and *The Electric Horseman*; Dustin Hoffman of Punch Productions for *Tootsie*; and the Academy of Motion Picture Arts and Sciences for a photograph from the 58th Academy Awards ceremony. Consent to reprint was also granted by all actors whose likenesses are depicted herein.

All stills and photographs used in this text were provided through the courtesy of Sydney Pollack.

You are always trying to sneak in your own personal view of the world.... That's what mainstream movie-making is...: in the guise of pure popcorn entertainment [to] see if you can work relatively intelligently and make a film about something that concerns you, without revealing that is exactly what you are doing.

— Sydney Pollack
South Bank Show
March 1994

Contents

xii CONTENTS

Preface

My interest in Sydney Pollack began with a master's program in humanities at California State University, Dominguez Hills, in 1990. After taking a course in film, I became aware that I had somehow developed over time a love for the medium as an art form. As I reflected on the possibilities of pursuing independent study projects for my coursework, I realized that among the films of American directors I seemed to gravitate toward those of Pollack.

With more reflection on specific films, I recognized the director's consistent attention to the theme of freedom, his interest in cultures in conflict and his respect for his female protagonists. These elements had attracted me to his work and ultimately led to my first project. Through the gracious assistance of Jeanine Basinger and William Taylor, I was able to arrange an interview with Mr. Pollack.

A year later, the project became the basis for my thesis, *A Humanistic Analysis of the Films of Sydney Pollack*. The thesis, in turn, became the basis for this book, which has been expanded to include an exhaustive filmography and Mr. Pollack's additional contributions to film, television and theater.

I have employed the principles of humanistic film criticism as described by Bywater and Sobchack, as I believe this theory best serves the director's cinematic style. According to Bywater and Sobchack, this form of criticism when applied to film "looks for representations of general human values ... the truths of human experience as they relate to the common and universal aspects of existence."[1] Based on the general principles of aesthetic inquiry, the humanistic approach to reading film seeks to comprehend the ideas, symbols and themes and the film's universal significance, as well as to identify and understand the artist behind the art form.

In Chapters 3 through 19, the films directed by Sydney Pollack are analyzed from this perspective. The emphasis is on values in conflict and human behavior — Pollack's main areas of interest — rather than on cinematic technique.

This book is not intended to be biographical. Consequently, details of Pollack's personal life are limited and are offered largely to provide a context for the discussion of his career in the industry.

As far as my personal contributions to this book are concerned, I concur with Pollack's revelation (from a 1970 interview with Aljean Harmetz) that in any creative project, the representations herein are "not the whole truth, just your truth, and it isn't even all of your truth."

J.M.
May 1998

Introduction

DURING THE 1960S, a new wave of American film directors emerged in Hollywood. Disillusioned with the "studio system" and its classical narrative, these new filmmakers — among them Robert Mulligan, Sidney Lumet, George Roy Hill, John Frankenheimer, Elliot Silverstein and Sydney Pollack — were looking for innovative and exciting ways to "expand the perimeter of the craft."[1] In a December 1966 interview with Peter Bart, Pollack explained that American filmmakers were still relying on "horizontal filmmaking" or "straight-line melodramatic narration of external event." According to Pollack, competing with European artists such as Truffaut, Fellini and Antonioni would require the synthesis of the "Hollywood" narrative with the vertical approach to filmmaking that the Europeans had taken to extremes.

> They've taken a single experience or incident and have explored it vertically to its most basic nuances, focusing on interior reactions. This has created a whole new cinematic vocabulary and a new range of visual techniques.

Pollack cautioned that the Europeans had in many cases "completely lost their ability to communicate with the mass audience; something no Hollywood filmmaker can either afford to do or would want to do."[2]

Pollack's understanding of the challenge facing contemporary American filmmakers of the 1960s, as well as his experiences with acting mentor Sanford Meisner, influenced the development of an intelligent cinematic style and his successful 30-year career in the film industry.

Cinematic Style

All of Pollack's films bear his signature. While most critics have described his pictures in terms of their slow and deliberate pace, contemplative mood, circular structure, ambiguous endings and metaphorical love stories, some elements of his style are more subtle. Pollack has often stated that he is not particularly adept at using the cinematic techniques or "tricks" that are often attributed to directorial style. Instead, he seeks an overall visual effectiveness,

3

a strong narrative line, and emotionally honest performances from his actors to reveal the truth of the controlling principle in each film.

The controlling principle is the cultural or political dialectic or social dilemma that fascinates him and provides the armature for his cinematic exposition and the vertical development of his pictures. Although Pollack works within established genres, he consistently extends cultural topics beyond stereotypic representation and characterizes his male and female protagonists as multidimensional, thereby raising his films above their genre formulas.

Early in his directing career, Pollack gravitated to an A-B-A, or circular, structure. He generally uses this in two ways: by opening the story in the present and using flashback to develop his themes, then returning to the present as in *This Property Is Condemned* and *Out of Africa*; at the end of the film, returning his characters to a place that is both physically and psychologically similar to where they began, as in *Jeremiah Johnson*, *The Way We Were*, *Havana* and *The Firm*.

The circular structure Pollack employs coincides with the director's philosophy about human nature: though people have experiences that move them and affect some change, they are never really different people. Thus, at the conclusion of the films, Jack Weil in *Havana* remains a gambler, albeit with an increased awareness of the human condition; Jeremiah Johnson continues his journey into the wilderness as a seasoned mountain man; Katie Morosky in *The Way We Were* returns to her activism and her ethnic environment.

In each of Pollack's films, a love story is employed as a metaphor for opposing world views. Even in a thriller such as *Three Days of the Condor*, the director created a tentative love story between Joe Turner and his female hostage, Kathy Hale, in order to explore the theme of suspicion. Pollack explains that the relationship between men and women is the only thing that really interests him, because "it's a metaphor for everything else in life."[3]

The languid pace of Pollack's narratives, which is responsible for the contemplative mood in his pictures, is especially notable in *This Property Is Condemned*, *Castle Keep*, *Bobby Deerfield*, *Jeremiah Johnson*, *They Shoot Horses, Don't They?* and *Out of Africa*, which are slow, thought-provoking films, laced with melancholy.

The director's subject matter further reflects his style. Pollack's interest in cultural relations has provided the backdrop for nine of his 17 films. In *The Slender Thread*, *The Scalphunters* and *Jeremiah Johnson*, the director explores race relations; *The Way We Were* involves a Jewish girl and a WASP boy; *The Yakuza* discusses Japanese and American values in the context of honor; *Bobby Deerfield* involves an American man and a European woman; *Out of Africa* examines cultural values in Danish, African, British and American circles; *Havana* explores the cultural relationships between Cubans and Americans during the Batista regime; and *Sabrina* discusses merging the wealthy with the working class, albeit briefly, while contrasting the personas of the European artist and the American entrepreneur.

In Pollack's remaining films, sociopolitical issues provide the backdrop: war and its destruction of culture in *Castle Keep*; freedom of the press in *Absence of Malice*; ethics and the law in *The Firm*; exploitation in *The Electric Horseman*, *They Shoot Horses, Don't They?* and *This Property Is Condemned*; gender issues in *Tootsie*; and covert operations in *Three Days of the Condor*. Many of these films overlap, touching upon both cultural and sociopolitical issues, as in *The Way We Were*, *Out of Africa*, *Havana* and *The Firm*.

Pollack's film settings often reflect the psychological conflicts of his characters. For example, the deteriorating Southern town in *This Property Is Condemned* visually comments on the destruction taking place in Alva's life; the circular dance floor in *They Shoot Horses, Don't They?* mirrors the personal imprisonment experienced by the characters during the Depression; and the landscape of Africa in *Out of Africa* emphasizes Denys Finch Hatton's obsession with freedom.

The director is drawn to the 1930s, 1940s and 1950s, which he describes as particularly rich periods from a cinematic point of view, and he reveals the special character of those times in *This Property Is Condemned*, *They Shoot Horses, Don't They?*, *The Way We Were*, *Castle Keep*, *Out of Africa* and *Havana*. As he explained in an interview with *American Film*, "Things seemed simpler than they do now. That innocence fascinates me, and the loss of it moves me."[4]

All of Pollack's films are infused with a distinctly American spirit. As he noted in an interview on the *South Bank Show* in 1994, "There is a spirit or character in this country founded on the sense of leaving and starting something new."[5] This spirit has informed the central character in each of Pollack's films.

Finally, Pollack is an actor's director. "Committed to the creation of pragmatically constructed imaginary circumstances that ... serve as dramatic bedrock for true behavior,"[6] he consistently and successfully derives emotional truth from the performances of his actors.

On a popular level, Pollack says he is committed to making movies that he would like to see. He stated (in a 1989 interview with Bob Costas) that his films have not been highly cultured, and he has never made an art film. However, one might argue that *Castle Keep*, a surrealistic war picture, was an attempt to integrate elements of art cinema into an established American genre.

Pollack says his midwestern upbringing helped create his point of view as a filmmaker. He describes a "suspiciousness of sophistication" in midwestern culture during his youth, and he has translated that theme into his motion pictures. Moreover, the director is able to live in the "gray area" as a filmmaker, which often presents a dilemma for critics, who search in vain for a strong point of view in his pictures. Pollack defends his ambiguity because it allows the emergence of different sides of an argument, the opportunity to explore facets of each side without making a moral judgment.[7]

Pollack's world view is further reflected in the conflicts of his characters. In several of his films, the central female character — for example, Katie Morosky (*The Way We Were*), Dorothy Michaels (*Tootsie*), Karen Blixen (*Out of Africa*), Bobby Duran (*Havana*), Abby McDeere (*The Firm*), Sabrina Fairchild (*Sabrina*) — is invested with interior wisdom which the male protagonist must learn, whereas male characters such as Jeremiah Johnson, Hubbell Gardiner (*The Way We Were*), Sonny Steele (*The Electric Horseman*) and Mitch McDeere (*The Firm*) are often victimized by their own choices.

Every Pollack film except *Sabrina* is concerned with flawed human beings whose nobility lies in their personal struggles and perseverance — characters forced by their circumstances to rise to moments of heroism, then return to a place psychologically and physically similar to where they began, faced with an uncertain future. Only with the remake of *Sabrina* did Pollack diverge to a modern fairy tale with a happy "Hollywood" ending.

Technologically, Pollack has made a significant change in his filmmaking. In 1985, with the shooting of *Out of Africa*, the director abandoned widescreen and now works exclusively in the spherical medium.[8] In a KCET interview with Hugh Hewitt on *Life and Times* in May of 1994, he explained that this change was motivated by his unhappiness with the way widescreen pictures are compromised when aired on television and transferred to videocassette. According to Pollack, the audience loses the sense of environment, which is as important as the characters.

Integration of Other Art Forms

In his directing, Pollack draws from art forms other than cinema, such as dance, poetry, architecture and sculpture. Early in his career, dance and poetry offered him insights into the interplay of structure and content. Pollack credits Martha Graham and Louie Horst with his appreciation of dance and its application to his skill as a director. During his time at the Neighborhood Playhouse, Pollack learned preclassical dance forms from Horst. These forms gave him a sense of structure and variation, and he eventually integrated this experience with scriptwriting. The result is often an A-B-A structure in his films.

This A-B-A structure, which inevitably brings Pollack's film characters back to their beginning, albeit with a slightly altered worldview, is also a reflection of Pollack's love for poetry and his identification with T.S. Eliot's *The Four Quartets*:

> We shall not cease from exploration
> And the end of all our exploring
> Will be to arrive where we started
> And know the place for the first time.[9]

As for architecture, Pollack believes it is analogous to film in that both art forms are a combination of the technical and the aesthetic.

In additive sculpture, armature is defined as "a framework serving as a supporting core for clay." According to Pollack, in film, the director's "idea" or theme provides the same framework. Once the armature is defined, each scene is developed as a function of that armature and "tacked on," just as clay is added and blended together to create the final form of a sculpture.

Artistic Control

Once he settles on his "idea" or "armature," Pollack takes control of every creative aspect of the film, including editing and scoring.

Though not a musician, Pollack has developed a keen sense of rhythm and sound. He finds pieces of music that are particularly evocative and adds them to the cut as signposts to the composer. Then, as he sits in on the scoring session with composer and orchestra, he continues to make suggestions with regard to shape (orchestration) and texture (instruments). This process enables the composer to understand just what Pollack wants to pull emotionally from the literary and cinematic union he has so carefully created.

Pollack's artistic control is perhaps greater than that of many directors, due to his extensive interest in, and knowledge of, the technical side of filmmaking. Moreover, his experiences as an actor and producer have given him a reputation for being able to "do everything on the movie." David McGiffert, assistant director on *Tootsie*, explained: "I've seen him paint sets and take apart microphones. He at all times has an overall schematic in his head ... to know not only what should happen with scenes, what has happened before and after, and how to modulate all that."[10]

Author, playwright and television writer Susan Dworkin, in her 1983 film study, *Making Tootsie*, summarized Pollack's artistic and technical abilities by describing him as a "rampaging autodidact ... [with] none of the learning neuroses that plagued the formally educated. He could do art and he could do technology. You could teach him anything; therefore, you couldn't tell him much."[11]

Chronology

(Productions are listed by air or release date)

1934	Birth of Sydney Pollack on July 1 in Lafayette, Indiana.
1952	Graduation from South Bend Central High School.
1952–54	Acting student: Sanford Meisner's Neighborhood Playhouse, New York City.
1954	Lead role in *Stalag 17* (summer stock).
	Stage appearance in *A Stone for Danny Fisher*, Downtown National Theater, New York City. Opened 10/21.
1954–57	Returned to Neighborhood Playhouse as instructor.
1955	Stage appearance in *The Dark Is Light Enough*, American National Theater and Academy Theater (ANTA), New York City. Opened 2/23.
1956	Acting role in "The Army Game." *Kaiser Aluminum Hour*. Aired: 7/3.
	Acting role in "Time Lock." *Kraft Television Theater*. Aired: 11/28.
1957–59	Served in the U.S. Army.
1958	Married Claire Griswold, 9/22.
1959	Acting role in "For Whom the Bell Tolls" for *Playhouse 90*. Aired: 3/12 and 3/19.
	Acting role in "Family Man." *Brenner*. Aired: 6/20.
	Acting role in "The Case of Julia Walton." *U.S. Steel Hour*. Aired: 9/9.
	Dialogue director for television special "The Turn of the Screw." Aired: 10/20.
	Acting role in "35 Rue du Marche." *Armstrong Circle Theater*. Aired: 10/28.
1960	Acting role in "The Fifth Column." *Buick Electra Playhouse*. Aired: 1/29.
	Dialogue director for feature film *The Young Savages*. Comes to California for the first time and meets Burt Lancaster.
	Pollack and his family move to California. Observes the film industry for six months at Universal Studios.

9

(1960)   Acting role in "The Contest for Aaron Gold." *Alfred Hitchcock Presents*. Aired: 10/18.

Acting role in "The Trouble with Templeton." *The Twilight Zone*. Aired: 12/9.

1961   Acting role in "The Chrysanthemums." *Robert Herridge Theater*. No air date found.

Acting role in "A Quiet Night in Town." *Have Gun Will Travel*. Aired: 1/7 and 1/14.

Acting role in "Spoken in Silence." *The Deputy*. Aired: 4/29.

Television directorial debut. "Something to Die For." *Shotgun Slade*. Shot: November 9–11, 1960. Aired: 6/4/61.

Directs "The Smallest Target." *Frontier Circus*. Aired: 10/12.

Directs "King of the Mountain." *Cain's Hundred*. Aired: 10/24.

Acting role in "Compulsion to Confess." *The New Breed*. Aired: 10/31.

Directs "Karina." *Frontier Circus*. Aired: 11/9.

Directs "The Fixer." *Cain's Hundred*. Aired: 12/12.

1962   Directs "The Big Trouble with Charlie." *Ben Casey*. Aired: 1/29.

Directs "Rio Doloroso." *The Tall Man*. Aired: 2/10.

Directs "The Wrecker." *Target: The Corruptors*. Aired: 3/2.

Directs "For the Ladybird, One Dozen Roses." *Ben Casey*. Aired: 3/5.

Directs "The Inheritance." *Frontier Circus*. Aired: 3/15.

Directs "Monument to an Aged Hunter." *Ben Casey*. Aired: 3/19.

Directs "Incident at Pawnee Gun." *Frontier Circus*. Aired: 5/24.

Directs "Phoebe." *The Tall Man*. Aired: 5/26.

Directs "When You See an Evil Man." *Ben Casey*. Aired: 5/28.

Acting role in *War Hunt*. Meets Robert Redford. Released in Los Angeles: 7/25.

Directs "Mrs. McBroom and the Cloudwatchers." *Ben Casey*. Aired: 8/1.

Directs "The Night That Nothing Happened." *Ben Casey*. Aired: 8/8.

Directs "Go Not Gently Into the Night." *Ben Casey*. Aired: 8/29.

Directs "Black Curtain." *Alfred Hitchcock Hour*. Aired: 11/15.

1963   Directs "Kill or Be Killed." *The Defenders*. Aired: 1/5.

Directs "I'll Be Alright in the Morning." *Ben Casey*. Aired: 1/7.

Directs "A Cardinal Act of Mercy." Part I and II. *Ben Casey*. Aired: 1/14 and 1/21. Five Emmy nominations: 1962/63 season.

Directs "The Hollister John Garrison Story." *Wagon Train*. Aired: 2/6.

Directs "Suffer the Little Children." *Ben Casey*. Aired: 2/25.

Directs "Diagnosis: Danger." Pilot for CBS. Aired: 3/1.

(1963) Directs "The Dark Labyrinth." *Alcoa Premiere*. Aired: 3/21.
Supervised Burt Lancaster post-synch and English dub on Luchino Visconti's *The Leopard*. Released: 8/16.
Directs "Solo for B-Flat Clarinet — Part I." *Ben Casey*. Aired: 9/9.
Directs "Solo for B-Flat Clarinet — Part II." Pilot for *The Breaking Point*. Aired: 9/16.
Directs "Something About Lee Wiley." *Bob Hope Chrysler Theater*. Aired: 10/11. Emmy nomination for Best Director: 1963-64 season. Meets David Rayfiel.
Directs "The Quality of Justice." *Arrest and Trial*. Aired: 11/17.
Directs "The Name of the Game." *Kraft Suspense Theater*. Aired: 12/26.

1964 Directs "War of Nerves." *Bob Hope Chrysler Theater*. Aired: 1/3.
Directs "Two Is the Number." *Bob Hope Chrysler Theater*. Aired: 1/31.
Directs "Fear Is a Handful of Dust." *Mr. Novak*. Aired: 2/25.
Directs a theatrical production for UCLA entitled *P.S. 193*. April 3–May 10.
Directs "The Watchman." Pilot for NBC. *Kraft Suspense Theater*. Aired: 5/14.
Directs "Man on a String." *The Fugitive*. Aired: 9/29.
Directs "Murder in the First." *Bob Hope Chrysler Theater*. Aired: 10/9.
Directs "Question: What Became of the White Tortilla." *Slattery's People*. Aired: 10/26.
Directs "A Candle in the Window." *Dr. Kildare*. Aired: 11/5.

1965 Directs "The Fliers." *Bob Hope Chrysler Theater*. Aired: 2/6. Pilot for NBC.
Directs "The Last Clear Chance." *Kraft Suspense Theater*. Aired: 3/11.
Directs "The Game." *Bob Hope Chrysler Theater*. Aired: 9/15.
Directs first feature film, *The Slender Thread*. Released: 12/23.

1966 Receives "New Director of the Year" award from Interstate Theater Chain.
Receives Emmy for Outstanding Directorial Achievement in Drama for 1965-66 season for "The Game." Award presented 5/22.
Directs *This Property Is Condemned*. Released: 8/3.

1968 Directs *The Scalphunters*. Released: 4/2.
Directs one sequence of *The Swimmer* with Burt Lancaster. Released: 5/15.

1969 Directs *Castle Keep*. Released: 7/23.
Receives production credit and directs *They Shoot Horses, Don't They?*. Nominated for Best Director. Released: 12/11.

1971   Creates Sanford Productions with Mark Rydell.
1972   Directs and produces *Jeremiah Johnson*. Released: 12/21.
1973   Sanford Productions is dissolved.
        Directs and produces *The Way We Were*. Released: 10/17.
1975   Directs and produces *The Yakuza*. Released: 3/19.
        Directs *Three Days of the Condor*. Released: 9/24.
1977   Directs and produces *Bobby Deerfield*. Released: 9/29.
1979   Directs *The Electric Horseman*. Released: 12/21.
1980   A founding member of Robert Redford's Sundance Institute.
        Produces *Honeysuckle Rose*. Released: 7/18.
        Mirage Enterprises is created.
1981   Directs and produces *Absence of Malice*. Released: 11/19.
1982   Directs and produces *Tootsie*. Acting role in *Tootsie*. Released: 12/17.
        Nominated for Best Director.
1984   Produces *Songwriter*. Released: 10/12.
1985   Directs and produces *Out of Africa*. Released: 12/13. Wins Academy Awards for Best Picture and Director.
1986   Mark Rosenberg joins Mirage Enterprises.
        Appearance on *Barbra Streisand—Putting It Together: The Making of a Broadway Album*. HBO. Aired: 1/11.
        Appearance on *West 57th*. No air date found.
        Recieves Commander of Arts & Letters Award from French Minister of Culture
1987   Appearance on "Starring Natalie Wood." *Crazy About the Movies*. TV special. Aired: 10/9.
        Appearance on *Hello Actors Studio*. No air date found.
1988   Produces *Bright Lights, Big City*. Released: 4/1.
        Produces *Scrooged*. Released: 11/23.
1989   Produces *Major League*. Released: 4/7.
        Appearance on *Later in LA*. Aired: 6/14.
        Produces *The Fabulous Baker Boys*. Released: 10/13.
        Mark Rosenberg leaves Mirage.
1990   Produces *King Ralph*. Released: 2/90.
        Produces *Presumed Innocent*. Released: 7/27.
        Executive produces "Sanford Meisner: The Theater's Best Kept Secret." *American Masters*. PBS. Available for broadcast: 8/27.
        Produces *White Palace*. Released: 10/19.
        Lindsay Doran joins Mirage.
        Appearance on *Robert Redford and Sydney Pollack: The Men and Their Movies*. TV special. Aired: 12/9.
        Directs and produces *Havana*. Released: 12/9.
        Narrates *The Forest Through the Trees*. Documentary. Video recording.

1991   Appearance on "Robert Mitchum: The Reluctant Star." *Crazy About the Movies.* Aired: 3/17.

Produces *Dead Again.* Released: 5/91.

Appearance on "Jessica Lange: It's Only Make Believe." *Crazy About the Movies.* Aired: 8/13.

Appearance on "One Foot In; One Foot Out." *Naked Hollywood.* Aired: 8/25 and 8/31.

1992   Acting role in *The Player.* Released: 4/92.

Produces *Leaving Normal.* Released: 4/92.

Appearance on *Street Scenes: New York on Film.* TV Special. Aired: 6/9.Produces *A Private Matter* for HBO. Aired: 6/20.

Acting role in *Death Becomes Her.* Released: 7/92.

Acting role in *Husbands and Wives.* Released: 9/92.

1993   Appearance on "John Barry's Moviola." *Great Performances.* Aired: 3/29.

Appearance on *Willie Nelson The Big Six-O: An All-Star Birthday Celebration.* TV Special. Aired: 5/22.

Directs and produces *The Firm.* Released: 6/30.

Produces *Fallen Angels* for Showtime. Six segments aired: 8/1, 8/15, 8/29, 9/5, 9/19, 9/26. Emmy award nominee.

Produces *Searching for Bobby Fischer.* Released: 8/93.

Produces *Flesh and Bone.* Released: 11/93.

1994   Appearance on *South Bank Show.* Aired: 3/18.

Appearance on *Life and Times.* Aired: 5/10

Acting role on *Frasier.* NBC. Aired: 11/8.

1995   Appearance on "The Hollywood Style." *American Cinema.* Aired: 1/23.

Appearance on *Salute to the Top 10 Comedy Movies of All-Time.* TV Special. Aired: 7/9.

Produces *Sense and Sensibility.* Released: 6/25.

Appearance on *Inside the Actor's Studio: The Craft of Theater and Film.* Aired: 11/95.

Directs and produces *Sabrina.* Released: 12/15.

1998   Appearance on *Mad About You.* Aired: 2/24.

Produces *Sliding Doors.* Released: 4/24.

Acting role in *Eyes Wide Shut,* directed by Stanley Kubrick. No release date given.

Current and future projects from Mirage Enterprises:

The Talented Mr. Ripley, feature film for Miramax and Paramount Pictures. Projected May 1998 start.

Random Hearts, feature film projected September 1998 start. Produced and directed by Sydney Pollack.

(Current and future projects)

For Love of the Game, feature film for Universal Pictures. No start date.

Up at the Villa, independent feature film with Intermedia. No start date.

Grand Concourse, television pilot for CBS. No airing date.

Poodle Springs, feature for HBO. Projected to air in 1998.

Chapter 1

A Brief Biography

BORN IN LAFAYETTE, Indiana, on July 1, 1934, Sydney Pollack spent his youth in South Bend. His parents, David and Rebecca, attended Purdue University, and his mother's artistic talent was passed on to the three Pollack children: Sydney, Bernie (a costume designer) and Sharon (a choreographer). Raised in a Midwestern "town without culture," Pollack endured the hardships of prejudice and the illness and early death of his mother.[1]

While attending South Bend Central High School, Pollack became interested in theater. He appeared in a variety of high school productions, including *L'Aiglon*, *Tobias and the Angel*, *Harvey*, *Everyman*, *Lady in the Dark*, *Central Standard Time* and *Ali Baba and the Forty Thieves*, which were directed by James Lewis Casady.

Pollack's interest in theater evolved into a desire to study acting in New York. David Pollack wanted his son to attend Northwestern University after graduation and become a dentist. With the Korean War in progress, Pollack tried to convince his father that he would be drafted in two years, and when he returned from the Army, he would be eligible for the G.I. Bill with which he could complete his college education. In the meantime, he would go to New York.

In 1952, against the wishes of his father, Pollack left South Bend and enrolled in Sanford Meisner's Neighborhood Playhouse in New York City. He describes his two-year intensive course in theater at the Neighborhood Playhouse as "unequaled anywhere." After graduation, Pollack was invited to return on a fellowship as Meisner's assistant. He was 19 years old.

While Pollack had no aspirations to teach (or to direct, for that matter), the opportunity to continue to learn from Meisner was impossible to refuse. Pollack summarizes the effect his relationship with Meisner had on his career:

> When truths about one art are deep enough, they become true about all art. ... I was, without knowing it, absorbing the foundation of what would become a very specific approach to directing. The fact is that every area in which I function as a director—writing, production design, costume design, casting, staging, cinematography, even editing—is dominated by, and concerned with, the principles and ideas I've learned from Meisner.[2]

15

Pollack in an early publicity photo.

While teaching at the Neighborhood Playhouse, Pollack appeared in theater and television. In 1954, he played the lead in a summer stock production of *Stalag 17*, directed by Edward Binns, and was also cast in Harold Robbins' off–Broadway production *A Stone for Danny Fisher*, starring Zero Mostel and Sylvia Miles. In 1955 he appeared in Christopher Fry's *The Dark Is Light Enough*, starring Katherine Cornell and Tyrone Power. Among his television roles were "The Army Game" for *Kaiser Aluminum Hour*, which starred Paul Newman, and "Time Lock" for *Kraft Television Theater*. Pollack continued to work with Meisner until he was drafted in 1957. During the two years Pollack served in the Army, Meisner offered master classes in California. A participant in those master classes was one of the behind-the-scenes stars of 1950s television, John Frankenheimer, who would influence Pollack's career in television and film.

After Pollack was discharged in 1959, he read for a part in Frankenheimer's two-part *Playhouse 90* production "For Whom the Bell Tolls." Impressed with Pollack's association with Meisner, Frankenheimer offered him a role in the production.

In 1959, Frankenheimer hired Pollack to coach two children in the television special *The Turn of the Screw*, an adaptation of the 1950 Henry James novel. While his title was dialogue director, Pollack actually functioned as an acting coach for the children. The production marked the American TV debut of Ingrid Bergman.

Frankenheimer continued his collaboration with Pollack on the feature film *The Young Savages* (1961), which starred Burt Lancaster, Shelley Winters and Telly Savalas. Frankenheimer hired two young men for the production who had no acting experience, and he brought Pollack to California to coach them.

While Pollack was involved in *The Young Savages*, Lancaster became curious about him. Convinced that Pollack possessed the talent to direct, Lancaster arranged for him to meet Universal Studios executive Lew Wasserman. According to Pollack, Wasserman was not terribly interested in him because he lacked directorial experience. Nevertheless, he offered Pollack a salary and the run of the studio for six months in order to learn and observe.

Pollack in his high school production of *Ali Baba and the Forty Thieves,* **South Bend Central High School, South Bend, Indiana, 1950.**

During his "observation period," Pollack took acting roles in episodes of *Have Gun Will Travel, Buick Electra Playhouse, Robert Herridge Theater, Alfred Hitchcock Presents, The Deputy, The New Breed* and *The Twilight Zone.* When the syndicated series *Shotgun Slade* was canceled with four shows remaining to be produced, Pollack was given the opportunity to direct one of the episodes.

Pollack (center, standing) in a 1954 summer stock production of *Stalag 17*. Standing at right is Tige Andrews.

He told author William Taylor regarding his 1961 television directorial debut: "I screwed it up royally, but I did learn a lot from the editor, Dick Belding ... about the mechanics of film."[3]

During his five years in television, Pollack directed episodes of *Frontier Circus*, *Ben Casey*, *Dr. Kildare*, *The Fugitive*, *The Alfred Hitchcock Hour*, *The Defenders*, *Target: The Corruptors*, *Arrest and Trial*, *Kraft Suspense Theater*, *The Breaking Point*, *Slattery's People*, *Cain's Hundred*, *Bob Hope Chrysler Theater*, *The Tall Man*, *Mr. Novak*, *Alcoa Premiere*, and *Wagon Train*.

Pollack was recognized for his accomplishments as a director in television with an Emmy and two additional nominations for Best Director. Many actors whom he directed also received nominations and awards.

Pollack earned his first Emmy nomination for a two-part episode of *Ben Casey* entitled "A Cardinal Act of Mercy" which aired in January of 1963 and introduced Kim Stanley in her first television appearance. Stanley and Glenda Farrell won Emmys for their roles.

The *Bob Hope Chrysler Theater* production of "Something About Lee Wiley," which aired in October of 1963 and starred Piper Laurie and Claude Rains, won three Emmy nominations, including one for Best Director. Rains came out of retirement to do the part, and it was the last role he played before he died. It was during this production that Pollack met David Rayfiel, who has since collaborated on most of the screenplays for Pollack's films.

Pollack (standing, center) in "The Fifth Column," an episode of *Buick Electra Playhouse,* **1960. Seated at right is Richard Burton.**

In 1964, Shelley Winters won an Emmy for her role in "Two Is the Number," directed by Pollack and produced for the *Bob Hope Chrysler Theater.* The production also won First Prize at the International Festival of Television Programs at Monte Carlo.[4]

During his final year in television, the 1965–66 season, Pollack won an Emmy for directing "The Game" for the *Bob Hope Chrysler Theater.* The production garnered five nominations, as well as an Emmy for Cliff Robertson.

In addition to television, Pollack directed the West Coast premiere of *P.S. 193,* under the auspices of the Theater Group of the UCLA Extension. *P.S. 193* ran from April 3–May 10, 1964, and was written by David Rayfiel and produced by John Houseman. The theatrical production starred James Whitmore and Cloris Leachman.

In the early 1960s, Pollack maintained a link to the film industry through Burt Lancaster. Through Lancaster's association with the production of *The Leopard,* Pollack was hired to supervise the English dub and the Lancaster post-synching for the 1963 release. Working on *The Leopard* allowed Pollack to observe the work of Italian director Luchino Visconti.

After directing in television for five years, Pollack had his first opportunity to direct a feature film with the 1965 Paramount Pictures release *The Slender*

Pollack (second from left) at a script meeting for an episode of *Ben Casey*. Vince Edwards is seated to Pollack's left.

Thread. Thirty years later, Pollack has 17 films to his directorial credit and a respected reputation in the movie industry as a successful mainstream director. His films have received 46 Academy Award nominations, including two for Best Picture and three for Best Director, as well as numerous other awards and acknowledgments. For the epic love story *Out of Africa* (1985), Pollack won Academy Awards for Best Picture and Best Director. In 1986, he was honored by the French Minister of Culture with the Commander of Arts and Letters award.

In 1969, Pollack received his first production credit* for *They Shoot Horses, Don't They?* As of 1997, Pollack and his production team have garnered credits for 25 feature films and several television specials. Since the 1981 release of *Absence of Malice*, his productions have appeared under the banner of Mirage Enterprises.

Between directorial projects and Mirage productions, Pollack has appeared as an actor in *Tootsie* (1982), *The Player* (1992), *Husbands and Wives* (1992) and *Death Becomes Her* (1992). His most recent role is in Stanley Kubrick's *Eyes Wide Shut*, awaiting release at the time of this writing.

Pollack received production credit through Sydney Pollack Productions, but he did not receive a producer's credit.

Pollack and his wife, Claire (Griswold), reside in Pacific Palisades, California. They were married on September 22, 1958, during his tenure in the U.S. Army and lived in Fort Carson, Colorado, until his military discharge in 1959. Claire was an actress who later developed an interest in architecture. Her work on the couple's Los Angeles and Utah properties was featured in *Architectural Digest* in 1988.

The couple had three children: Steven, Rebecca and Rachel. Steven was killed in a plane crash in Santa Monica on November 26, 1993, at the age of 34. Rebecca Pollack Parker is currently a senior vice-president at United Artists and married to Hutch Parker, an executive at 20th Century–Fox. Rachel Pollack Sorman is employed in the International Video Division of MGM. Rachel is also a professional singer who regularly appears with her own band at the Troubadour, Roxie and Luna Park clubs in Los Angeles.

In addition to directing, producing and an occasional acting role, Pollack is a founding member and continues to serve on the Board of Directors of the Sundance Institute, a non-profit organization established by Robert Redford in 1980, which provides opportunities for aspiring independent filmmakers to collaborate with industry veterans. Pollack also served for seven years as chairman of the board of American Cinémathèque, a non-profit, community-supported entertainment organization in Hollywood. A founding member and currently on the board of directors of the Film Foundation, Pollack maintains an involvement in the film preservation and restoration movement, working with other industry directors and president Martin Scorsese. He also continues as executive director of the Actors Studio West. In addition, Pollack is often invited to give lectures and participate in symposia.

Pollack as Producer
and Actor

POLLACK BECAME involved with the production of motion pictures in 1969 with the release of *They Shoot Horses, Don't They?*. Initially serving as a self-defense mechanism for pictures he was also directing, producing affords Pollack several advantages.

Producing feature films fills Pollack's time creatively between directorial roles and facilitates the making of pictures which he deems valuable contributions to the art form — material for which he feels some personal identification but not a passion to direct.

In addition, producing motion pictures enables Pollack to locate and help develop new directors as well as make the kinds of films that he does not direct: small films, out-of-the way films, art films and films that might not be made if Mirage did not take a hand in the process.

As a producer, Pollack's position is one of supervisor and facilitator. He allows producing credits to go to his staff of producers, currently Bill Horberg and David Rubin at Mirage, and most often assumes the role of executive producer. As Pollack stated:

> There isn't any sense in me doing the work that someone else can do.
> [For my producers] it's everything they do. It is good for them to be
> rewarded for their hard work. I don't make a living as a producer.

Pollack and his team of producers are creatively involved in their projects, normally maintaining a "hands-on" relationship except with productions such as *Presumed Innocent*, where the director (Alan Pakula) is highly experienced.

As a producer, Pollack tries to support and facilitate the director's vision. His own experience as a director has made him considerate of the director's territory, and he is careful to refrain from intrusion. Pollack retains final cut authority on all pictures he produces, which can serve either as a threat or a comfort to the director:

> I have never exercised it, but I use it as protection against a studio
> or somebody else. If there is a conflict, legally I have the final cut,

but I will not insert my authority on a director. If I did, no director would work for me.

Pollack summarizes his role as a producer:

> Whatever the circumstances surrounding the picture, the job is the same ... to be a sort of godfather, oversee it, facilitate in getting it made, to put my two cents in when it's needed and keep my mouth shut when it's not.

Pollack's production credits have appeared under three banners: Sydney Pollack Productions, Sanford Productions and Mirage Enterprises/Productions.

Sydney Pollack Productions

They Shoot Horses, Don't They? (1969), *The Way We Were* (1973), *The Yakuza* (1975) and *Bobby Deerfield* (1977) are Sydney Pollack productions for which he also received director's credit. Other Pollack productions include *Honeysuckle Rose* (1980) and *Songwriter* (1984).

Pollack produced *Honeysuckle Rose* (1980) from the first draft screenplay written by Carol Sobieski. He became involved due to his former association with country singer/songwriter Willie Nelson in *The Electric Horseman* (1979). Warner Bros. believed that Nelson was going to be successful as an actor, and that country music would be of growing interest to the movie-going public. So the studio executives went to Nelson with the script. Since Nelson did not know much about the film business, he asked Pollack to advise him and Warner Bros. to try to sign Pollack to direct. Pollack was not interested in directing, but he agreed to produce it in order to work with Nelson.

In 1983, Pollack took a year off to help his friend and attorney Gary Hendler start TriStar Pictures. During the first year, TriStar garnered Academy Award nominations for *The Natural* and *Places in the Heart*. During this time, Pollack produced *Songwriter*. Alan Rudolph directed the picture, which also starred Willie Nelson. Pollack describes *Songwriter* as "a wonderful, underrated film." According to Pollack, the country/western star concept, while successful in music, has not found its audience at the movies.

In addition to feature films, Pollack served as executive producer for "Sanford Meisner: The Theater's Best Kept Secret," which aired as a segment of PBS's *American Masters* in 1990.

Sanford Productions

Sanford Productions was created in 1971 in partnership with Mark Rydell. Named after Pollack's acting mentor Sanford Meisner, the company developed or produced five films before its dissolution in 1973. *Jeremiah Johnson* was released in 1972, directed and produced by Pollack; *The Cowboys* was released in 1972, directed and produced by Rydell.

Scarecrow (1973) was Pollack's first production effort which he did not direct. The film was entered in the Cannes Film Festival. Since Pollack was selected for the jury, he withdrew his association with the production of the picture. The film received the Golden Palm Award at Cannes. It was directed by Jerry Schatzberg and starred Gene Hackman and Al Pacino.

Pollack and Rydell developed the script for *Night Moves* (1975), which was directed by Arthur Penn and also starred Gene Hackman. When the production company was dissolved, the script was sold to Sanford Productions president Bob Sherman as part of the settlement agreement.

Sanford Productions also developed *The Spikes Gang*, a 1974 release originally titled *Harry Spikes*. *The Spikes Gang* was produced by Walter Mirisch, written by Irving Ravetch and directed by Richard Fleischer. The film starred Lee Marvin and Ron Howard.

Mirage Enterprises/Productions

Absence of Malice (1981), which co-starred Paul Newman and Sally Field, was the first film billed as a Mirage Enterprises production. Since 1981, Mirage has produced 17 additional feature films: *Tootsie* (1982) with Dustin Hoffman and Jessica Lange; *Out of Africa* (1985) with Meryl Streep and Robert Redford; *Bright Lights, Big City* (1988) with Michael J. Fox; *Scrooged* (1988) with Bill Murray; *Major League* (1989) with Charlie Sheen and Tom Berenger; *The Fabulous Baker Boys* (1989) with Jeff Bridges, Beau Bridges and Michelle Pfeiffer; *King Ralph* (1990) with John Goodman; *Havana* (1990) with Robert Redford and Lena Olin; *Presumed Innocent* (1990) with Harrison Ford; *White Palace* (1990) with Susan Sarandon and James Spader; *Dead Again* (1991) with Kenneth Branagh and Emma Thompson; *Leaving Normal* (1992) with Meg Tilly and Christine Lahti; *Searching for Bobby Fischer* (1993) with Joe Mantegna, Laurence Fishburne and Ben Kingsley; *The Firm* (1993) with Tom Cruise and Gene Hackman; *Flesh and Bone* (1993) with Meg Ryan and Dennis Quaid; *Sabrina* (1995) with Harrison Ford and Julia Ormond; *Sense and Sensibility* (1995) with Emma Thompson; and *Sliding Doors* with Gwyneth Paltrow.

In 1992 and 1993 respectively, Mirage produced the HBO special *A Private Matter*, starring Sissy Spacek and Aiden Quinn, and the six-episode anthology *Fallen Angels* for Showtime. Two additional television productions are in the wings for Mirage: *Grand Concourse* is a pilot for CBS, and *Poodle Springs* will be aired on HBO.

"Production Only" Credits

The following discussion does not include films for which Pollack also received director's credit. Those films are discussed in detail in Chapters 3–19.

Bright Lights/Big City was a 1988 release which Mirage produced for MGM/UA. Mark Rosenberg and Julie Bergman were the producers at Mirage, and the novel upon which the film is based was "a hot book." Pollack, however, was not enamored with the film script partially due to the central character (played by Michael J. Fox), who is a cocaine addict. Pollack believed it would be difficult for the audience to sympathize with this character.

In 1988, Mirage also produced *Scrooged* for Paramount. Bill Murray and agent Michael Ovitz wanted Pollack to direct the picture, but he declined, and Richard Donner was hired to direct.

Major League, produced in 1989 for Paramount, was the first significant financial success for Mirage. The picture starred Tom Berenger and Charlie Sheen. First-time director David Ward and the original cast reprised their roles in the sequel *Major League II* (1994), produced by Morgan Creek.

Pollack originally considered directing *The Fabulous Baker Boys*, which was produced in 1989 for 20th Century–Fox. Since he was considering the director's role, Pollack engaged in a lot of script work with Steve Kloves, the screenwriter. As they collaborated, Pollack discerned the intelligence with which Kloves dealt with the material. When Pollack decided not to direct, he and Rosenberg encouraged Kloves to direct, and Pollack stepped back to the role of executive producer. Producers' credits were given to Mark Rosenberg and his wife, Paula Weinstein. Weinstein had originally optioned the script, then brought it to Mirage in the hope of getting it made. Pollack takes a great deal of pride in the picture, which starred Beau Bridges, Jeff Bridges and Michelle Pfeiffer.

In 1990, Mirage produced *White Palace* for Universal. Pollack had purchased the rights to the book and developed the screenplay in partnership with Amy Robinson, who had her own production company (Doubleplay Productions). Pollack took executive producer credit for the picture, which starred Susan Sarandon and James Spader. Luis Mandoki directed and Ted Tally and Alvin Sargent also collaborated on the screenplay.

In the same year, Mirage also became involved in a second project with Universal, *King Ralph*, starring John Goodman and Peter O'Toole.

Pollack wanted to do a picture with Bill Murray. David Ward had been so successful with *Major League* that another collaboration was imminent. Pollack and Ward sat down one day to talk about an original script. They imagined Bill Murray as the King of England. It happened that Pollack's younger daughter, Rachel Sorman, who works in the International Video Division of MGM, suggested that he do a movie with Mikhail Baryshnikov and Bill Murray as co-stars. She thought it would be a great combination. Intrigued by the idea, Pollack and Ward began to create a story about a man who inherits a ballet company. In the meantime, a friend of Pollack's told him about a book in which a man who owns a hot dog stand becomes King of England. Since the second idea seemed more workable, the script for *King Ralph* was written. An undistinguished film, *King Ralph* gave David Ward another opportunity to direct.

Presumed Innocent (1990), starring Harrison Ford, was a successful film for Mirage and Warner Bros. Veteran Alan Pakula directed, and the screenplay was written by Frank Pierson. It is one of the highlights of Mirage's production credits to date.

Pollack and Rosenberg convinced the studio to purchase the screen rights to the book. When the screenplay was completed, Pollack offered the script to Pakula. Due to Pakula's experience as a director, Pollack remained in the background while the film was being shot, only reviewing the dailies. After Pakula showed him the first cut, Pollack offered suggestions.

In opposition to Pakula and Warner Bros., Pollack believed the original book ending should be used. What fascinated Pollack about the story was its ending:

> [T]he painful and terrible irony of this man having to live the rest of his life knowing that his wife was a murderer, but that he in fact had caused the murder to happen ... through his infidelity.

The studio and the director were convinced that the audience would not accept "letting a woman who is the mother of a young child and who is also a murderer go unpunished." But to Pollack, the ending was special precisely because of this element. When the test audiences did not react favorably to Pakula's first ending, Pakula agreed to go back to the book.

After Mark Rosenberg left Mirage, Pollack hired Lindsay Doran from Paramount. A year later, her assistant at Paramount, Bill Horberg, also joined the production company. *Dead Again*, released in 1991, was Doran's first production credit under Mirage.

With *Dead Again*, Mirage brought Kenneth Branagh and Emma Thompson to the attention of American audiences. Branagh directed and starred in a dual role in the picture. His wife Emma Thompson co-starred, also playing a dual role. Through this production, Pollack and Doran became acquainted with Thompson, which led to their subsequent collaboration on *Sense and Sensibility* (1995). *Dead Again* was written by Scott Frank and also starred Andy Garcia.

Leaving Normal was a project which Lindsay Doran developed with Ed Solomon for Universal in 1992. Ed Zwick (*Legends of the Fall, Glory, Thirtysomething*) wanted to direct it. Since Zwick had a production team of his own, Mirage only became involved at the editing stage and attending the previews. It was a troubled picture, according to Pollack, but he liked the acting. Meg Tilly and Christine Lahti starred.

In 1992, Mirage produced *Searching for Bobby Fischer* for Paramount. The story of chess protege Josh Waitzkin, this picture did not find the audience Pollack had expected. Based on the book by Fred Waitzkin, it was written and directed by Steve Zaillian. Bill Horberg functioned as producer, and the cast included Joe Mantegna, Max Pomeranc, Joan Allen, Laurence Fishburne and Ben Kingsley.

Flesh and Bone (1993) was a collaborative effort with Mirage and Paula Weinstein's company, Spring Creek, for Paramount. Mirage's second picture with director Steve Kloves, the film starred Meg Ryan and Dennis Quaid.

Out of Mirage's association with Emma Thompson in *Dead Again* came the Jane Austen classic *Sense and Sensibility* (1995). Perhaps the most important roles Pollack and his producers played in *Sense and Sensibility* involved serving as both facilitator to find backing for the picture and protector for director Ang Lee and screenwriter Thompson.

A new director, Lee had never worked with a studio, and Thompson had, until recently, lived in the shadow of Kenneth Branagh. Pollack noted that Mirage had a difficult time finding anyone to make the picture: "In 1991, most studio executives didn't know who Jane Austen was ... and no one knew Emma Thompson."

Lindsay Doran received producer's credit and was "hands on" during the entire shooting period. Pollack was involved at a distance since he was shooting nights on *Sabrina*. He would come home at 5:00 A.M. from the set of *Sabrina*, run the dailies from *Sense and Sensibility* and e-mail notes back and forth to Doran. According to Pollack, the process worked beautifully, especially with Doran on the set. Pollack and Doran made several trips to New York to participate in the editing of the picture with director Lee.

The latest completed project for Mirage is *Sliding Doors*, which premiered at the Sundance Film Festival in January 1998 and was released in April. The film marks the directorial debut of British television actor, Peter Howitt, and stars Gwyneth Paltrow, John Hannah, John Lynch and Jeanne Tripplehorn.

Current and future film projects for Mirage include *The Talented Mr. Ripley*, a Miramax and Paramount release which will star Matt Damon and Gwyneth Paltrow; *Up at the Villa*, an independent film with Intermedia in association with October Films, based on the novella by W. Somerset Maugham, starring Kristin Scott Thomas and Sean Penn; and Universal Pictures' *For Love of the Game*.

Acting Credits

Pollack gave up acting following his first film role in *War Hunt* (1962). Twenty years later, he reluctantly agreed to play the part of George Fields, Michael Dorsey's agent, in *Tootsie* (1982), a role which would bring him a myriad of acting offers.

During the shooting of *Tootsie*, Pollack and Hoffman were having some difficulty. Dabney Coleman had been cast in the role of the agent, but Hoffman wanted Pollack to take the role. Being a pragmatic actor, Hoffman told Pollack it would be easier for him in terms of motivation to "put on the dress" if Pollack

Publicity portrait, 1996.

played the part of the agent. Coleman was his peer — another actor — and Hoffman was convinced only Pollack, as a director, could motivate him.

Pollack did not believe Hoffman was serious. Michael Ovitz, Pollack's agent, called the director regularly, encouraging him to take the role. Pollack, however, was worried about the movie. It was a stretch for him, a style he had not worked in for a long time, and he did not want to be concerned with learning lines, makeup and acting.

But since he was having various arguments with Hoffman, Pollack came to the conclusion that it would be wise to concur. Though he did not enjoy the experience, Pollack noted that he was pleased with the result and that Hoffman "deserves either the credit or the blame."

Due to his performance in *Tootsie*, Pollack began receiving offers for roles in more feature films but repeatedly turned them down. Finally, as a favor to long-time friend Robert Altman, Pollack stepped in for Blake Edwards to play the lawyer in *The Player* (1992). (Pollack had been associated with Altman in television, and when Edwards became ill, Pollack filled in.)

Robert Zemeckis was also a friend, and Pollack admits he agreed to do a bit part in *Death Becomes Her* (1992) "on a weak day." He recalls:

> I tried to get out of it. I even called the casting director saying that I didn't want to take a role away from an actor. There are a lot of actors out there who can do the same role. They make a living out of it. It was kind of a joke for me. But the casting director said Zemeckis really wanted me to do this. And it did give me the chance to work again with Meryl Streep — only this time as an actor.

Pollack played a major role in Woody Allen's *Husbands and Wives*, also released in 1992. Allen asked him to read for the part, since he had only seen Pollack in *Tootsie*.

Since directors do not often have the opportunity to see each other work, Pollack thought the experience to work with Allen would be an educational one. He admired Allen as a director, and he loved the script, even though he was not fond of the character he played. Pollack described the script as "smart, well-defined," offering "true observations about relationships."[1]

Pollack attributes the tragic coincidence of the Woody Allen–Mia Farrow scandal, which surfaced at the time of release, to the picture's poor performance at the box office. Nevertheless, he thought it was a wonderful movie and enjoyed working with the cast.

Pollack made a "guest voice" appearance on the popular television sitcom *Frasier* during its second season. In an episode entitled "The Candidate" (aired November 8, 1994), Martin (John Mahoney) appears in a political candidate's television commercial, drawing disapproval from Frasier and Niles. Pollack played the voice of Holden Thorpe.[2]

Recent acting roles include a guest appearance on NBC's television sitcom *Mad About You*, which aired February 24, 1998. Pollack appeared as an amiable psychiatrist whose outrageous fees drive Paul and Jamie back to their former neurotic therapist.

During 1997, Pollack replaced actor Harvey Keitel in Stanley Kubrick's production of *Eyes Wide Shut*. Because of the secrecy surrounding the project, access to credits and storyline has been limited. No release date has been set.

The Slender Thread
(1965)

About the Production

SHOOTING COMMENCED June 7, 1965, in Seattle, Washington. *The Slender Thread* was the first feature film shot on location in Seattle since the 1962 release of *It Happened at the World's Fair*, which starred Elvis Presley.

A thousand local citizens were employed as extras, and the daily overhead averaged $12,000. Forty University of Washington students were drafted for the opening sequence. Aerial scenes were filmed by helicopter, using a Mark II camera with a 10-to-1 zoom lens, range 25-250mm.

The interior of the Crisis Clinic was created on a Paramount sound stage where Sidney Poitier remained for most of the picture, linked to Anne Bancroft, who spoke with him via a connecting telephone line in her dressing room.

The dramatization of the first suicide attempt revealed in the film could have been a costly one. Bancroft was wearing the bottom of a wetsuit under her costume. As she waded off shore to dramatize the suicide, the wet suit became saturated and pulled her underwater. Pollack and other members of the film crew had to rescue her.[1]

Source Material

The picture is based on the *Life* magazine article, "A Decision to Die," written by Shana Alexander, about an actual incident. The article tells the story of a woman (pseudonym "Nell J"), who called 11 persons for help before taking an overdose of pills.

First-time producer Stephen Alexander was moved by the article his wife had written. Believing there was "a picture in that article," he showed a draft to Stirling Silliphant, who wrote the screen treatment. Meanwhile, Alexander acquired the film rights to the article from *Life*. After Sidney Poitier read the screenplay, he agreed to play the role of the crisis clinic volunteer. The property was offered to all major film companies, and Paramount picked it up.[2]

Synopsis

Inga Dyson (Anne Bancroft) is a married woman with a 12-year-old son. Her husband Mark (Steven Hill) is a commercial fisherman. Alan Newell (Sidney Poitier) is a college student at the University of Washington who volunteers at a crisis center.

The Slender Thread focuses on one hour in the lives of Inga and Alan, who become involved through a suicide hotline. After repeated attempts to find someone to talk with about her feelings of guilt and fear, Inga relinquishes hope and drives to a motel to carry out her suicide. She ingests barbiturates, then calls the Crisis Clinic advertised on the front page of the newspaper in a final attempt to connect with a compassionate and caring person. Newell, her only link to life, remains on the telephone with her while emergency personnel attempt to locate her.

Analysis

The Slender Thread is a unique love story, one which fascinated Pollack principally because the two central characters never meet. Brought together through a coincident chain of events, Inga and Alan forge a tentative but passionate relationship within the course of an hour-long telephone conversation.

The film is shot in the present — 1965. Inga and Alan are individuals who under normal circumstances would have nothing in common. In the opening sequence of the film, the viewer is introduced to the racial, gender and generational "differences" between the characters. Alan is a black student at the University of Washington, characterized as unusual by the myriad of white students on campus. Alan appears to be about 22 years old and is apparently unmarried.

Inga is a married woman in her early thirties with a son. She is white and middle class. Her employment and social circles appear to be racially homogeneous. With their "differences" established, the "crisis" which brings the two characters together catalyses an intimacy based on mutual vulnerability which leads to trust and a unique type of love story.

A series of aerial shots during the title sequence provides the audience with clues to the characters' identities in relation to each other and their environment. The University of Washington campus, the Crisis Clinic, the wharf and the Space Needle serve as backdrops and guideposts for what is to follow.

The story begins with Inga Dyson driving erratically through Seattle. On the passenger seat in her car lies a model sailboat, Provider III, an image which serves as a time linkage to a similar scene repeated later in the film. The model, which belongs to Dyson's son, is suitably named as it is a replica of Provider II, the commercial fishing boat owned by Mark Dyson. The model symbolizes the lineage within the family which is shattered after Mark Dyson discovers the boy he thinks is his son is the product of a pre-marital affair.

The viewer is then introduced to Alan Newell, who leaves the University of Washington for the Crisis Clinic where he volunteers to "man" the hot line. After arriving at the clinic, Newell discovers that he will be unsupervised for the evening, setting up the environment through which Alan and Inga are forced to rely only upon each other's communication skills and humanity. The lack of a support team also serves to promote an intimate environment for the two strangers.

After Inga makes the call to the hotline, Pollack dramatically creates through their telephone conversation two complex characters who build a brief but intense relationship and learn to care about each other.

Newell is determined to keep Inga talking, hoping that she will want to abort her suicide and reveal her location. In an effort to keep her on the telephone, Newell tries to elicit information as to what has driven her to end her life. He repeatedly asks her what went wrong "today." Inga's relationships with her husband and son and the encounters she had on the day of her suicide attempt are then revealed in flashback as she tells the stranger her story.

Inga explains that the source of her guilt and shame is an affair she had prior to her marriage. She concealed this secret from her husband and son for 12 years. The secret was inadvertently discovered by Mark Dyson when the boy received a $263 check from his biological father.

As Inga relates these intimate details, the viewer is introduced to a penitent, submissive woman — a woman who describes herself as evil. Through Inga's work associates, Pollack further reveals a passive woman with low self-esteem. She is non-assertive, accommodating and timid in the presence of her husband, son and co-workers — the individuals she most wishes to please.

Pollack creates a sense of the character's painful need for affirmation on the day of her suicide attempt. In a scene at her workplace, Inga receives a call from her boss, who has extended his skiing vacation. He asks if there is anything important she needs to tell him. Inga replies that she fixed his squeaky chair — all by herself. He ignores the comment and asks if there is anything "important."

Inga then asks a co-worker to join her for lunch, but the co-worker has prior plans, and it is obvious from Inga's facial expression that she feels rejected.

Her need for affirmation and usefulness continue to be thwarted. Inga leaves work and sees four children on the beach, concerned for a sick bird. In an effort to save the bird, Inga puts aside her own pain, her instinct to save a life compelling her to take action. She runs to a nearby liquor store to buy

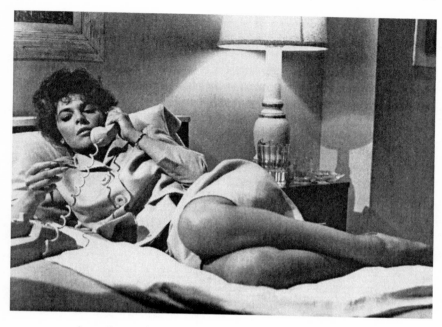

Anne Bancroft in *The Slender Thread* (Paramount, 1965).

some brandy. When she returns, the bird has been buried by the children in a marked grave in the sand. For the first time, Inga unleashes her repressed anger by reacting to the meaningless death of the bird — more likely the meaninglessness of her own life — and repeatedly kicks the grave.

Inga then visits the wharf where she finds her son playing with the model sailboat. Hoping to spend time with him, Inga is disappointed that he must leave for a baseball game. She takes his model and places it on the passenger seat of her car as she moves closer to taking her life.

In a final attempt to solicit help, Inga drives to the hospital where she was previously admitted for a prior suicide attempt. She asks to speak to the doctor who helped her, but he is no longer employed there. The resident on duty speaks with her briefly, and requests that she admit herself to the hospital. Inga explains that she just wants someone to talk to about her feelings. When no one will listen, Inga leaves the hospital and proceeds to the motel to prepare for her suicide.

After Inga connects with Newell on the telephone at the Crisis Clinic, the viewer sees a different personality unfold. Committed to her course of action and drugged, Inga responds to Newell with a self-assurance and intelligent perceptiveness that were not apparent in her other interactions which were revealed in flashback. She is a stronger, more confident person in Newell's presence — a woman who has taken control of her life. She is a woman at peace.

Newell's character is vivid and passionately played by Sidney Poitier. Once he discovers that Inga is going to be difficult to persuade, Newell admits to her that he is ill-prepared to deal with her situation. He bluntly reveals his inadequacy and his inexperience to the dying woman. He tells her that he is not a trained clinician but volunteers at the clinic for academic credit. Newell is afraid, because he knows he cannot save her.

It is Newell's expression of vulnerability that enables Inga to trust him, and she remains on the line. As Inga's physical condition deteriorates, Newell moves through stages of impatience, frustration and finally anger when he cannot elicit the woman's whereabouts. The two individuals argue and bond through this painfully intimate experience.

In the end, the police are able to locate Inga by tracing the call. Her husband has been summoned and appears at the Crisis Clinic just as Inga is removed from the motel and taken to the hospital. Of course, Newell is ecstatic over the outcome. When the physician who operates the clinic, Dr. Coburn (Telly Savalas), asks if he would like to meet Inga, Newell declines. While professionally valid, Newell's refusal to meet Inga is disappointing. Newell, however, has the wisdom to understand the temporary nature of their relationship in a moment of crisis. The two are never supposed to meet.

After the woman has been rescued, Newell remains at the Crisis Clinic ready to take the next caller — his life seemingly uninterrupted and unchanged by his critical encounter with Inga Dyson.

The Slender Thread discusses the issue of trust in relationships. Honesty is explored in various ways with regard to the relationship between Inga and her husband, son and Newell. As to the outcome of the relationships within the family, Pollack's ambiguous ending is consistent with the director's ability to present characters in opposition without declaring them "right" or "wrong."

The film also exposes the irony of communication, as Pollack juxtaposes the coordination efforts of the civic network of police, the Coast Guard and utility companies with the ineffective communication between individuals in the relationships which have made the mobilization necessary. As Brendon Gill states in *The New Yorker*:

> It is the demonstration, thanks to admirable photography and still more admirable cutting, of how the conventional apparatus of a big city ... can be mobilized and all their diverse technical resources brought to bear upon the saving of a single life that makes the picture fascinating.[3]

The title suggests the fragile nature of the telephone line which connects the suicidal woman to the clinic volunteer. What if the power goes out? What if she is cut off? Technology could fail, and all would be lost.

While the telephone line is the literal representation of the "slender thread," the symbolic application of the title would suggest the fragility of the relationship established between Inga and Alan — strangers who must create an immediate thread of humanity between them, one which could be cut off at any moment due to any number of verbal exchanges which could block successful communication.

Pollack's circular structure is evident even in his first feature film, as the director 1) uses flashback to tell his story, and 2) brings Inga back to an undetermined future within the confines of a broken marriage, just as the viewer encountered her in the early moments of the film.

The Slender Thread is an entertaining character piece offering its audience energy, passion and suspense within the context of interpersonal communication.

Chapter 4

This Property Is Condemned (1966)

About the Production

THE FILM was shot on location in Bay St. Louis, Mississippi, a railroad town on the Gulf Coast. The boarding house used in the film was the vacant former home of Mayor John Scafide. Stores and houses were shot on Third Street, where the transformation to 1934 required false fronts, old automobiles and assorted props.

In New Orleans, ten days of shooting in the French Quarter required the masking or removing of television aerials, window-mounted air-conditioners, traffic lights and billboards. Shooting took place near historic settings such as Pirates Alley, Jackson Square, Court of the Two Sisters and St. Louis Cemetery No. 1 on Basin Street. The local Horseless Carriage Club provided 45-year-old cars.

Color was muted throughout the film to evoke the mood of the 1930s. Muted costume effects were produced by bleaching the costumes. Interiors were designed with faded curtains. Exterior shots were cast with a smoke pall.

Natalie Wood's "nude" outdoor swimming scene was shot inside a Paramount studio sound stage. The tank was filled with warm water which was dyed black to hide the flesh-colored suit she was wearing. The scene was shot with a floating, sealed camera with its lens at the water line.

The production brought an estimated $200,000 in revenue to New Orleans and $345,000 to the community of Bay St. Louis.

Robert Redford did his own stunt work in the fight scenes.[1]

Source of Material

This Property Is Condemned is loosely based on a Tennessee Williams one-act play. Although only the prologue and epilogue maintain a connection to Williams' play, the conversations between Willie and a friend inspired Pollack and his writers to develop the central character, Alva Starr.[2]

36

Synopsis

Natalie Wood stars as Alva, the beautiful older daughter of Hazel Starr (Kate Reid), who runs a Mississippi boarding house for railroad men during the Depression. Robert Redford (Owen Legate) and Charles Bronson (J.J. Nichols) round out the cast in their respective roles as a railroad efficiency expert and an earthy boarder. Both men represent potential salvation for Alva, who dreams of another life away from the decaying railroad town. However, Alva destroys her chances for happiness when, in a drunken stupor, she marries J.J. When she awakes and realizes what she has done, she steals J.J.'s money and takes a train to New Orleans to find Owen. Reunited with Alva, Owen begins to plan for their life together, a dream which is shattered by the arrival of Alva's mother, who discloses the details of her daughter's secret marriage. After Alva runs out into the rain to escape the humiliation of the moment, her younger sister Willie concludes the story in an epilogue, explaining that Alva died some time later back at the boarding house when illness overtook her.

Analysis

This Property Is Condemned is a character study with existential literary themes and universal appeal. The film captures the lyricism of the playwright, while discussing themes which parallel Williams' most autobiographical play, *The Glass Menagerie.*

In *This Property Is Condemned,* Alva Starr draws men to the center of the all-female household at the Starr boarding house in the deteriorating Mississippi railroad town of Dodson. Alva's role is to entertain the boarders and accommodate their romantic advances. As the younger sister Willie states: Alva is the "main attraction."[3]

Hazel Starr is the matriarch of the household, an aging and desperate woman who controls and uses her daughters to keep her rooms rented and to try to secure a financial future for the family.

Willie, Alva's younger sister and the narrator of the story, spends her time keeping the men at bay (to protect her older sister) or working as a servant at the boarding house.

In *This Property Is Condemned,* the male characters function as both the causes of the women's condemnation and their possible salvation. The absent father has condemned the women to "fend" for themselves however they can, resulting in a life of drudgery and prostitution for the Starr women. Mr. Johnson and J.J. offer the women a potential escape, but simultaneous emotional and/or economic condemnation.

Owen Legate has the dual role of villain and potential savior. His purpose

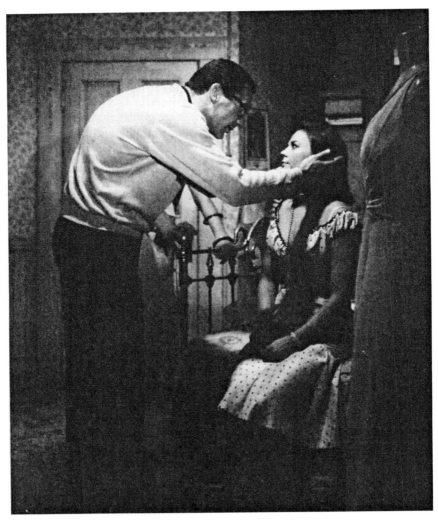

Pollack coaches Natalie Wood for *This Property Is Condemned* (Paramount, 1966).

in visiting Dodson is to reduce the rail activity, thereby simultaneously condemning the town to economic destruction and the Starr women to financial
ruin. Owen's role as a replacement figure for the absent father is established
immediately upon his arrival in Dodson, as Hazel Starr assigns him to "Papa's"
room. The father's art-work adorns the walls and his personal effects remain
as he left them, underscoring the illusion that he is still "living" in the house.
With Owen's arrival, the "protector" and "provider" has come to life.

Like other Pollack films, the environment in *This Property Is Condemned* serves as a reflection of the central character's psyche. In addition, the environment in this film also can be seen as a determining influence in the development of the central character, Alva Starr.

As the title of the film suggests the economic destruction of the Southern town, it also reflects the personal destruction of Alva — a piece of property exploited by her mother and used by the boarders to fulfill their fantasies. Alva is condemned to spiritual and physical death, just as the town and its citizens are likewise condemned by the loss of their jobs on the railroad.

As a determining influence, Alva's environment confines her to a life she would gladly shed. Daydreams provide Alva with a daily escape from her environment. She creates imaginary circumstances in her empty life in order to elevate her surroundings and her self-image, supporting the view that if she were removed from her environment she would not behave as she does. Alva displays a kindness, sympathy and gentility which in a different milieu would afford her the properties of a respectable lady.

Pollack creates a lyrical beauty in the innocence he ascribes to Alva and her world of make-believe. In reality, Alva prostitutes herself to keep the rooms full and her mother in the company of men. However, the film elevates her out of the conventions of that role, and she is presented as an innocent victim of her mother's desperation.

The railroad car which Alva's father decorated and named "Miss Alva" is a concrete symbol of her world. It rests next to the stationhouse, serving as a monument to Alva; it is filled with dust and is in disrepair. The car has not been attended, just as Alva has been left unattended by her father. It is here that Alva and Owen begin to discover each other, and Owen's role as protector and provider is developed.

Within the confines of the railroad car, Alva becomes fanciful and pretends to be on an imaginary trip. Owen challenges her fantasies in an attempt to bring her into the reality-driven world to which he is confined. He tries to ground her, but he fails to break her world of illusion. She brings dreams into his desolate life, and Owen begins to appreciate the joy that dreams can bring to an individual. He admits he has never had a dream.

As with other Pollack characters, Alva is victimized by her choices. A misunderstanding leaves Owen and Alva estranged, and he returns to New Orleans without her. Drunk and in the depths of despair, Alva lashes out at the cruelty of her mother and marries J.J., a boarder with whom her mother is involved. Realizing the destructive nature of her choice, she abandons her new husband and goes to New Orleans.

Alva is reunited with Owen, but her decision not to tell him about her marriage leads to the destruction of their relationship. Unable to face the humiliation of her own deceit, Alva chooses isolation over an attempt to seek Owen's forgiveness, condemning herself to a life of despair.

Alva's punishment and subsequent loss of possible happiness with Owen

Natalie Wood in *This Property Is Condemned* (Paramount, 1966).

Legate is consistent with Tennessee Williams' pathetic victims. The protagonists in Williams' plays seem predestined never to escape their circumstances, condemned to a life without hope.

This existential element is only one of the common threads shared by *This Property Is Condemned* and *The Glass Menagerie*, Williams' kindest and one of his most memorable plays. For example, the absent father figure is integral to understanding the circumstances of the families in both plays, along with issues of confinement, escape, illusion, potential rescue by a male suitor and a domineering mother figure.

The Wingfields in *The Glass Menagerie* are confined to their apartment during the Depression with only a fire escape as a symbol of some form of exit from their circumstances. In *This Property Is Condemned*, the Starr family is confined to their boarding house during the Depression as well, with the railroad their one possibility of escape. The central character in both families — Alva in *Property* and Laura in *Menagerie* — survives by living in a world of illusion. Moreover, part of the illusory world involves a concrete symbol of the protagonist's psychological state as well as an attachment to the absent father.

Laura Wingfield clings to her delicate glass figurines and the phonograph records which her father left behind, while Alva Starr withdraws to the railroad car her father memorialized in her name and lives in her daydreams.

The overbearing mother in each story, Hazel in *Property* and Amanda in *Menagerie*, manipulates the introduction of a male suitor. While each suitor potentially represents an economic solution to the families' problems, he is also permanently lost to the protagonist, resulting in despair and the continued confinement of the central character.

The use of the motif is another characteristic of Tennessee Williams' plays which Pollack preserved in *Property*. First, the railroad is a recurring symbol. The film begins and ends with Willie walking along the tracks in front of the boarding house. Owen Legate enters the story when he disembarks from the train, and he and Alva leave town, separately, on the train bound for New Orleans. Everyone in the film enters or exits Dodson, Mississippi, by rail, thereby indicating the importance of the railroad to the survival of the town, as well as the only means of escape.

"Breath" is also a motif in the film. Alva periodically refers to the fact that she can't catch her breath, reflecting how her very life force is being destroyed. When Willie explains in the epilogue that Alva died of tuberculosis, it can be understood that Alva has succumbed to her environment.

The "inability to breathe" motif is also consistent with Tennessee Williams, as he created in his plays the element of claustrophobia which reflects the psychological trauma endured by the characters imprisoned by an environment they cannot escape. The ambience of heat, discomfort and a lack of air, help create the milieu of confinement in *Property*. Only Alva experiences discomfort in the film; Owen admits he has never been "breathless."

The viewer is told in the epilogue that Alva returned to the boarding house where she lived until her death from a lung "affection." In the epilogue, Willie, as narrator, is wearing Alva's clothes and jewelry, reflecting her identification with her dead sister. Thus, Alva died retaining the only identity she knew: that of the "main attraction." Willie memorializes her sister by living alone in the condemned boarding house, confined by the same destructive elements assigned to her sister, destined to meet the same end.

In *This Property Is Condemned*, Pollack employs a circular structure, utilizing a prologue/epilogue format and revealing his story in flashback. Cinematically, the director used several aerial (helicopter) shots and zooms in the film which add a sense of movement, provide some change of perspective and open up the film to contrast its claustrophobic elements.

Released in 1966, *This Property Is Condemned* continues to maintain its validity and resonance. The song "Wish Me a Rainbow," which is sung by Natalie Wood and Mary Badham, while dated, supports the central character's illusory nature. The strength of the film lies in the exploration of its existential themes and its sympathy for the pain and ultimate destruction of its characters. The association the film maintains with the personal demons attributed to Tennessee Williams and reflected in his plays supports its contemporary and universal appeal.

The Scalphunters
(1968)

About the Production

THE SCALPHUNTERS previewed at the Academy Award Theater in Beverly Hills, California, on February 16, 1968, as a fundraiser for the Transport a Child Program. The event was hosted by Mrs. Burt Lancaster.

Filmed on location in Mexico, *The Scalphunters* was the first film Pollack shot in Panavision. (Panavision is a trade name which is often used to denote widescreen processes. While Panavision provides equipment for both widescreen and spherical processes, when used in this text, it refers to widescreen, unless otherwise noted.)

Source Material

The original story and screenplay were written by William Norton.

Synopsis

Joe Bass (Burt Lancaster) is a white trapper whose furs are stolen by a band of Kiowas, led by Two Crows (Armando Silvestre). Against the wishes of Bass, the Kiowas trade a black slave, Joseph Lee (Ossie Davis), whom they picked up from the Comanches, for the furs. As Bass attempts to reclaim the furs from the Kiowas, white scalphunters attack the band of Indians, killing and scalping several of them. The scalphunters, led by Jim Howie (Telly Savalas), escape with Bass' furs, which are still attached to his pack horse.

Bass makes a series of attempts to reclaim the furs from the scalphunters, which leads to several action sequences. Meanwhile, the slave, an unwilling participant in the action, joins Howie's band and endears himself to the scalphunter and his girlfriend Kate (Shelley Winters). After gaining her trust through a discussion about astrology, Lee convinces Kate to release the horse with the furs. However, Kate and Lee are caught. Failing in his attempt to regain the stolen furs, Lee becomes a captive and continues to travel with the scalphunters and their entourage until he once again reunites with Bass in the climax of the film.

In the end, as Bass regains ownership of his furs from the scalphunters, the Kiowas return and kill the white mercenaries, taking the women, wagons and Bass' furs as bounty. The film concludes with Bass and Lee scheming once again to regain the furs, this time as equal partners who have come to respect each other rather than as master and slave.

Analysis

According to Pollack, one cannot claim to be a "real movie director" in Hollywood until one directs a Western. Regarded as a parlor director because of his previous work in television and the fact that his first two films were strong character pieces, Pollack was launched by *The Scalphunters* into the Western/comedy genre with veteran actors Burt Lancaster, Telly Savalas and Shelley Winters.

The meeting of a variety of cultural dissidents and the metaphor of possession which the "stolen furs" represent in the film add texture and depth to an otherwise mundane storyline. *The Scalphunters* also allows for the exploration of salient sociological issues.

The light-hearted tone of the film is set in the opening titles with humorous sketches, reminiscent of the sketches used in the 1991 Billy Crystal comedy/quasi–Western *City Slickers*. The film's tone allowed Pollack to visit sensitive racial issues without alienating the audience.

The Scalphunters was produced in 1968 at a time when the civil rights movement and women's rights were certainly on the minds of many Americans. The film uses satire, humor and action sequences to deal with possible resistance from the rising sensibilities of the audience. Racism, prostitution and violence are strong themes.

For the action-driven Western fan, Pollack employs brawls, chases, an avalanche and a hand-to-hand mudfight-to-the-finish between Bass and Lee, representing the equivalent of the Western showdown or gunfight between the forces of good and evil. Rather than one of the forces being destroyed, however, the director blurs the racial differences between the two men in the beige mud, and the two emerge as equals rather than slain or victorious heroes.

For those interested in social commentary, the controlling principle or armature of the film concerns ownership, with slavery and prostitution providing the context for its discussion. A similar armature was also created in the 1985 Pollack film *Out of Africa*, yet the later film is more literary, aesthetic and allegorical in its execution, exploring ownership within the context of colonization, materialism and intimate relationships.

On a literal level, *The Scalphunters* describes Bass as a trader who skins beavers in order to sell their hides for profit. The Indians and the scalphunters want to own the hides for a similar reward. The Indians are willing to trade for them; the scalphunters are willing to kill and steal for them. Similarly, the scalphunters kill Indians in order to sell their scalps for profit. They also "own" the women who travel with them and serve as prostitutes and servants for the band of mercenaries.

In contrast, the runaway slave merely wants to be free and yearns for Mexico, where he can escape the bondage of ownership. As the storyline unfolds, Lee assumes the role of a bargaining chip — owned by prior slave masters, traded by one tribe of Indians to another, enslaved by Bass, and held for sale by the scalphunters.

In effect, the script presents Lee, the furs, the scalps and the prostitutes as commodities which continue to be traded and stolen, exploited for their commercial or sexual value. As the plot advances, the morality of each group involved is revealed in stark contrast, providing the director with the opportunity to present differing points of view among stereotypic individuals who inhabited an uncivilized region of the country during the second half of the nineteenth century.

The banter between Lancaster and Davis — white man against black man — is demeaning. Pollack maintains the balance in the viewer's sentiments by casting Ossie Davis as the moral and intellectual superior to the insensitive white man. In every scene, Lancaster's character is revealed for what it is and the runaway slave comes out on top. Somehow the viewer knows that Bass is going to learn from this "black Comanche" — a nickname the white trapper has bestowed on Lee.

Unable to see the slave as an equal, Bass relies on the principle of ownership to maintain control of the relationship between himself and his newly acquired property. Just as his "ownership" of the furs drives him to risk life and limb to regain possession, so Bass assumes possession of Lee, another "hide" to be sold.

Howie, aptly portrayed by Telly Savalas, is the leader of the scalphunters and the true villain in the film. He is a murderer, a mercenary, an abuser and a liar. He wants the slave for one purpose: to sell him for $1500. Howie is not redeemed in the film.

Bass, however, is a redeemable character. In the beginning, he does not want the slave to accompany him, and until Lee physically engages in a fight with him at the end of the film, Bass refuses to respect him. To Bass, being a man means being willing and able to fight and kill another. The former slave, who is an intellectual, does not see it that way.

Lee shows an amazing lack of animosity toward his Indian and white

Burt Lancaster in *The Scalphunters* **(United Artists, 1968).**

captors. Perhaps Pollack concluded that it was logical for the slave to be pacifistic for two reasons. First, Lee is an educated man and lives by his wits instead of his fists. Lee absorbs knowledge like a sponge, using it to empower himself and to ingratiate himself to the individuals he encounters. He avoids conflict and seeks peaceful resolutions. He has to be pressed to attack Howie in order to bar him from killing Bass. Lee finds it difficult to use a knife or gun against those who would harm him.

Secondly, Lee had to be submissive to survive as a slave, so it was a learned behavior for him to capitulate in the face of hostility. This trait is emphasized in the conversation between Lee and Bass, when Lee responds that "you [Bass] wouldn't last one minute [as a slave]."[1]

Whatever the case, Burt Lancaster was cast as a cruel, self-centered racist in the role of Joe Bass. The opposition established by these two characters in terms of cultural differences creates a tension in the film which propels it through its conclusion.

Bass does a lot of posturing in the film in an attempt to remain in control and maintain his own sense of self, which is strongly challenged by Joseph Lee. Lee is wise and self-educated, where Bass is simply experienced in the art of survival. To maintain his false sense of superiority in the slave's presence, Bass repeatedly reminds Lee that he is master. Undaunted, Lee maintains his centeredness, trying to build a sense of equality between the two men, through which respect can emerge.

During the mud fight, the two men "meet" at a junction where there is a sense of bonding and mutual understanding. Beige is a popular color for director Sydney Pollack, and he uses it metaphorically in many of his films.* In *The Scalphunters*, the beige color created by the mud eliminates the skin color which separates the two men. Now equal in color, and having drawn Lee into a physical fight, Bass is able to relinquish his ownership of Lee, represented by the gesture of allowing him to ride with him on his horse. In return, Lee repeats the line Bass uttered early in the film about waiting until nightfall when the Indians would be drunk to reclaim the furs, thereby indicating that Lee has gained equality with Bass and willingly consents to ride with him as his friend.

There are situations within the film which might offend the sensibilities of some viewers. In addition to the dehumanizing comments Bass makes toward Lee, one scene involves violence against women, which while never shown is intimated and might prove offensive rather than humorous.

Kate (Shelley Winters) has been manipulated by Lee to free the horse upon which are mounted Bass' beaver furs. The next morning, Kate is seen nursing a black eye and Lee has a rope tied around his neck as the wagon train with the scalphunters continues on its route. While cleverly providing shorthand for the film, so that an encounter between Howie, Kate and Lee are not necessary, this scene, in light of present-day feminist consciousness, might be read as condoning violence against women.

The overall representation of women in the film as prostitutes and servants also dates the picture. The "ownership" of the women parallels the "ownership" of the slave, reflecting a hegemonous mentality toward both groups — attitudes which Pollack seems to be exposing rather than exploiting. Everyone who is not white or male is treated as property, just like the furs, and passed from one group to another. The women are kidnapped by the Kiowas at the end of the film, and the attitude expressed by the Winters character is one of amiable resolution. To Kate, men are men, no matter what their race, character or culture.

Pollack's concerns in *The Scalphunters* appear to be focused on balancing racial issues among men, but the gender issues are just as important. In portraying the Winters character as a strong-willed, capable woman, Pollack carefully avoids presenting her as a victim. However, little sympathy can be gained for her position in life, as she is dressed and adorned with accoutrements of wealth for the time and the environment in which she is placed. Her lifestyle appears comic rather than pathetic, and the indifference with which she rides off with the Indians and continues her life of sexual favors further underscores her role as property.

The director attempts to balance the representation of the Indians in the

Beige is used in The Way We Were *to dress Redford's blonde girlfriend; beige is used for Faye Dunaway in* Three Days of the Condor *to represent her change from suspicion to trust.*

film. Pollack gives Two Crows an honest and compassionate character. He is willing to trade, not steal the furs from Bass, and he will not leave Bass without a horse, a rifle and his cookery in the desert. Pollack has created a friendly atmosphere between the two rivals, which foreshadows the likelihood of Bass coming to terms with the cultural differences which separate him from the slave.

Overall, the film discusses some issues which, 30 years ago, needed discussion. Today, the film feels dated and would more than likely only appeal to die-hard Western fans who enjoy slapstick comedy and the work of talented actors such as Burt Lancaster, Telly Savalas, Shelley Winters and Ossie Davis.

As serious commentary on social issues, the film makes important progress, especially for its time, with regard to the representation of minorities as equal, if not superior, in wit, intelligence and humanity. However, the film is stereotypic in its representation of its villain, and the film's treatment of women is likewise stereotypic and could raise the dander of a few feminists.

Pollack uses his circular structure in *The Scalphunters*, bringing his co-protagonists physically back to where they began on a quest to regain the beaver skins. The love story between Kate and Howie, the prostitute and the scalphunter, does not work as a metaphor for the attraction of opposites as in Pollack's later films. Rather, the growing relationship between Bass and Lee as "buddies" substitutes for the director's usual heterosexual love story.

Castle Keep (1969)

About the Production

THE NOVEL *Castle Keep* found its way to producer Martin Ransohoff while it was still in galleys. The book was "acclaimed on both sides of the Atlantic for its remarkable wit, satire and dramatic power." Ransohoff purchased the film rights to the novel and principal photography commenced in January 1968.[1]

The tenth-century castle, which serves as a barracks, refuge and principal metaphor, was constructed in Yugoslavia.

Source Material

The film was based on the novel *Castle Keep* by William Eastlake.

Synopsis

Major Falconer (Burt Lancaster) leads a unit of American infantryman to intercept the Germans at a tenth-century Belgian castle during World War II. Taking up residence at the castle, which is inhabited by the Comte de Maldorais (Jean Pierre-Aumont) and his wife Thérèse (Astrid Hereen), the eight American soldiers philosophize about the meaning of war, sex and art. Among the soldiers are found a would-be preacher, an art connoisseur, two writers, a baker, an Indian and a cowboy. Lancaster, the seasoned, one-eyed leader of the unit, views war in expedient terms. Cpt. Beckman (Patrick O'Neal) portrays the "art expert" who wishes to save the artwork embellishing the castle from destruction.

Lancaster soon becomes involved with the Countess and impregnates her — an action supported by the impotent Count, who wants a son. As the Germans advance to take the castle, the unit pulls together to defend it. Only Therese and Private Benjamin (Al Freeman, Jr.), the black writer, escape death as the castle and its artifacts are destroyed.

Analysis

This surrealistic war film, was released in 1969 in the midst of the Vietnam conflict, when anti-war sentiments raged across college campuses. It is also a cult film, and an ambitious one for director Pollack.

Pollack described this war drama as a "strange movie that [occasionally] plays on the late show." He noted that Michael Radford, British producer, director and screenwriter (*1984, White Mischief, Il Postino*), studied *Castle Keep* while at the London Film School (the film remained a key study subject in this school for years). About his first attempt at surrealistic filmmaking, Pollack remarked:

> Americans don't do surrealism very well. Although Nichols tried it with *Catch 22* and George Roy Hill tried it with *Slaughterhouse 5* … and they were more or less successful, depending on your point of view … this was the first time we tried to make an American surrealistic war film. It had its fans and detractors. It got some of the best and most interesting reviews I've every had. Audiences were bewildered by it; they couldn't follow it.

Pollack noted that throughout the film he tried to reinforce a sense of imbalance which gave rise to the surrealistic quality inherent in the work. Framing and lighting were used against convention to produce an uncomfortable, albeit unconscious, effect in the viewer.

> The traditional framing, particularly in an anamorphic set-up, is that when a character is looking from the left side of the frame toward the right side, you keep a lot of space in the direction that they're looking. In *Castle Keep* I did the reverse, which tends to make the viewer feel slightly uncomfortable.
> We also tried to light the film in a non-realistic way. So if an actor walked into a close-up where the left side of his face would be very close to a lamp, we would key-light him from the right…. When you look at it, you don't quite know what's different, but you respond on an unconscious level.[2]

Pollack, fascinated by the technical side of filmmaking, readily experiments with lighting and color to effect a mood. In *Castle Keep* he used warm tones, moving toward rose for shots inside the castle and cold tones in the exterior shots.

In an interview with *Film Comment* in 1975, Pollack defined the central question in *Castle Keep* as "whether it is worth saving man or the best that man can do." Pollack continued:

> Sooner or later you have to take a stand, no matter what is destroyed; otherwise you have Nazi Germany. It doesn't matter what has to go. What matters is that man survives. In a sense, Major Falconer's point of view wins out, but … it's not ever so simple.[3]

The holocaust at the end of the film, where both sides sustain heavy losses and the castle is destroyed, accented the director's point of view that "neither side was right and there has to be another way — a better way."[4]

The metaphor implied in the relationship between the Count and Countess and Major Falconer's role as sire to the Belgian heir deserves consideration. The marital relationship is unconventional, as Therese is actually the Count's niece as well as his wife. The procreative act between Falconer and Therese appears to symbolize the merging of the Old World with the New World through the seed of the American soldier. Rather than the survival of the Old World, which would be represented by maintaining the pure lineage through the Count, the act of procreation displaces the purity of the line, just as war and the intermixing of soldiers with the local women creates the displacement of lovers as well as progeny. This "mixing" alters the culture, representing another element in the destructive power of war.

The film opens and closes with strong imagery, through which Pollack employs his circular structure. As the film begins, the director displays the artwork at the castle and its eventual destruction. At the end of the film, he flashes before and after shots of the statuary intact, alternating with shots of the castle in fiery ruin.

Castle Keep is a film which tries hard to be intellectual. It is unexpected that soldiers, in the midst of conflict, would discuss such universal questions as the meaning of war, the destruction of culture, art and beauty. Pollack revealed that he and writer David Rayfiel were so enamored with the beauty of the book that they kept adding passages from it to the script. The result was in some way a "talkiness" which has been noted by critics as detracting from the piece. On the other hand, it is courageous of the filmmakers to attempt such a fusion of battle scenes and philosophy. In a surrealistic drama, realism can be suspended, and in *Castle Keep*, there are scenes which are positively antithetical to the reality of a war zone.

Consider the flute scene. While a soldier would probably be discouraged from playing a flute to avoid tipping off the enemy as to his position, here the scene is employed to allow a statement to be made. Two American soldiers are on watch in the woods looking for Germans. One soldier begins to play the flute, only to discover a kindred spirit in the German soldier hiding in the forest who hears the flute's defects. The German offers to fix the flute; when he does, the other American soldier expedites the kill. Fusing music (i.e., culture) with the killing punctuates war's expediency and its destruction of culture. It also raises the possibility that individuals could find alternative ways to view the enemy, i.e., through art we can rise above our political differences.

There is much energy given to the issue of "bread" throughout the film. Metaphorically, bread represents life. It provides nourishment and sustains life, while the sharing of it offers the opportunity for community and the bonding between individuals. Sgt. Rossi (Peter Falk) is a baker. He leaves the

Burt Lancaster (left) and Al Freeman, Jr., in *Castle Keep* (Columbia, 1969).

"war" temporarily to practice his trade in the village near the castle, an act which in essence gives him a renewal of life. He assumes the role of husband to the baker's wife as well. Later in the film, he shares his bread with his fellow soldiers, and they all leave the baker's shop to defend the castle with bread in their hands, signifying their desire to "live."

Imagery is a bit heavy with regard to the screaming eagle, which symbolizes destruction or "the world coming to an end." The scream is juxtaposed with a sculpture of an eagle-like bird.

The symbolism of the Volkswagen is obtuse. Cpl. Clearboy (Scott Wilson) finds a Volkswagen to which he becomes attached. Some of the other American soldiers try to destroy it by tossing it into the moat. Fortunately, the car floats, and it is not destroyed. Perhaps the floating Volkswagen foreshadows the American unit's inability to destroy the Germans, or perhaps the car represents some Freudian attachment of the corporal's. Alex Keneas of *Newsweek* referred to the "Volkswagen theory" as "a bit of autoeroticism."[5] Mostly, it is just unclear.

In preparing for the final battle to defend the castle and its artifacts, the Americans set up strongholds in the garden among the statuary and atop the walls of the castle. The soldiers in the garden clear the trees, presumably to remove obstacles which would inhibit the movement of their stolen German

Burt Lancaster in *Castle Keep* (Columbia, 1969).

tank, or perhaps to symbolize the environmental destruction of war. As the battle ensues, the men defending the castle from the garden are wounded. Pollack envelops them in a surrealistic haze, framing them with red roses. In a dream-like state, the men talk about their rescue, how they will find the bridge lowered across the moat and the castle will protect them from death. But it is just a dream — for they all die in the "forest of dead roses."

Meanwhile, from atop the castle walls, Major Falconer commands what is left of his unit. Amid the exchange of platitudes about the soldiers abandoning their private wars to defend the castle and its artifacts, Private Benjamin is exhorted to write about the incident and describe the heroism of the American soldiers.

Richard Schickel noted in his *Life* magazine article and film review of *Castle Keep* how Eastlake "showed us that each man has his own castle — an idea or ideal — that he will defend with his life once he finishes the really hard job, which is finding out what and where it is." Schickel continues to describe the irony which emerges in the story when in "the course of defending the castle, [Eastlake's] characters all die within moments of acquiring this self-knowledge."[6]

In the final sequence of the film, the drawbridge is destroyed, and Pollack distorts the image of the German soldiers advancing to take the castle. Fire engines arrive and hoist their ladders up the walls of the castle. (The counterpoint established between a tenth-century castle and modern fire engines is stunning.) Major Falconer asks Sgt. Benjamin to escape and take Therese with him while Falconer and Beckman remain behind to defend the castle. With machine gun perched atop the castle wall, the two soldiers make a final stand against the German assault. The battle scene fades out to white as the castle burns.

Many scenes are designed in counterpoint to represent the opposing points of view in the film. The viewer meets the Count and Countess riding on horseback on a hunt as the American soldiers appear, individuals from two worlds gently colliding at a fateful intersection. This intersection might be read as one of culture and war, the destiny of both the castle and the unit of soldiers to be determined by the advancing German army.

Bruce Dern leads a group of American conscientious objectors through the streets of the nearby village, singing and calling upon God to save the fornicating soldiers from the temptation of the brothel. Briefings which describe German troop activities are held in the Castle's chapel, a map draped in front of the altar. In the final battle, two men are pinned down in the "forest of dead roses." Surrounding these wounded men, with gunfire and enemy troop movement all around them, are red roses in full bloom standing out amidst the greenery.

The title of the film is also metaphorical. While it represents the location of the barracks for the enlisted men within the castle walls, i.e., within the "keep" or tower, it also speaks of a safe haven for the men as well as their concern to protect the historic structure and all of its artwork, i.e., culture, from harm.

Pollack on location in Yugoslavia for *Castle Keep* (Columbia, 1969).

Arthur Knight in his film review summarizes his own reading of the central issues presented in the material. *Castle Keep* explores "the essential horror of war [in] ... its indiscriminate disposition of a cultural heritage in the name of expediency."[7] In addition, the film addresses the timelessness of war, that the destruction of "ideals, art and human beings" has accompanied all wars.[8] By juxtaposing a tenth-century castle with a twentieth-century war, Eastlake created this association of which Knight speaks.

Schickel discusses two valuable sociological elements in *Castle Keep*. First, he noted that the film successfully dramatizes how men try to "maintain their humanity, their sense of priorities and proportions in the crunch of battle, bitter reminders of war's absurdity." Furthermore, he comments on the way the film captures the sense of "displacement," which realistically must accompany the individual's initial experience of war. This sense of displacement is absent in most war films, which depict war as necessary and therefore acceptable.[9]

Castle Keep is unique among anti-war films. Since it escaped the appreciation of American audiences in the year it was released, it is unfortunate that it is not available for those interested in surrealism today. The film has never been released on video.

Chapter 7

They Shoot Horses, Don't They? (1969)

About the Production

PRODUCTION BEGAN February 17, 1969, on location in Santa Monica. The piers at Ocean Park and Santa Monica were used for the exterior shots and the Oregon Ballroom provided the set for the interior facsimile of the Aragon Ballroom. Pollack used an old (circa 1930s) rotating/oscillating crane camera borrowed from MGM to film the marathon sequences.

In 1994, not a single negative of the original film had survived. Pollack undertook the project to restore *Horses* in letterbox format on videocassette and laserdisc. John Simon, guest critic in residence at the 1994 Telluride Film Festival, chose *They Shoot Horses, Don't They?* as his favorite film, and Pollack attended the festival to introduce the restored print.

Source of Material

The film was based on Horace McCoy's novel, *They Shoot Horses, Don't They?*

In a 1975 interview with *Film Comment*, Pollack told Patricia Erens that, prior to his taking the project, the property had been owned by "some 20 people ... the first of them was Charlie Chaplin."[1]

Synopsis

They Shoot Horses, Don't They? is set in a dance hall in California in 1932. The contestants for the dance marathon represent a wide range of types, all hoping for the $1500 cash prize at the end of the weeks of physical and mental exhaustion. The purpose of the marathon is entertainment, and the promoter (Gig Young) creates artificial relationships between the audience and the participants as a means of maintaining audience interest in the marathon experience.

Gloria (Jane Fonda) is a cynical, down-on-her-luck actress who meets a hopeful and optimistic man in Robert (Michael Sarrazin), her dance partner. They learn to depend on each other to survive the rigors of the marathon, creating an opportunity for trust. Robert destroys that trust when he appears to have engaged in a sexual encounter with another woman during a break.

Gloria responds to Robert's betrayal by initiating a meaningless sexual encounter with the promoter. This estrangement results in Gloria and Robert switching partners. Eventually their partners drop out, and they are reunited to finish the race. At this point, however, Gloria and Robert discover the truth about the marathon: the prize money is a lie. The promoter will deduct the living expenses of the winners from the prize money, leaving them with nothing.

Both individuals abandon hope, and choose not to finish. Standing on the pier outside the dance palace, Gloria asks Robert to kill her. The optimism with which he began the contest has long since dissipated and in his empathy for Gloria's condition, he accommodates her request.

The film ends with Robert being charged with Gloria's murder and the remaining couples still struggling to win the elusive prize.

Analysis

Based on Horace McCoy's novel, the film resurrects the exploitation and inhumanity of the dance marathons of the Depression. The film generated such anger from audiences and critics that Pollack was surprised. In an interview with Aljean Harmetz in March 1970, Pollack responded:

> There is a poverty of spirit today as well as a poverty of body. Human nature doesn't change. The elements in human nature that produced the dance marathon still exist. That kind of exploitation still goes on. But today it isn't expressed in the form of a dance marathon ... [The film] disturbs people, and yet I didn't intend for it to disturb them as much as it does ... I don't really believe there's no justice ... I don't find man's situation hopeless. Basically the film shows a girl who blows her brains out because she can't bear the pain of living. Painful as life is, I can't imagine getting out of it.[2]

In Pollack's film art, life is never hopeless. While the director does not fail to present life as harsh, ambiguous and painful, Pollack imbues his pictures with a sense of possibility — with another way out, illustrating the director's belief in the stamina of the human spirit against impossible odds. Pollack loved the film because he loved the nobility of the characters and their instinct for survival. It is their perseverance that Pollack celebrates in *They Shoot Horses, Don't They?*.

The allegorical content of the film was unintentional but inherent in the structure of the film. As Pollack commented:

> When you put a group of people in one room for two hours, you're making an allegory. You can't help it. If you put them in a dance hall, the dance hall becomes a microcosm.... What you put on the screen isn't the whole truth, it's just your truth, and it isn't even all of your truth.[3]

Artistically, Pollack succeeded in pushing the sense of desperation of the marathon participants to its limits. Through his use of slow motion, real time and the expression and movement of his actors, the reality of physical, mental and emotional exhaustion was harshly established.

The endurance with which the characters have been invested is a powerful statement in *Horses*. These individuals are willing to die, or to lose a baby, to win the prize money, which for a rational audience may be difficult to comprehend. Nevertheless, Pollack's characters make the risk of death and, in Gloria's case, the deliberate choice of death and ultimate loss of hope a believable option. What is most notable is that he did so without ever having to establish levels of motivation with elaborate back stories and character development.

The director relied on the stereotypes associated with the Depression era to inform the viewer's sense of the characters' imaginary circumstances which could lead to their irrational and desperate choices. The audience knows little about the characters, but it has no need to know more.

Pollack establishes a sense of entrapment in the dance hall through dim lighting and little exposure to the outside world. Robert would occasionally seek out the sun through the skylight, or attempt a brief view of the ocean when the garbage was removed. Only at the beginning and end does the director open up the film to the pier and the ocean outside the dance hall.

To further enhance the sense of entrapment, Pollack created red exit signs much larger than normal, which are visible in many of the scenes. For Pollack, those exit signs symbolized that "somewhere there was still a little promise — a way out."[4]

Since time was a concern for the director, he structured the narrative to maintain literal time, which helped create feelings of claustrophobia and exhaustion. To further accentuate those feelings, Pollack filmed the first dance sequence for eight-and-a-half minutes without a break, and shot the derby races just under real time.[5]

An imaginary scenario with a horse is employed to inform the metaphorical meaning of the film. In a crosscutting sequence, the director begins the film in the country, where a horse runs in slow motion through a meadow. A boy and a man with a gun are running after the horse. Cutting to a scene on the beach outside the dance hall, the viewer encounters Robert, enjoying the ocean view. In the background can be heard the voice of the marathon promoter/emcee, detailing the rules of the dance marathon. The director cuts back to the meadow where the horse falls, is injured and is subsequently shot, then cuts to the dance hall where the contestants are lining up to register for the marathon.

Pollack equipped himself with roller skates and hand-held camera to capture the dance marathon in *They Shoot Horses, Don't They?* (Palomar, 1969).

Michael Sarrazin and Jane Fonda in *They Shoot Horses, Don't They?* **(Palomar, 1969).**

At the end of the film, Robert shoots Gloria. At this point, Pollack cuts back to the meadow and instead of the horse falling to the ground, the image is that of Gloria. The continuity of the analogy has been established and the statement completed. Robert's only defense when the police ask him why he shot Gloria remains: "They shoot horses, don't they?"[6]

Pollack employed an unusual technique to prepare the audience for the ending of the film. Rather than take Robert through a trial after the death of Gloria, Pollack interspersed scenes from his arrest, interrogation and trial intermittently as "flashforwards" throughout the days of the marathon.

Shooting in Panavision, which Pollack states is the only medium he likes to use, the director maintained a sense of environment. As Pollack explained:

> [Panavision] is so structured that even in the tightest closeup you spill off the edges of the face and you spill off to a sufficient degree to know where you are.... Essentially Panavision is a two-shot medium. It's a terrific medium for relationships. In a closeup of one person you always get the sense of the other person ... the presence is always there.[7]

The exploitative elements of the marathon were exposed through Gig Young's portrayal of the promoter/emcee. Rocky is a man concerned with public relations, and his decisions center on selling tickets and keeping the stands filled. He often refers to the fact that the spectators come to see a show, they want to see the contestants' misery, and they must have people with whom they can sympathize.

To illustrate his point, the promoter steals a dress and makeup from the actress/contestant so that she does not look like a "star" but just another person with whom the audience can identify.

The promoter encourages the audience to "sponsor" their favorite couple. The couple, in turn, wears the insignia of the business which is sponsoring them. This artificial relationship, which is built between the sponsor and the couple, places added pressure on the dancers to drive themselves beyond their limits. They are not only pushing to win for themselves, but also for the approval of the sponsors.

The flavor of exploitation is further developed when Rocky asks Gloria and Robert to get married on the dance floor "for effect," after they are reunited as partners near the end of the film. The absurdity of his request, linked with their decision to quit, elicits the truth from the promoter, that he will charge the winners of the marathon what is on their "tab," effectively reducing the prize money to nothing.

While Rocky is the personification of exploitation and inhumanity, his character reveals redemptive qualities. A manipulator of human behavior, he is unremitting in his goal to maintain this form of popular entertainment. Nevertheless, he shows compassion and understanding for those marathoners who crack under the pressure. Ultimately, while he will drive these individuals to the end of their endurance, he will rescue them when they fall. The viewer has the sense that under different circumstances, the promoter would be a more redeeming character, and that he, too, is a victim of the economic desperation of the time.

The derby races are cruel. The state of exhaustion which the couples endure is exploited by the advent of a three-minute derby, where the contestants "walk" a race. The derby is an elimination round (the three couples who finish last are disqualified). The cruelty of this process is emphasized by the slow motion sequence, focusing on the agony of the participants as they literally drag each other around the track, some collapsing, others holding on — just barely — until the finish.

The characters of Robert and Gloria are central to an appreciation of the themes of the film. Robert is a kind soul, victimized repeatedly by his own choices, a man blown about by the will of others. At first, he is an optimistic lad who inadvertently enters the dance hall to watch the goings-on. Since Gloria does not have a partner, Robert is enlisted. He patiently endures Gloria's cynicism and his kindness toward her eventually brings her to trust him. Robert succumbs to the advances of the starlet, however, and loses Gloria's faith and trust in the process. Furthermore, Robert is willing to be manipulated by the promoter in a mock marriage, then follows Gloria's order to shoot her. Ultimately, Robert pays for his choices by being convicted of murder.

Gloria is an angry and cynical woman who keeps everyone at a distance by her viciousness. Obviously she has been repeatedly hurt and trusts no one. She has lost all faith and hope. The marathon is the end of the road for her, but there are moments during the grueling ordeal when Gloria actually believes she can win. Her brief episodes of hope, however, are destroyed first in Robert's betrayal, then in the final betrayal of the non-existent prize money, leaving Gloria with only one way out — suicide.

While initially there is no clear-cut sense of community, circumstances of the dance marathon force the women and men to rely upon each other. Survival as a couple is dependent on one's partner and one's own strength and determination. While some of the partners are married couples or lovers, others are total strangers as in the case of Gloria and Robert. In desperation, they hold each other up physically and emotionally, knowing that their individual victory lies in the ability of the other partner to persevere.

In addition, the men and women live together in a dormitory setting, facilitating their reliance on one another to some extent. In viewing the dormitory quarters, one is reminded of a concentration camp or prison, where mistrust can occur as easily as friendship. This forced intimacy which is prevalent as a result of the circumstances of the marathon environment serves as a breeding ground for hostility, rivalry and compassion, allegorically representing the larger society which engenders the same traits in an increasingly competitive world.

Controversial in subject matter, yet insightful in terms of the interplay of human needs in conflict with social values, *They Shoot Horses, Don't They?* earned Pollack an Oscar nomination for Best Director of 1969.

Chapter 8

Jeremiah Johnson
(1972)

About the Production

JEREMIAH JOHNSON was originally Robert Redford's project. Due to Redford's special interest in the story (which took place near his home in Utah), Pollack collaborated with him on the structure and content of the picture.

The film was shot on location after Pollack negotiated with Warner Bros. The studio restricted Pollack's budget, however, to what it would cost to shoot the film on the studio lot.[1] In the end, the director put up personal assets for the money to complete the picture.[2]

Pollack shot two weeks of pre-production work in St. George and Provo, Utah, to capture the changing autumn colors.[3]

Jeremiah Johnson premiered at the Cannes Film Festival on May 9, 1972. The film was critically and commercially successful, especially in Europe, because of its mythic overtones.

Source of Material

Jeremiah Johnson relates the legendary story of a mountain man (Robert Redford), a composite figure drawn from a fictional character in the novel *Mountain Man* by Vardis Fisher and the story "Crow Killer" by Raymond W. Thorp and Robert Bunker.

The project developed from an original screenplay by John Milius. Pollack worked secondarily from the Thorpe and Bunker story, and finally read Fisher's novel, *Mountain Man*. While Pollack used some lyrical passages from *Mountain Man*, he conceived the Jeremiah character quite differently from the author. Fisher was more interested in the "killer" aspect of the protagonist, whereas Pollack was drawn to the illusion of trying to escape from life and how a man's choices can ultimately victimize him.[4]

Synopsis

Through his patient exploration of the protagonist's experiences as he moves through his initiation in the wilderness, Pollack reveals the thoughtful story of Jeremiah Johnson, a deserter in the early part of the nineteenth century, who abandons civilization for the isolation of the Rocky Mountains.

The director dramatizes Jeremiah's search for freedom by comparing the protagonist's physical and spiritual journeys. This comparison generates a complex iconography, which suggests additional levels of symbolism beyond the spiritual. Thus, the film is accessible as a simple Western, a spiritual quest or rite of passage and an allegory.

Analysis

As Jeremiah leaves the outpost to embrace a new culture — that of the mountain man — the viewer has few clues about his past. While the protagonist wears a military uniform, it can be assumed that he is a deserter whose disillusionment with society has led him to seek a life apart from it.

During his journey, the initiate encounters an environment which is unfamiliar, sometimes hostile, occasionally friendly, and challenges his physical and moral strength at every turn. Jeremiah must deal with the difficulties of providing food and shelter for himself as well as adapting to the elements of weather, an unfamiliar Indian culture, and predators. At the beginning of his journey, he does not have the proper equipment nor adequate knowledge to succeed, but it is apparent that he has the will and determination to persevere in this environment.

As Jeremiah's journey unfolds, he meets individuals who "educate him" in ways appropriate to his survival, as well as engage him in a series of social relationships. Repeatedly faced with choices which challenge his intent to isolate himself from society, the protagonist becomes husband, father, friend, ally, adversary and eventually a legend in his own right.

Jeremiah's physical journey is paralleled by a spiritual one, and the spiritual dimensions are often revealed through the other characters. While the male characters in the film serve as extensions of his persona, the women awaken his sense of duty and his humanitarian instincts, as he is moved to compassion, respect for the dead and religious ritual, develops sensitivity to his Indian wife, builds a home to protect and comfort his family, and finds simple joy in play.

Jeremiah's initial encounter on his pilgrimage is with death as he meets a mountain man frozen in the snow. The encounter not only foreshadows the probable demise of the protagonist, but engages him in a familial relationship with the dead man with whom he shares the bonds of identification (as a mountain man) and inheritance (through his will). On a practical level, Jeremiah inherits the rifle he needs to improve his chances for physical survival.

Continuing his ascent into the mountains, Jeremiah meets Bear Claw, the seasoned mountain man, who offers moral as well as physical tools needed for the initiate's survival, thus serving as both mentor and shaman. Bear Claw repeatedly refers to Jeremiah as "pilgrim" (i.e., one who sets out on a quest with some moral purpose), revealing the spiritual tone of their relationship, as well as the spiritual meaning of the protagonist's journey. It is Bear Claw who provides Jeremiah with his initial socialization in the wilderness, teaches him to hunt, and who identifies with his loneliness and need for a woman. As the veteran mountain man, Bear Claw embodies what Jeremiah will become following his initiation: wise and adaptable. More than a survivor, Bear Claw has made an art out of adaptation.

Jeremiah leaves the company of Bear Claw and returns to his isolation. Soon he encounters a crazy woman and her son. Witnessing the devastation this family has suffered at the hands of the Indians, Jeremiah's compassion for the woman and her son overrides his desire for isolation. He helps the woman bury her family, repairs the cabin and offers to take them to the outpost. When the woman refuses to leave the dead and demands that Jeremiah take her son, he reluctantly assumes the role of father figure and returns to his journey accompanied by the mute boy, whom he names Caleb.

Caleb's symbolism is multi-faceted. First, his youth parallels Jeremiah's inexperience as a mountain man. Second, his muteness, which symbolizes "that which is unspeakable," parallels Jeremiah's silence about his own past. The viewer is led to believe that Caleb does not speak because of the trauma he suffered when he witnessed the atrocities rendered upon his family by the Indians. Thus, Caleb's silence mirrors the silence Jeremiah maintains about his former associations, in which we can only assume he witnessed similar atrocities inflicted by his own people.

With Caleb in his company, Jeremiah comes upon a trader named Del Gue. Portrayed as amoral, the trader swindles and connives, and while he reveals some understanding of Indian culture, he shows no respect for it. Del Gue is an anti-hero, seen in stark contrast to Jeremiah, but also projecting the elements of Jeremiah's personality which could come into play if the survival instinct were to overpower his conscience. It is through Del Gue's association with the Indians that the protagonist errs and wins an Indian wife.

As a result of both his choices and his blunders, Jeremiah is faced with the responsibility to protect and care for a woman and child. Submitting to his newly acquired level of domestication, he builds a home for his family. As love begins to flower among the family members, the cavalry arrives and confronts Jeremiah with a dilemma, which ultimately leads to the climax of the film and his moral deterioration.

Asked to assist in the rescue of a group of settlers, Jeremiah is at first reluctant to associate with the cavalry, but his consideration for the settlers overrides his caution. When the search party reaches a Crow burial ground, Jeremiah, the army officer and the chaplain discuss their options. Unsure of what retaliation would lie in store for them if they desecrated the burial ground and realizing that the search party can neither afford to go a different route nor continue alone and still succeed in their quest to save the settlers, Jeremiah chooses to lead the group through the burial ground. After reaching the settlers, Jeremiah returns home through the same route, and as he moves through the remains of the dead, he senses danger. Upon reaching his cabin, he finds his family murdered.

Overwhelmed by his emotional pain, Jeremiah enters a state of spiritual transformation. With lighting, the director describes the passing of time as the protagonist sits in his cabin at first trembling, later transfixed. Once he emerges from his catatonic state, Jeremiah prepares Swan and Caleb and sets fire to the cabin, which serves as a funeral pyre as well as the symbolic representation of the annihilation of the familial, the domestic and, as we soon discover, the civilized aspects of his life. Blurred in the waves of heat generated by the fire, the face of Jeremiah is surreal, symbolizing the level (unconscious) and the irrationality of the protagonist's interior transformation.

It is at this moment that Jeremiah's parallelism with Caleb is most significant. When Caleb dies, Jeremiah loses both his innocence and his silence, and his muteness is assuaged in the acting out of his vengeance. No longer "deserting" the violence and savagery of war that he knew in his past, he becomes what he has despised. Choosing his destiny, he denies his sense of social order and expiates his guilt in the retaliation he pursues with the Indians, searching out and killing all who have participated in the death of his family.

Jeremiah's retaliation leads to a cycle of attacks from the Crow, coming at him when he least expects them, one at a time, leaving him in a continuous state of fear and uncertainty. By the time Jeremiah again encounters Bear Claw — his mentor and shaman — he is nearly unresponsive to human conversation. Jeremiah is spiritually and morally dead.

The Significance of the Environment

The environment (the Rocky Mountains) emerges as a primary character in the film and engages the protagonist in a multi-dimensional relationship.

Physically, the wilderness serves as Jeremiah's home, providing resources for food and shelter and occasional socialization. On a moral level, the wilderness provides Jeremiah with a testing ground for his perseverance, endurance, and courage. Spiritually, the wilderness is the power which gives and the power which takes away. As human encounters, whether white or Indian, may become a friend or foe, so too the wilderness becomes both his adversary and his ally, as well as his teacher. Jeremiah's discovery of the frozen man with the rifle comments upon the spiritual relevance and dual nature of his environment, i.e., that nature preserves as well as annihilates — while simultaneously forcing the protagonist to come to terms with the eventuality of his own death.

Pollack comments on the relationship between Jeremiah and his environment by altering cinematic perspective. In the beginning of the film, the protagonist is a novice, cinematically dominated by the landscape. As the film progresses, his image enlarges in relation to the landscape. By the end of the film, Jeremiah dominates the foreground and the landscape has diminished, representing the maturity he has attained in relation to his environment.[5]

As a character representing an extension of the protagonist, the mountain environment symbolizes the unpredictable, spontaneous aspect of Jeremiah as well as the destructive and protective elements that co-exist within his psyche.

The Allegory

Jeremiah Johnson is also accessible as an allegory. The classical compositions used by the director cinematically comment on the universality of the film's themes. Limited camera movement produces the sense of the picture being complete inside the frame. Thus, the result of the frame composition is that the whole world is contained within each shot, enabling the viewer to experience the universal message of the film as well as the significance of its sociological elements.[6]

The dramatic content of the picture underscores the futility of the search for isolation, as participation in society and in the good of others continuously interrupts Jeremiah's journey. The film also reveals that even in isolation, "everyone" is subject to the laws of the natural environment. Through Jeremiah's experiences, the viewer is able to reflect on the consequences of choice, the desire to be cleansed from social evil and the illusory nature of freedom.

White/Indian relations provide a backdrop for the film, and the metaphorical love story between Jeremiah and Swan allows for Pollack's exploration of the differences between the two cultures and the similarities in human nature which allow bridges to be built. Despite language barriers and incongruities of custom, Jeremiah and Swan are able to create a true community with each contributing their own unique skills.

Pollack's circular structure is evident in the ambiguous ending of the film, where Jeremiah, isolated once again, begins another journey with his destination unknown. One of Pollack's more contemplative films, *Jeremiah Johnson* engages the viewer through its universal themes and striking cinematography, joining *They Shoot Horses, Don't They?* as one of the director's successful allegories.

Chapter 9

The Way We Were (1973)

About the Production

THE WAY WE WERE has gained respect in retrospect. Initially, the film was not well received by critics, though it was successful at the box office. Robert Redford made an observation on the critical rebuff of the picture in *Film Comment*:

> Critics had trouble with *The Way We Were* because they won't own up to their own emotions. They feel that it's got to be off-center or bold before they can accept it.... Intellectually, you know [Katie and Hubbell] shouldn't be together, but on a gut level you want them to make it because you like them and because they like each other. That's a fair emotion.[1]

According to Pollack, critics recently have started to recognize the merits of the film, regarding it as a "classic" love story with redeeming social value.

Principal photography began on September 15, 1972 at Union College, Schenectady, New York. (Originally, the Cornell University scenes were to be shot at Williams College in Williamstown, Pennsylvania.) The production crew moved to New York City for a week of shooting, then to Burbank Studios. The film cost $5 million. It opened October 24, 1973.[2]

Source of Material

The film was based on Arthur Laurents' novel *The Way We Were*. Laurents had directed Streisand on Broadway in "I Can Get It for You Wholesale" (1962). Her fiery spirit reminded him of a girl he knew in college, which inspired him to write the novel.

Producer Ray Stark, who had worked with Streisand on *The Owl and the Pussycat* (1970), wanted to do another film with her. He purchased the screen rights to Laurents' novel and sent Streisand a 50-page treatment. After she agreed to do the part, Pollack was hired in November 1971 to direct the picture.

67

Synopsis

This romantic period piece stars Streisand as Katie Morosky and Redford as Hubbell Gardiner.

A strong-principled political activist, Katie joins the Young Communists on a college campus circa 1940. On campus, she meets Hubbell, the consummate college athlete. The two are ethnic, political and moral opposites who eventually enter upon a doomed love affair. After many attempts to survive their differences over several years of marriage, Hubbell leaves Katie and a new baby. The two return to lives similar to the way they were when the lovers first met.

Analysis

In Pollack's description of the film, Redford played the all–American athlete to whom everything came easy. He had talent, intelligence, looks and charm. Streisand, on the other hand, was cast in the role of the outsider, the misunderstood radical, the ugly duckling. What pleased Pollack was that both sexes in the audience could identify with either character depending on their own experiences.[3]

Pollack told James Lipton in a 1994 interview that the "spine" of the film involved the opposition of "living in the passion of the moment versus the wisdom of a longer view." The director admits there was difficulty in making Redford's "longer view" argument valid.[4]

Katie Morosky is one of Pollack's multi-dimensional female characters. An intelligent, strong-willed Jewish woman, Katie clings to her idealism and activism hoping no one will notice her social inadequacies. Her passion for changing the world gives her purpose and vitality, while her assertiveness and inflexibility keep people at a safe distance. Katie works in the intellectual milieu because of her fear of the emotional one, reflecting a fear of rejection and abandonment. Finally, Katie holds a tight rein on her political principles, unable to allow disagreement or compromise, as though her opinions were personal defenses against a cruel and uncaring world.

As the quintessential outcast, Katie is drawn in strict contrast to the other female characters in the film. She does not present the softness of femininity expected of women in her era. She does not come from the advantaged class of Hubbell's social set. Neither does she present the shallowness of her female counterparts in the film, who are objectified for their beauty and exist for the validation of the male members of their circle.

Hubbell Gardiner, in contrast to Katie, is intellectually, physically and emotionally attractive. He is the successful, all–American athlete who easily wins the hearts of the girls who wish to objectify him as a trophy to obtain.

Hubbell is not particularly interested in politics or anything *else* of a serious nature. He takes life as it comes and is unconcerned and uncommitted to anything except his writing.

In the opening title sequence of the film, the contrast between the two characters is set. In this montage, Hubbell is seen competing in sports (crew, track, javelin, discus) and playing football with his friends. In contrast, Katie is always working, whether in the diner, running off flyers or preparing for a peace rally. Hubbell and his girlfriend frequent the diner where Katie works as a waitress. They talk, laugh and enjoy themselves, something Katie never seems to do. To underscore Katie's alienation from the "popular crowd," she passes by a sorority house. She longingly looks up at the window, as if to wonder what it would be like to be part of this circle.

To further illustrate the polarity of the two characters, Katie and her friend Franke set up a banner at the base of a statue on campus advertising a peace rally. As a prank, Hubbell and his friend J.J. place a fishing pole with a fish dangling from it in the statue's hand.

The backstory is revealed in flashback when Katie meets Hubbell in a nightclub a few years after college graduation. As she looks at the handsome man in a naval uniform, she remembers back to their college years, when she admired him from a distance.

Their story begins at a peace rally on their college campus in the late 1930s, where Katie is introduced as president of the Young Communist League. It is her passion and dynamism at that rally that captivate Hubbell. She convinces the students to take an oath refusing to support the United States government in any war it might conduct.

Katie and Hubbell share an English class. Determined to excel on a paper required for the course, Katie is hurt when Hubbell's paper wins the praise of the professor. As the professor begins to read the essay, Katie realizes that Hubbell is not what he seems.

In the opening lines of "The All American Smile," Hubbell reveals his self-reflection: "In a way he was like the country he lived in, everything came too easy."[5] The story continues to describe how the author often saw himself as a fraud. It is here that the superficial characterization ascribed to Hubbell begins to be dimensionalized.

When the plotline returns to the present, i.e., the nightclub, Katie invites Hubbell to her apartment, knowing that he has been unable to find a hotel room in New York. Drunk and not terribly interested in Katie, he goes to her apartment and passes out in her bed.

Katie sees the opportunity to live out her college fantasy with Hubbell and slips into bed with him, hoping that he will make love to her. Here Pollack creates a memorable and insightful love scene, all through the imagined emotions of his female star, who the viewer realizes has replayed this fantasy innumerable times. Now Hubbell is really there.

Barbra Streisand and Robert Redford in *The Way We Were* (Columbia, 1973).

The relationship between the two individuals develops slowly over a period of months, until finally they fall in love and eventually marry. As their relationship grows, however, the differences in their world views collide, making their harmony an artificial one.

After the war, Hubbell is offered the opportunity to write a screenplay based on his first novel, *A Country Made of Ice Cream*. Katie and Hubbell move to Malibu and join his best friend J.J., who has become a Hollywood producer. When conflicts arise between Hubbell and the director over the integrity of the story, Hubbell struggles with his desire to succeed versus his artistic integrity. While he does not sell out too quickly, Hubbell eventually meets the director's demands in order to keep his job.

Katie is an avid supporter of Hubbell's writing talent, but she is also a harsh critic of his willingness to settle for less than artistic integrity. However, Hubbell's view of the world is much more pragmatic than Katie's. He decides to play the game.

Hubbell's politics of success are held up in ironic counterpoint to Katie's dogmatic political principles. While Katie is rigid and uncompromising, Hubbell is practical and flexible. Neither one of these individuals is able to change. Finally, it is Hubbell who gives it up. Frustrated and tired of trying to keep the relationship harmonious, he moves on to a meaningless liaison with a former girlfriend, then leaves Katie after their baby is born.

Years later, the couple reunites momentarily on a street in New York City. The viewer learns that Katie has returned to her activism and her roots, and is now married to a man who shares her ethnic background. As usual, Hubbell appears to be smooth and successful, adorned by another "plastic" blonde.

Pollack spoke of the emotional independent activity within the actors that served this final love scene:

> Look at the ... emotional activity ... that's got to be going on in those two people, who were so much in love with each other at one time and have not seen each other in so long.... His life has gone downhill. He knows that, and she knows that, but she's not going to comment on it. He talks about all the television work he's doing. He knows he's been caught with the same kind of girl he's been with all his life — another beige girl. Meanwhile, she is married to David X. Cohen, and her hair is frizzy again. He has got to be looking at her and thinking that's exactly the way she looked the first time I saw her on the campus.[6]

As the ex-lovers meet in the final scene, Katie invites Hubbell to her home to see their daughter. Of course, Hubbell declines. He shows concern for his daughter by asking if "he" (Katie's new husband) is a good father. But Hubbell is unable to become a part of his daughter's life. With tears in his eyes, Hubbell admits he is not a good loser, but then he has not had as much practice as Katie.

Pollack stated that *The Way We Were* was written for Barbra Streisand. Redford and his agents did not want him to do the picture. As Redford explained for *Film Comment* in 1975:

> In the book, [Hubbell] is shallow and synthetic. It was written by a man who didn't understand men and didn't know how to write about a real man-woman relationship. We also thought the politics were phony, but Sydney felt the material had great possibilities as a love story.... One of the reasons Sydney wanted to do it was that he identified with the character of an uncommitted man. Finally, I just took the part on faith. Together we totally reworked the character of Hubbell.[7]

In Pollack's eyes, Redford represents the metaphorical American male. Consequently, Pollack believed that Redford's persona, i.e., the easy, smooth, charming exterior with a darker and more complex personality inside, would serve the character of Hubbell Gardiner well.

Pollack brings a radiance and attractiveness to Streisand that is very appealing, and it is easy to identify with her in both intellectual and emotional terms. The director's circular structure is present in the film, as the two lovers return to their former associations at film's end. The film is contemplative, and the director's languid pace and his sense of melancholy combine to elicit a mood of love and loss.

Cinematically, Pollack's frame composition reflects the lovers' relationship, as the director places Katie in a dominant position in all but the love scenes, where he allows Redford's screen persona to predominate.

Streisand's hairstyle was used as a symbol of change throughout the film. The kinky hairstyle was employed when she was in harmony with her ethnic background and activism. Pollack straightened her hair for the more feminine, romantic look necessary for Redford's character to fall in love with her. At the end of the film, Katie's hair returns to the kinky state, indicating her realignment with her true self.

There is an obvious hiatus in the center of the picture. After Katie and Hubbell break up in New York, she convinces him to try their relationship again. The narrative leaps from this scene to Malibu without any marriage proposal, wedding or family involvement. The viewer has to think through the jump in the storyline, and the believability of their marriage at this point in their relationship is difficult to accept.

With regard to a "hole" in the storyline, Pollack explained to interviewer Patricia Erens that a large section of the film was eliminated from the final cut at the request of producer Ray Stark:

> [T]he section dealt with the backgrounds of both characters, Hubbell's parents, Katie's father and her other men ... [In one scene] Katie asks Hubbell if he loved his parents and it occurs to him, as though for the first time, that he has never thought about it.[8]

The viewer can only assume that the scenes that were cut initially served the logic of the picture in the couple's transition from estrangement to marriage.

The Way We Were is a sad film, precisely because of the truth it engenders about many love relationships, in which the values of one party contradict the values of the other, making it impossible to preserve both the integrity of the relationship and the integrity of the individuals.

An acting vehicle for Streisand, the film was a box office success. Pollack used World War II and Hollywood blacklisting as temporal and political backdrops for the film, although he was criticized for not delving deeper into the political issues suggested by the storyline. Presumably, Pollack would defend his approach to the film, because the film was not about the politics of the McCarthy era. It was about the opposing views of living in the moment versus making decisions based on a longer view and an understanding of the shifting priorities of life.

As with all Pollack films, social and political issues are introduced but not explored in depth, because the director's personal interest lies in the dynamics of human relationships.

Chapter 10

The Yakuza (1975)

About the Production

THE PRODUCTION crew on *The Yakuza* included 15 Hollywood and 55 Japanese technicians setting up locations in Tokyo, Kyoto, Osaka and Kobe. Pollack employed a Japanese cameraman (Okozaki Kozo) for Japanese scenes and an American cameraman (Duke Callaghan) for American scenes.

Pollack noted stylistic differences between the two cinematic traditions. In Japan, not only does the cameraman operate the camera himself, but in lighting a scene, the Japanese light the way, one unit at a time, since they do not have the large lighting units of American film crews. Pollack explained that with the Japanese lighting style, "by the time you finish [lighting a shot] there will be thousands of very small units."

Screenwriter Paul Schrader (*Taxi Driver, Obsession, Hard Core*) reportedly was paid $300,000 for the script, which was subsequently retitled *Brotherhood of the Yakuza*. Schrader and director Pollack are purported to have had conceptual differences with regard to the film. Schrader was quoted as saying that Pollack directed against the grain of his script. Schrader described his script as a "violent, underworld film about blood, duty and obligation." According to Schrader, Pollack romanticized it into a rich, transcultural film, causing the picture to fall "between those stools," neither of "those films" being fully realized in the Pollack version.[1]

Part of Pollack's preparation for directing the film involved talking with actual yakuza.

Source Material

The film is based on a story by Leonard Schrader and a screenplay by Paul Schrader and Robert Towne.

73

Pollack with his family—wife Claire, son Steven, and daughters Rachel (left) and Rebecca—during the filming of *The Yakuza* (Warner Bros., 1975).

Synopsis

American businessman George Tanner (Brian Keith) swindles his Japanese friend and yakuza businessman Tono (Okata Eiji) out of a shipload of guns. In retaliation, Tono kidnaps Tanner's daughter, who attends a Japanese university in Tokyo. In an attempt to secure his daughter's release, Tanner enlists his old army buddy Harry Kilmer (Robert Mitchum). Kilmer goes to Japan to seek the aid of a former yakuza member, Tanaka Ken (Takakura Ken), who is no longer involved in the organization, but owes a debt to Kilmer.

After Kilmer and Ken reunite and determine their plan, Tanner's daughter is rescued, Kilmer murders Tanner (who has double-crossed him) and Ken and Kilmer destroy the yakuza gang involved in the plot.

A police investigation of Kilmer and Ken is averted due to Kato's intervention (he is an important government official and Ken's brother). The police are satisfied that the yakuza gangs have expiated their revenge upon each other and the issue is closed.

Analysis

The Yakuza has been described as "a combination of an Oriental Mafia story overlaid on a formula international business swindle, mixed up with an interracial love story."[2] Confusing at times in the narrative development, *The Yakuza* nevertheless presents some powerful images of Japanese culture with its backdrop of gambling dens, tattooed swordsmen, cemeteries, temples, baths and brothels.

In *The Yakuza*, Pollack presents an original, American interpretation of the Japanese "yakuza" genre, popular in Japan and other parts of Asia, though not well known in the United States. This genre has more substance and morality than the formula kung fu or karate films which have emerged in recent years. The "yakuza" are expert swordsmen who live by a strict code of morality, which is highly ritualized and based on honor and obligation. The "yakuza" genre combines the ancient samurai tradition with contemporary gangster themes.

Rex Reed commented that *The Yakuza* teaches the audience many salient social and anthropological facts about Japan and its culture. He compared it to "an underground tour, the kind you never get at Japan Air Lines." Reed continued that the originality of the film, its many-layered plot, and its lack of superficial humor elevated it above the standard samurai "flick."[3]

Despite the high praise *The Yakuza* received from some reviewers, the film opened to mostly negative reviews and was considered a financial failure.

Donald Richie of *Newsweek* compared the yakuza genre with the American Western, with its stylized violence culminating in "the Japanese version of the final shoot-out," i.e., the swordfight. Other similarities, according to Richie, include "rigid ethical truisms" and "machismo violence which is explained and excused by platitudes about obligations and the rightness of revenge."[4]

At the same time, Richie praised *The Yakuza* as "restrained, intelligent, thoughtful ... and one of the most serious and entertaining yakuza films ever made."[5]

The form of the "yakuza" genre is preserved in the Pollack version. The film opens with a "jingi" or introduction scene.[6] Here the central characters meet and the picture moves logically through its plot points to a bloody denouement.

In the beginning of the film, there is an explanation of the term "yakuza" for the purpose of educating the non–Japanese audience. From that description emerges a clue as to the psyche of the gangsters, who chose this name to describe themselves. The Japanese Kana for "yakuza" is 893, which equals the number 20. The number 20 is a losing number in gambling.[7]

Pollack described the three principal characters in the film, who are portrayed by Robert Mitchum, Brian Keith and Tanaka Ken:

> They are very much alike even though they come from different countries. They are really three antiques ... people who are over the hill and existing in a world that has passed them by. They still live by a set of moral standards which have become outmoded.[8]

Though this film is quite violent and hard-to-follow at times, the subtext allows this standard action movie to transcend its mixed genre formula. The film works in counterpoint both in its characterizations and in its pace. Pollack interweaves slow languid sequences with blunt, fast-paced action.

In the action sequences, gunfight and swordfight scenes are edited to provide maximum impact. With regard to these scenes, Pollack explained that his interest was in their counterpoint:

> I kept cross-cutting between Mitchum and Takakura Ken. Mitchum is an absolute bull and Ken is like a matador. They're both doing the same thing, but Mitchum is going about it in a pragmatic way while Ken is much more artful.[9]

Honor and obligation ("giri"— the burden hardest to bear) are the core of the film's message as well as the motivation for the action, and the director contrasts these moral attributes with the corruption and violence of the gangster element.

From an aesthetic point of view, *The Yakuza* shows enormous reverence for cultural differences and those attributes of a man which, in Japanese culture, make him a man: honor and fulfillment of his own obligations. A grisly portrayal of the ritual of penitence (the cutting off of the little finger) is repeated twice: once by Ken in atonement for the killing of his nephew, and, at the end, by Kilmer in atonement for his love affair with Eiko.

Pollack believes he chose to do the film precisely because of the atonement scene between Kilmer and Ken. For the director, this scene represented the ultimate connection and reconciliation of two people of opposite cultures (eastern and western). As Pollack stated for *Film Comment*:

> It was a kind of understanding, totally emotional and non-verbal....
> [I]n my terms it was just tremendous respect and the limits to which one will go to keep one's word.[10]

Due to the somewhat confusing storyline, it is helpful in the analysis of *The Yakuza* to offer here expository information, as it was divulged at intervals throughout the film. This additional information will allow the reader to comprehend more clearly the meaning of the film.

During the occupation of Japan by American military forces at the end of World War II, Harry Kilmer, an army MP, saved Eiko and her child from a firestorm. The two fell in love. Unwilling to marry Kilmer due to her loyalty to her Japanese husband, Eiko agreed to live with him until he returned to the States. In 1951, her husband Ken returned home, only to discover that his wife and child were saved by Kilmer, thereby placing him in debt to his American enemy. Despite the debt, Tanaka Ken (who poses as Eiko's brother) was angered and humiliated by the liaison between his wife and Kilmer and remains permanently separated from his wife.

Americans Kilmer, Tanner and Oliver Wheat (Herb Edelman) were friends who served in Japan during the occupation. Kilmer and Tanner returned to the States, Tanner developed ties with the yakuza and "Ollie" remained in Tokyo.

The plot rests on the swindle and subsequent attempt to secure the release of Tanner's daughter. Several subplots are introduced, all of them centering on relationships.

The first subplot involves Eiko and Kilmer, an interracial love affair unchanged by time, separation and distance. During his visit, Kilmer again asks Eiko to marry him, but she refuses. By the end of the film, Kilmer discovers the truth behind Eiko's refusals: that she is married to Ken.

A second subplot emerges in the relationship between Kilmer and Tanner. While Tanner recruited Kilmer to rescue his daughter, Tanner tries to have him killed in a bath house. With his old friend now turned against him, Kilmer must expedite Tanner's death in order to ensure his own survival.

One subplot that begins but never develops involves Hanako, Eiko and Ken's daughter, and Dusty, an American bodyguard. Another interracial love relationship is building when the couple is murdered in a shootout at Ollie's apartment.

Ken's relationship with his brother Kato creates an additional element of tension within the film. Actually, Kato's role is important to the dramatic content of the film. Kilmer initially visits Kato in an attempt to locate Ken. Through their conversation, Kilmer discovers that Ken has remained alone, having broken away from his family. Kato is willing to help Kilmer because he views him as a Westerner whose values are consistent with his and his countrymen. A successful government official, Kato influences the outcome of the plot, and condones the elimination of the gangster unit. His only request is that Ken spare his son Spider, who has become aligned with the yakuza.

During the climactic swordfight, Ken recognizes his nephew from the spider tattooed on the boy's head. As he pauses to spare his life, images of the yakuza taking his daughter's life revisit him. Avenging her death, Ken breaks his word to Kato and kills his nephew. Since Ken has wronged his brother, he feels obliged to fulfill the right of penitence by severing his little finger. Though Kato protests, Ken fulfills the obligation and asks forgiveness in the killing of the boy. The two brothers are reconciled through this act of atonement.

The most salient subplot, however, involves the relationship between Kilmer and Ken. The two men love the same woman, are indebted to each other, join forces to eliminate the yakuza gang and struggle to come to terms with their cultural differences and human similarities. Kilmer, who was present during the atonement scene between Ken and his brother Kato, is so moved by the level of honor and respect which it symbolized that, to assuage his own guilt for his affair with Ken's wife, he goes to Ken's apartment to seek forgiveness. Kilmer likewise severs his finger, and the two men share a personal bonding which is both deeply moving and unbearable to witness.

Pollack employs several cinematic techniques in this film to provide the drama. In an especially notable sequence, Kilmer has learned that Tanner is trying to kill him. Kilmer decides that the only solution is for him to kill Tanner first. Pollack uses a hand-held camera to follow Kilmer down the hallway to Tanner's office, creating the sense that Kilmer is stalking Tanner. Once face to face with Tanner, Kilmer fires several shots into Tanner's body. Rather than maintaining continuous action during this shot, Pollack edited the scene by cutting after each shot is fired, propelling the dramatic impact of Kilmer's act.

Although *The Yakuza* succeeds in dramatizing a respect for Japanese culture as well as the yakuza honor code, Pauline Kael criticized it for its lack of dramatic content. She stated in *The New Yorker* (March 1975): "Pollack isn't a violent director, and he has even lost his bearings on what he is usually good at. He doesn't seem to know where emotions stem from."[11] Kael is referring to the director's usual excellence in promoting dramatic content from within his narrative and actors, rather than through the editing tricks he employs in *The Yakuza*.

Louis Black of *The Daily Texan* called *The Yakuza* a "painfully underrated and amazingly eloquent film" in which the exploration of interpersonal relationships is more important than the narrative" and Mitchum's character, which undergoes the most subtle evolution, is both "intellectual and instinctual, erotic and brutal, intelligent and oblivious."[12]

Overall, *The Yakuza* is a creative and unusual film which transcends its genre through its thoughtful examination of honor among two men of different cultures.

Three Days of the Condor (1975)

About the Production

POLLACK AND his writers made considerable changes from the book *Six Days of the Condor*, upon which the film is based. While the director was not enamored with the novel, which was about heroine smuggling, he liked the pace and the contemporary themes it presented.

Lorenzo Semple, Jr., wrote the first draft of the screenplay. Pollack credits Semple with making *Condor* work as a film. Pollack then called upon David Rayfiel, with whom he has collaborated on most of his screenplays, to do an extensive rewrite which led to the idea of a radical CIA group within the CIA. Pollack describes the backstory:

> The group feels crippled by the exposure of what's happened as a result of Watergate and has decided to continue operations secretly. In this case, it was a tentative plan for an invasion in the Middle East.[1]

Pollack and Rayfiel also changed the characters. One character who was significantly altered was the international assassin Joubert, portrayed by Max Von Sydow.

> In the book, the villain is a horrible, horrible man — a pure mercenary who kills strictly for money ... the kind of mustache-twirling villain that just bores me. So we began to create a character whose amorality was more solvent than the CIA morality.[2]

In the Pollack version, Joubert becomes a man who isolates himself from society and creates his own morality, relying only upon the exercise of his own talents.

Pollack cast John Houseman in the role of the CIA chief. Their relationship goes back to *This Property Is Condemned*, when Houseman was the producer.

John has this tremendous kind of authority and dignity. It's almost European. It's impossible not to listen to him when he talks ... We wrote in a part for the top CIA official and we needed someone who could really carry the weight. I knew I wanted Houseman all along.[3]

Source of Material

The film is based on the book *Six Days of the Condor* by James Grady.

Synopsis

Joe Turner (Robert Redford) is employed by the CIA through a front organization called the American Literary Historical Society. Turner reads books and feeds the texts onto a computer in order to uncover leaks, codes, and new ideas, and check the plots against actual CIA operations. One day he goes out for lunch, and when he returns, he finds his fellow workers systematically executed. Turner's attempt to contact the CIA and arrange for his own safety is futile, and he remains a target—"unfinished business," so to speak. Although he has escaped the fate of his co-workers, a corrupt unit within the CIA is determined to exterminate him since he has stumbled on a plot to invade the Middle East.

For three days Turner eludes the assassins, led by free-lance professional Joubert (Max Von Sydow). With the help of a female hostage (Faye Dunaway), Turner uncovers information which leads him to identify the man behind the plot. After confronting Deputy Director Atwood (Addison Powell), Turner realizes that the counter-agency's mission involves oil. In an effort to expose the corruption within the "company," Turner turns the story over to the *New York Times* and finds himself faced with an uncertain future.

Analysis

Turner, whose code name is "Condor," was described by Rob Edelman as "a humanist employed by the Central Intelligence Agency. Turner is an intellectual, an antistereotypical character, who resents that he cannot tell others what he does." In contrast to his co-workers, Turner "trusts a few people."[4]

Pollack displays Turner's antistereotypic nature in several ways. He rides a scooter to work, wears blue jeans (unlike his associates), is continually late, bypasses chain of command within the office and refuses to use standard security procedures to enter and exit the building.

The key to the logic behind the film is Turner's photographic mind. Since

Robert Redford and Sydney Pollack confer on the set of *Three Days of the Condor* **(Paramount, 1976).**

he has absorbed much of the detail of the books that he reads, he is capable of drawing upon an enormous body of knowledge. The film demonstrates Turner's broad grasp of subject matter as he predicts the weather, solves a murder mystery, identifies the ailment of an indoor plant, discusses the backgrounds of Van Gogh and Mozart with men at the lunch counter, and fixes the copy machine in the office. This ability to recall information enables Turner to escape the fate of his co-workers and outwit the assassins.

Both thriller and a spy story, *Condor* is good entertainment. It is one of Pollack's more literal films, similar to *Absence of Malice* and *The Firm.* Thus, while there is some elevation of theme, it remains a basic genre picture. Pollack explained to *American Film* that *Condor* required a different kind of work than his previous films — it forced him out of his usual languid pace, requiring him to move fast and not allow the film to settle into a contemplative mood.

As the storyline unfolds, Turner arrives at the office one morning and follows his usual routine. The viewer learns that he is waiting for a response to an inquiry he has made through another employee, Heidegger (Lee Steele). Since it is his turn to order lunch for the staff, Turner exits through a back door to escape the rain and visits a local lunch counter. In his absence, Joubert, a freelance assassin, and his two accomplices (one disguised as a mailman) enter the building and execute the employees.

When Turner returns to his office, he finds the front door ajar and discovers the bodies of his co-workers. He takes the .45 automatic handgun the receptionist kept in her desk, exits onto the street, calls the CIA from a telephone booth. "The Major" (Jess Osuna) instructs Turner to resurface in two hours and call again. Turner visits an art gallery, goes to see Heidegger, whom he finds murdered in his apartment (and barely escapes two agents), then returns to his own home to learn that two other men are waiting for him. Turner vanishes and calls the CIA. He speaks to Higgins (Cliff Robertson), Deputy Director in New York, and they set up a meeting in order to bring Turner in to safety.

Suspicious of these CIA operatives whom he does not know, Turner is lured to an alley by the promise that one of his good friends will be there to pick him up. Sam Barber (Walter McGinn) is a social friend as well as an agent, and he willingly arrives with Wicks (Michael Kane), the Deputy Director from Washington, D.C., to "pick up" "Condor." When Turner approaches the alley and recognizes his friend, Wicks shoots at Turner, then executes Sam Barber. Turner in self-defense wounds Wicks, who is hospitalized. Joubert is hired to kill Wicks in his hospital room.

Turner is again on the run. Entering a clothing store, he decides to take a hostage. He follows a customer to her car, forcing her at gunpoint to drive him to her apartment, where he can hide until he can organize his thoughts. Once in Kathy Hale's apartment, Turner tries to enlist her trust. He attempts to prove his identity by showing her an identification card for Tentrex Industries. He explains that the telephone number for this company and the CIA are the same number. Turner briefly tells her what he does and what has happened. He explains that he just needs a safe, quiet time to pull things together.

After watching the news on television, Turner realizes that there is a coverup of the alley killing in which he was involved. Concerned for the safety of Sam's wife Mae (Carlin Glynn), Turner ties up his hostage and takes her car to visit Sam's wife, who is preparing dinner and unaware of what has transpired. Turner tells her to leave the apartment and go upstairs to be with friends. As he leaves the building, he meets Joubert in the elevator. Turner is suspicious of the assassin and narrowly engineers an escape.

When Turner returns to Kathy's apartment, she begins to understand that he has no intention of harming her, and as she attempts to comprehend his predicament she allows herself to open up and begin to trust him. Turner notices Kathy's black-and-white photographs, and their discussion of her artwork leads to a tentative intimacy. Kathy's fascination with Turner grows into a sexual encounter, which transforms the hostage into an ally. Pollack symbolizes Kathy's role adjustment by changing her clothing from black to beige.

The next morning, as Turner works through the logic of what has transpired, a mailman appears at the door. The assassin gains entry to the apartment and a fight ensues. Turner then enlists Kathy to help him set up a meeting with CIA Deputy Higgins. After Turner abducts Higgins, he realizes that he has stumbled on an intelligence network. It seems that Turner had raised a question about a certain mystery that "didn't sell," sent in his inquiry through Heidegger to the CIA, and found that it was dismissed. In reality, Turner had uncovered a network within the CIA which was working on a plan to invade the Middle East. It was Turner's inquiry that sentenced his unit to be destroyed.

Turner then involves himself in an elaborate scheme to trace a hotel key (which he found in the pocket of the mailman), locate a telephone number and rewire the New York telephone lines in order to confuse the CIA conspirators. Through this elaborate undertaking, Turner discovers the name of the Deputy Director of Operations in the Middle East. With this information in hand, Turner no longer needs his hostage/ally, and Kathy boards a train to Vermont to meet her lover at a ski resort.

Turner confronts Leonard Atwood (Addison Powell), the Deputy Director of Operations in the Middle East, at his home. While Atwood tells him nothing, Turner figures out that the whole issue is about oil. Joubert, the freelance assassin, appears from behind and kills Atwood, who has become an embarrassment to the CIA. Joubert spares Turner, as the "company" does not know Turner is present at the scene and brings him back to New York City.

Turner and Joubert share some expository dialogue after Atwood's execution. It is here that the viewer learns the morality of the freelance assassin, as Pollack has described it. Joubert is a man who "has no cause to believe in, no side to take." Since economics determines the good guys from the bad guys, "today one country is right; tomorrow it's another."[5] The scene between Joubert and Turner also foreshadows Turner's future, as the assassin informs him that he will be eliminated when he least expects it.

The film concludes with Turner meeting with Deputy Director Higgins in front of the *New York Times* building. Turner explains that he has given the story over to the newspaper. In a moment of trust, Turner believes that through the press he can expose the counter element within the "company." The film ends in ambiguity, however, and suspicion is raised once again as Higgins asks Turner how he knows that the paper will print his story.

Pollack's goal in *Condor* was to take a story about heroin smuggling and transform it into a relatively intelligent thriller dealing with corruption within the CIA and attempt to discuss trust and suspicion within that context.[6]

Pollack wanted to show the destructiveness of suspicion and the necessity of trust in human relationships. Through Turner's metaphorical relationship with Kathy Hale, the director tried to create some vertical dimensions in the film's content.

Kathy is a suspicious person by nature; Joe Turner is trusting. After the massacre of his fellow workers and the subsequent attempts on his own life,

Turner finds he is not able to trust those to whom he turns. His abduction of the woman becomes a desperate attempt to enlist the assistance, as well as the trust, of another human being. Through conversations about her art — lonely black-and-white photographs — Joe and Kathy create a temporary intimacy, represented by a sexual encounter, which then transforms itself into a tentative friendship. Within the space of 24 hours, the two characters shift roles with regard to trust and suspicion.

For Pollack, suspicion is a "destructive emotion" which prevents an individual from "breathing or mating." It is "antithetical to procreation" and consequently to life. Turner is a man forced to turn from trust to paranoia for fear of being murdered. Likewise, Turner holds the woman at gunpoint, forcing her into her "worst fantasy"— kidnapping and possible rape and murder at the hands of a stranger.

Three Days of the Condor maintains an interesting storyline with well-executed action sequences. For the viewer, the relationship between Turner and Kathy is artificial and only useful for the purpose of plot development and an understanding of Turner's thought process. The obligatory sex scene barely escapes being gratuitous through a cross-cutting sequence with Kathy's existential photographs.

Pollack uses image-to-sound relationships in counterpoint to deal with the themes of good versus evil. The story is played out during the Christmas season, and Christmas music and the Salvation Army provide the backdrop as Turner lives in fear and suspicion while trying to evade assassination. In another example, a cheery jingle is heard on Kathy Hale's television while she remains a frightened hostage.

Overall, the film is suspenseful and entertaining, and while not very believable in spots, it is a good commercial thriller with a fine cast. Von Sydow is disarming as the assassin for hire, and John Houseman astutely executes his role as the brilliant yet cynical CIA chief, very much aware of the unpredictability of a man who reads books.

Bobby Deerfield (1977)

About the Production

BOBBY DEERFIELD was shot on location in Italy. Marthe Keller's apartment was the largest set constructed for the film.

Source of Material

Paul Newman owned the original script, which he commissioned after he optioned the novel, *Heaven Has No Favorites* from Columbia Pictures. The novel was written by Erich Maria Remarque. The Alvin Sargent script, however, is not a faithful adaptation.

Synopsis

Celebrity race car driver (Al Pacino) has abandoned his roots in New Jersey, lives with a woman in Paris and competes on the European circuit. After a race in which a driver is killed, Deerfield becomes obsessed with finding the cause of the accident. He is convinced that it was not driver error but a malfunction in the automobile.

His investigation of the accident takes him to a Swiss hospital where he visits Karl Holtzman (Stephen Meldagg), another driver who was injured. Holtzman is gratified by Deerfield's visit, thinking that he has come out of professional concern for his condition. However, Deerfield's purpose is not motivated by compassion but a latent fear of his own death.

While having dinner at the hospital with Holtzman, Deerfield meets Lillian Morelli (Marthe Keller), another patient. The following morning, Deerfield is leaving to go to Milan where the race car was manufactured, when Lillian requests a ride from him. While on the road, Lillian and Deerfield begin to discover each other. After spending the night in Bellagro, they arrive in Milan, where the two part. After taking care of business in Milan, Deerfield returns to Paris.

Fascinated by Lillian's drive for pleasure and zest for life, as well as her insights into his personality, Deerfield is drawn back to Italy to see her. They spend a day and night together before Deerfield returns to Paris. Following his return, he enters a race in which he crashes, but he is not seriously injured. As he recovers from his accident, Deerfield discovers from his live-in girlfriend in Paris, Lydia Picard (Anny Duperey), that she knows about his relationship with Lillian and that the woman is dying.

Deerfield returns to Lillian's side and they share the last days of her life together. Through Lillian, Deerfield is able to discover a level of comfort in revisiting his past, accepting his roots and assuming his real identity.

Analysis

"Unusual" and "oblique" are terms which best describe this love story set in Europe with Al Pacino and Marthe Keller cast as the romantic duo. Roughly based on Erich Maria Remarque's novel *Heaven Has No Favorites*, *Bobby Deerfield* is a slow, contemplative study of two jet-setters whose lives become intertwined, and who eventually bring each other wholeness and joy.

Lillian (Keller) is terminally ill; Bobby (Pacino) is a celebrity race car driver. Lillian lives a manic lifestyle as a way of coping with her impending death. Bobby is repressed — spiritually and emotionally. He fears nothing, believes in nothing and gives nothing. Intrigued by Lillian's elusiveness, Bobby cannot resist her, and through the turmoil of their repeated attempts to understand each other, they eventually bond.

Pollack spoke of the criticisms he received when *Bobby Deerfield* was released. The director challenged the criticism that he made a "European film." While the picture was shot in Europe, he believes that the film is distinctly American. He was also criticized for producing a film like *Love Story*, without the sentimentality. As Pollack noted:

> ... that's exactly what I wanted ... to make a love story without the sentimentality. But if you go to the theater with a box of Kleenex and want *Love Story*, of course, the film is not that. I don't necessarily see that as a liability.[1]

Pollack and Newman liked the Sargent adaptation of the novel, but they were both a bit skeptical of its commerciality. When Pollack was finally free to do the picture and *Three Days of the Condor* was making money in the theaters, Newman was unavailable to play the lead. Since *Condor* appeared to be on its way to success at the box office, Pollack felt he could take a chance with *Bobby Deerfield*. He hired Pacino for the lead role.

Heaven Has No Favorites provided "a springboard to deal with something quite different from what the novel deals with." The theme which interested

Pollack was "the idea of a man who has turned against his own past and therefore makes himself a totally isolated individual. He has constructed an identity that isn't organic to himself. But during a relationship with a girl, he learns to accept the reality of who he is and to accept his own roots."[2]

This theme, which served as the armature for *Bobby Deerfield*, was not in the book. It was created by screenwriter Alvin Sargent. The book describes a girl who is dying and attempting to come to terms with death, and a man who deals with death every day. In this tragic love affair, both characters eventually die.[3]

In the adaptation, Bobby's relationship with his roots is brought into focus through a scene with his brother Leonard (Walter McGinn), who has come to speak with him about his family back in the States. After repeatedly ignoring his brother's phone calls, Bobby meets Leonard at a restaurant. Leonard is visibly angry because he believes that Bobby does not care about his family. He tries to reminisce with him about their childhood, but Bobby pretends he does not remember the Mae West impersonation he used to do. Leonard explains to Bobby that their mother is 70 years old and she wants to give him some land, but Bobby's reaction is one of indifference, avoiding Leonard's questions. Leonard leaves some family pictures with Bobby, and the two remain estranged.

Pollack credits screenwriter Sargent with keeping the screenplay from becoming too intellectual by finding corollaries to deal with the theme. Rather than having the characters confront each other with the meaning of death, life and roots, Sargent had Bobby, for example, admit that he could do a Mae West imitation which he had done in his childhood, thus dramatizing his coming to terms with his roots.[4]

Critics also complained that Pollack did not identify the malady from which Marthe Keller's character was dying. Pollack defended his decision to "leave out" the clinical scenes. Since the director looks at his films from the perspective of a spectator, he wanted only to impress upon the audience the idea that she was dying — the cause was unimportant.

Pollack did try to be accurate, however, in portraying her symptoms. He assumed she had a tumor and consequently indicated that chemotherapy was a treatment by dramatizing her hair falling out. However, it was important to the characterization of Lillian that she appear "full of life, with a great appetite for living right to the end."[5] Consequently, Pollack cast Keller and, consistent with the symptoms of the illness, she did not look pale and wan.

It is important to note that Pollack had a problem with the ending of the film all along. As he told Janet Maslin:

> The thing I was always upset about was why does she have to be dying ... I didn't want to make a film about a girl dying, I wanted it to be about a guy who was resurrected.[6]

However, Pollack conceded that he was "stuck" with the ending or he would not have been able to do the picture. Lillian's death was locked in, both in the book and in the screenplay, and Pollack admits he just could not come up with anything better.

An earlier ending for the film introduced the issue of euthanasia. As Pollack described it, "[Pacino] killed her, he unplugged her.... At first I thought it was a very moving scene, but then I realized that it was wrong." Since this ending was not organic to the film and since it raised a lot of other questions, including whether or not Pacino's character might get caught, it was dropped.

Pollack and Pacino knew there should be another scene in the picture. Unable to identify it, Pollack pasted together some extra footage involving a tunnel scene and the picture of the two lovers taken by some tourists earlier in the film. According to Pollack, it was not a bad ending, so he decided to retain it.

Pollack loved the film, even though it was not commercially or critically successful. It remains one of his favorite projects. Pollack believed in the film's romantic mood and in the metaphor it presented for being true to oneself. Bobby Deerfield's attempt to assume another identity and discard his roots destroyed something in him, and the director wanted to dramatize this spiritual death.

Pollack remarked that films "have a funny way of finding their true value quite a while after they're made." The reviewers who initially discarded *Bobby Deerfield* are revisiting it and finding value within the story. With regard to any motion pictures, Pollack contends that one needs to wait ten years to see which ones can last.

In *Bobby Deerfield*, Pollack shoots exquisite European locations which provide the film with life and warmth. In contrast, the love scenes are dark, lacking in eroticism, and foreboding. More European in style than American (it tends to be understated and restrained) and devoid of sentimentality, *Bobby Deerfield* is not a film for everyone. Patience and thought are required to appreciate its substance.

Although auto racing provides a backdrop for the film, it is not an action film. The track scenes are employed to relate the falseness and emptiness of Deerfield's identity, as he walks through the ritual of preparation for each race. The viewer cannot ignore the cold, dull stare in Pacino's eyes. The car crashes also suggest the literal risk of death which Deerfield and his fellow drivers face with each race.

As in other Pollack films, the environment mirrors the psychological nature of each of the central characters. The sanitarium where Lillian first meets Bobby environmentally reflects and foreshadows her impending physical death. The race track environmentally reflects Bobby's spiritual death, since his racing (as well as his lifestyle) negates his true identity.

The tunnel scene can be read as an oblique symbol of death, where Pollack brings both characters together to create a claustrophobic, tomb-like environment. Here Lillian, having accepted the fate of her illness, does not hesitate to express her personal agony by her scream; whereas Bobby, who remains in a state of denial regarding his own spiritual death, cannot enter into this ritual with Lillian, let alone understand it.

The boundaries between the two genders begin to blur in the subtext of the film. When Bobby goes into a bar and talks to the magician who entertained the patients at the Swiss hospital, there are two women slow-dancing in the background. As they drive to Milan, Lillian and Bobby have discussions about the meaning of masculinity and femininity. Lillian comments on the manly size of her hands while noting that Bobby holds the steering wheel with a feminine touch. Clearly defined sex roles are being challenged as there is an assertion made that men and women share both male and female characteristics.

The gender issue may be drawn in counterpoint to the American machismo life-style of Bobby Deerfield, who races cars for a living. His female companion Lydia stands by dutifully while he races, then nurtures him when called for, but the two rarely speak. There is no depth or intimacy to their relationship. They are individuals whose boundaries do not appear to cross, each one distinct, one male, one female operating in traditional roles. Lillian, on the other hand, draws Bobby's attention to linkages between men and women, as well as trans-gender characteristics he has not previously considered. Lillian's ideas challenge Bobby's assumptions about the world and help him to expand his concept of himself.

Lillian lives a spontaneous lifestyle, always in the moment, with selfish abandon. After Bobby and Lillian spend the night together in her apartment in Italy, he awakens to find her gone. Lillian has left to join a regada of hot air balloons. When Bobby confronts her about leaving him, she invites him to join her in this life-affirming experience. She never answers his questions.

Lillian asks for nothing and desires no attachments; she sees many different men. However, Bobby's love for this unusual woman draws him to stay with her through the moment of her death. He begins to sense a wholeness when he is with her, and he is unable to abandon this awakening. Bobby is able to find and accept his real identity and his past through his relationship with Lillian.

Through Bobby's growing sense of self, Pollack has demonstrated the effect of the interior strength and wisdom of this female character, whose nobility and courage in the face of death serve as a model for Deerfield.

Pollack hoped that viewers would understand his intent in the film. Nevertheless, the director admitted, "Sometimes I lose track of the black and white, and I find myself falling in love with the gray areas."[7]

What Pollack wanted most was for audiences to appreciate the role which Al Pacino played so skillfully:

> It's a performance that doesn't call attention to itself ... Al had the guts to be obnoxious for the first hour of the film, to the point where you want to punch him. That's a level of truth very few actors are willing to give.[8]

The Electric Horseman
(1979)

About the Production

THE ELECTRIC HORSEMAN was filmed on location in Las Vegas, Nevada, and near St. George, Utah. Rising Star, the $12 million thoroughbred race horse, was played by Let's Merge.

According to Pollack, the story is actually a screen version of a three-act play. Act I concludes with Steele's kidnapping of Rising Star, Act II is the chase and Act III is the love story.

The production of Act I began at Caesar's Palace in November 1978. The convention scenes were staged in the Circus Maximus main showroom of the casino. Real tourists and gamblers were present during the shooting of the interior casino scenes. Off-camera signs were posted to alert the tourists that they were being filmed. When Redford's character, Sonny Steele, rode through the casino on Rising Star, 500 extras stood in for the casino patrons.

The Las Vegas scenes were completed by Christmas. In January 1979, Act II and Act III were shot near St. George, Utah.

Pollack's brother Bernie was costume designer for the picture. It was reported that the "electric suit" Redford wore in the film cost $35,000.[1]

Source of Material

The original screenplay was written by Shelley Burton in 1972. Pollack and Redford were both committed to other projects at the time. When they were available to seriously consider the production, Robert Garland and Paul Gaer were hired to rework the script.

Synopsis

Sonny Steele (Robert Redford) is a five-time championship rodeo star, who, like the horse in the film, has been put out to pasture and financially survives by doing commercial endorsements for a major conglomerate. AMPCO corporation employs Steele as a spokesman for their breakfast cereal, and Rising Star is their corporate symbol. Steele makes public appearances promoting "Ranch Breakfast" and wears an elaborate costume which is illuminated when plugged into his saddle. As Steele endures the media circuit, playing the hero for young children and appearing at second-rate sports events, rodeos and fairs, he often shows up inebriated to dull the pain of exploitation.

As a finale for a major media event and press conference celebrating the merger of AMPCO Corporation with Omni Bank, Steele is expected to ride AMPCO's ex-champion race horse Rising Star onto the stage. At rehearsal, Steele discovers that the horse is drugged and has injuries which have not been properly attended. It seems that Rising Star is also "under the influence" in order for him to tolerate the requirements of celebrity status.

Angered by the conglomerate's treatment of Rising Star, Steele promptly walks out of rehearsal. When it is time for the event, Steele mounts the horse, rides him across the stage through a bevy of chorus girls, down the ramp, through the casino and past the slot machines, out the door and up the Las Vegas Strip.

The abduction of Rising Star initiates a manhunt and media frenzy, but the undaunted Steele continues his mission to spare the horse from further abuse. He is able to elude the law enforcement agents on his trail, and with the help of an eccentric friend who lives in the desert, Gus Atwater (Will Hare), he transports Rising Star to the Utah mountains.

With the law and the media in full alert because of the horse's abduction, reporter Hallie Martin (Jane Fonda) is determined to locate Steele and the horse. Through Steele's friend Wendell (Willie Nelson) and estranged wife Charlotta (Valerie Perrine), Martin learns enough about the cowboy to uncover his likely whereabouts. Martin is able to track down the ex-rodeo star and confront him about his plan for the horse.

Steele's plan is to release the horse in a canyon to live in the wild. Martin, taken by the passion and heart of the man, offers to tape his story for broadcast. After Steele's plea is aired on the news, AMPCO executives, embarrassed by the exposure of their company as abusive to animals, relinquish their quest for Steele's arrest, and stage a media event to celebrate the animal's release.

Steele, of course, is too smart for the corporate executives and releases the animal far away from the staged celebration. At film's end, Steele and Martin, who have a brief romantic interlude, part company. While Martin returns to her television news reporting, Steele is last seen hitchhiking out of town, having freed the horse and himself from the bondage of ownership and exploitation.

Bernie Pollack adjusts Robert Redford's tie on the set of *The Electric Horseman* (Columbia, 1979). Sydney Pollack stands just behind Bernie.

Analysis

In *The Electric Horseman,* Pollack addresses the issue of commercial exploitation using an entertaining premise. Through his recurring circular structure, the director presents the sad plight of the two central characters: a free-living, ex-rodeo champion in Sonny Steele and a champion race horse in Rising Star. No longer capable of continuing their heroic deeds, Sonny and Rising Star are injured has-beens, living out their lives as advertising gimmicks for a food corporation.

The horse is not only a literal character in the film, but serves as the symbol of Steele's moral deterioration and subsequent imprisonment as well. Steele is depicted as a weak, drunken womanizer. He is a man who is lost, holding onto his broken marriage from a distance, a shell without purpose or direction. Like Rising Star, he suffered an injury, and it locked him out of the sport he loved. The "easy money" offered by AMPCO supports his vices, while he loses a little more of his dignity with each public appearance. Unable to face what he has become, Steele remains drunk much of the time.

What stirs him from his stupor is his outrage at the treatment of the horse, something left in the world that he still respects. It is through his identification with Rising Star that Steele finds himself, his sense of morality and his courage, which move him toward personal redemption. Unable to accept the exploitation of Rising Star, he frees the horse, an act which constitutes a vicarious escape for the protagonist. In the end of the film, Steele leaves town, discarding both the artificial world of Las Vegas and his artificial existence as an employee of AMPCO.

The environment of Las Vegas serves as a reflection of the empty life of the protagonist. Pollack has demonstrated the superficiality of Steele's life by placing him in the casino with its confining spaces and artificial lighting, and its promise of wealth, glamour and excitement. But the promise is an empty one. This point is underscored in the elevator scene, where Steele is reflected in a mirror, dressed in his electric suit, interiorly vacant.

In *The Electric Horseman*, Pollack takes a strong stand against commercial exploitation by dramatizing the victimization and dehumanization that are its trademarks. There is no ambiguity in his point of view. Cinematically, the director astutely uses light as a metaphor. The artificial lighting of the casinos is contrasted with the natural lighting of exterior shots where freedom awaits Rising Star (and Sonny Steele).

Continuing the light motif, Pollack represents Steele's dehumanization by rigging the cowboy with electric lights, which serve to enhance the crowds' enjoyment of his public appearances. When Steele is late for one of his appearances, another "cowboy" is substituted, lights flashing, riding a horse around the arena. The point is that no one knows the difference.

Jane Fonda portrays reporter Hallie Martin, who pursues Steele in an attempt to "get the story" and finds herself becoming involved with the man, as well as the freeing of the horse. Pollack creates his love story through the interlude between Redford and Fonda. In Pollack's metaphorical love relationship where opposing points of view are realized, Martin is employed to continue the theme of exploitation as a member of the media, thirsting for the "exclusive" story, while Steele and Rising Star remain the objects of exploitation.

This time, however, Steele does not allow himself or the horse to be victimized. Steele is no longer passive, and he is no longer drinking. In the rugged mountain terrain, Steele is in control and Martin is the novice. It is Steele who "uses" the media to serve his purpose — to make a plea for freedom for Rising Star. In the process, AMPCO executives are publicly humiliated and resort to damage control to protect their image.

Hallie Martin's characterization is more fully developed than the female co-stars in other Pollack films (*Three Days of the Condor* and *Jeremiah Johnson*, for example) where the central character is male. While Martin is basically employed for plot development, momentary sexual interest and to help the protagonist reach his goal, there is some fullness to her characterization. Martin is strong-willed, resourceful and fiercely independent. She does not allow

Steele to abuse her and readily stands up to him. Yet her sensitivity emerges as she grows to understand the decency in the man and his respect for the horse. Caught up in the beauty and drama of releasing the horse, Martin's focus begins to shift from her duty as a reporter to her own humanity.

Steele gives a moving speech for Martin's news broadcast, which they tape in the mountains of southern Utah. He speaks of Rising Star's accomplishments, the courage and determination the horse showed in races where he endured when there was nothing left in him to give. He calls the horse a champion with a heart and a soul. He acknowledges that AMPCO owns him, but there are some rights no one can buy. The horse, according to Steele, deserves a better life because of the gifts he has given the world.

Rising Star and Sonny Steele are mirror images. The story Steele tells about the horse parallels his own career. Both were champions, both gave their heart and soul to their sport. To continue the analogy, both were drugged — the animal with Butazolidine and steroids, Sonny Steele with alcohol. Both are victimized by the world of advertising.

Steele tells Martin that steroids cause sterility, rendering the horse incapable of passing on his genes. By analogy, Steele's own life has become sterile, i.e., unproductive, unfruitful, ineffective. The horse, however, is an innocent victim, unable to break out of his imprisonment. Though Steele's life has become meaningless and unproductive, he is not impotent. He has the power to be effective if he chooses it. Recognizing that he has lost his dignity and self-respect, Steele chooses freedom and with it an uncertain future.

The film is slow and plodding, and Redford's persona is underplayed for this role. He shows more warmth and humanity and down-to-earth realism in his performance in *The Electric Horseman* than in his other films, where he is distant and smooth. There is no smoothness in Sonny Steele, and the cowboy mannerisms and drawl create a Redford character who is more accessible. There is no hint of an icon here.

The Electric Horseman was the film debut of country-western singer and songwriter Willie Nelson, who plays Wendell, a member of Steele's entourage. Nelson also performs songs for the soundtrack, including "Mamas Don't Let Your Babies Grow Up to Be Cowboys" and "My Heroes Have Always Been Cowboys." To round out the cast, John Saxon portrays the ruthless, heartless AMPCO executive Hunt Sears.

While *The Electric Horseman* is little more than a basic genre movie, it does have something of value to say within its own "commerciality." The film confronts the world of product endorsement, which objectifies and exploits athletic heroes to extend their entertainment value by tying them to the sale of products. Perhaps there is even a hint that the public is "drugged" by the powerful forces of advertising and the associations made between media stars and products which promise to enhance the health and potential of those who consume them.

The Electric Horseman is stereotypic, replays the same ideology as many other films concerning the inherently decent individual versus the institutions of a capitalist society, and pits the "cowboy" against the urban elite.

The film exposes the empty promises of advertising which correlate with the empty lives of the endorsers. With financial gain as the sole purpose of the enterprise, the values of materialism override any human values as demonstrated by the corporate executives of AMPCO. As a backdrop for inhumanity, exploitation and greed, Las Vegas served the material well due to its reputation for encouraging all human vices and its own unfilled promises of wealth and the power that accompanies wealth.

Las Vegas creates an artificial world based on the manipulation of the public's perceptions. In stark contrast, Steele and Rising Star return to the natural world outside the casinos and away from the media and conglomerates, where life is simple, uncontrived and devoid of gimmicks and the image culture. The natural world is the place for Rising Star and Steele to begin anew.

Those viewers who see free enterprise as both a blessing and a curse can appreciate the statement that is made in *The Electric Horseman* about the inhumanity of commercial and media exploitation that is the result of a materialistic society.

Absence of Malice
(1981)

About the Production

ABSENCE OF MALICE was shot on location in southern Florida. Most scenes were shot in actual restaurants, bars, banks and government buildings in Miami and the newsroom at the *Miami Herald*. The exterior for the fictitious *Miami Standard* was created on the back of Flagship National Bank on Brickell Avenue. Newman's "Gallagher Imports" business was located in a warehouse on Biscayne Bay, and his boat, "Rum Runner," was actually a 46-foot cruiser built in 1941 called "The Optimist." The scene between Sally Field and Melinda Dillon was shot in the gardens of Vizcaya, part of an estate which belonged to industrialist James Deering.[1]

Source of Material

The original screenplay was written by Kurt Luedtke, former executive editor of the *Detroit Free Press* and reporter at the *Miami Herald*. *Esquire* reported that Luedtke came to Los Angeles in 1979 and pitched the story to an agent at Zeigler Diskant. George Roy Hill was initially assigned to direct the picture. When the script made its way into Pollack's hands, he recalls

> I read a 250-page screenplay by a man who ... had no experience writing for movies but who was a talented writer. It was so complex that your head ached from trying to figure out what was going on. Nothing visual at all about it, but the bones were good.[2]

Pollack, who does extensive research for his films, relied on personal conversations with Luedtke to fill in the elements about the newspaper business that he needed to understand in order to direct the picture intelligently.

Synopsis

Newspaper reporter Megan Carter (Sally Field) of the *Miami Standard* prints a story about a secret government investigation of the role of Michael Gallagher (Paul Newman), a liquor wholesaler and mobster's son, in the disappearance of a labor leader. The story is leaked to her by an unprincipled government investigator, Elliot Rosen (Bob Balaban), who believes that Gallagher knows or can locate information on the disappearance of Diaz. In his attempt to "squeeze" information from Gallagher, he leaves a file on his desk for Megan Carter to "discover." Believing that the file indicates that Gallagher is a suspect, she prints the story without corroboration.

The story that is printed turns Gallagher's life upside down. The story not only threatens Gallagher's reputation, but results in a longshoreman's strike which brings his business to a standstill, and tragically causes the death of Gallagher's long-time platonic girlfriend, Teresa Perrone (Melinda Dillon).

Gallagher sets up a plot—and uses Megan to ensure that the story is printed. This results in Rosen illegally wiretapping his own boss, Quinn (Don Hood), who is running for re-election as District Attorney. When the Department of Justice sends in an investigator, Wells (Wilford Brimley), from Washington to confront all parties involved, justice is served, Rosen and Quinn are fired, the newspaper must print the full story, Megan's career is ruined and Gallagher is vindicated.

Analysis

Absence of Malice is Pollack's most literal film. The director described the picture as "never really having an operative spine." It has a theme which concerns "reality and illusion, i.e., appearances and the failure of appearances." It is the least ambiguous of Pollack's films; the director noted that *Malice* is simply "about what it is about; there are no other meanings beneath the surface."

The film provides solid genre entertainment with an intricate plot. As such, the characterizations tend to be superficial and stereotypic, except for Melinda Dillon's character, Teresa Perrone, whose multi-dimensionality comes through even though her screen time is brief.

Teresa is a fragile and repressed individual for whom Gallagher has a special affection. Having known each other since childhood, the two have bonded as friends, and their platonic love for each other serves to support both of these lonely people.

Teresa is frightened that Gallagher will go to jail. Knowing that she can provide the alibi which could save him, she calls Megan Carter. In her attempt to clear Gallagher, Teresa reveals intimate details about herself, details which if made public would deeply humiliate her. She works for the principal of a

Catholic school, and she has had an abortion. Gallagher took her to Atlanta for the procedure during the time that the union leader disappeared, providing an alibi for Gallagher and eliminating him from suspicion.

Teresa fears her father and the school administration's reaction to her secret abortion. Yet, her love for Gallagher and her ability to free him takes her past her fear to trust Megan Carter to protect her anonymity. Unmoved by the woman's pleas and emotional state, Megan assures her that people will understand about the abortion.

Megan does grapple with printing the issue of the abortion and discusses it with her editor. The editor determines that it is the only factor that will make the reader believe in Gallagher's alibi. Seeing it as essential to the piece, Megan prints the girl's story, using her name rather than respecting her request for anonymity.

When the article is printed on the front page of the newspaper, the humiliation that Teresa experiences drives her to a vain attempt to hide her secret past by picking up the newspapers off her neighbors' lawns. Unable to face the world, Teresa takes her own life, neatly and quietly slitting her wrists in her bathtub.

Luedtke supports the realism of Megan Carter's scenario:

> I am startled and shaken by the information finding its way into print under the cover of unnamed sources. Combined with that is a suspension of reportorial interest in questioning the motives of the people supplying the information.... It's awfully difficult ... for readers to make a judgment about the quality of information they are being given. But without the name of the speaker, there is no possibility for the reader to make an informed judgment at all.[3]

When Megan learns of the suicide, she visits Gallagher at his place of business, where he angrily rebuffs her in a violent confrontation. Badly shaken, Megan reveals her source to him as she leaves the warehouse. Armed with the investigator's name, Gallagher devises a plan to expose the unsavory investigation, humiliate the ambitious district attorney and ultimately to seek revenge.

Paul Newman's role as Michael Gallagher is tightly played and well-acted, and he was nominated for an Academy Award. The audience is allowed to know little about Gallagher except that he is the son of an ex-mobster, who was raised to be law-abiding and that he is innocent of the crime for which he is being harassed.

To illustrate the point that his father wanted him to be an honest man, Gallagher relates the story of how his father locked him in a basement for three days after he and his friends went joy riding in a stolen car. His father wanted him to understand what the life of a criminal, should he choose it, would be like.

Gallagher's rough exterior is countered by his kindness and the sense of humanity he shows in his relationship with Perrone, which provides his character with some dimensional development.

Wilford Brimley portrays Justice Department investigator Wells, and literally steals the show with his outstanding performance. He is called in to evaluate the culpability of each of the players in the subplot which develops when Gallagher decides to seek his revenge. The strength and assertiveness of the Brimley character is drawn in sharp contrast to the political wheeling and dealing going on among the other characters. Wells gets to the heart of the matter; there are no illusions here. His role shines in dramatic contrast to the understated Newman persona as well.

As a character, Megan Carter (Sally Field) never reaches a resonance which seems organic. She oscillates between ambition and vulnerability, and the viewer becomes frustrated with her motivated yet hard-to-believe choices. Consequently, Megan Carter's character is difficult to care about, especially when she continues to make the same mistakes. However, Pollack believed that the repetition of these mistakes made the script work. "The reporter commits the same error three times. In order to make the audience care for her, the audience has to believe that she stumbles with it each time."[4]

The audience is asked to accept that at the age of 34, Megan lacks the good judgment required of an investigative reporter. The key to understanding her character, however, may be to associate her with a comment made by her editor; within this revelation may lie the core of her dilemma as a newswoman.

The editor of the newspaper tells Megan that he can be nice to people and he can tell the truth, but he has not learned how to do both at the same time. Perhaps this is Megan's problem as well. This raises the question as to whether these two elements are irreconcilable in the press.

Megan initiates a romantic relationship with Gallagher, which again shows her poor judgment, since she is writing about his investigation. However, Gallagher appears more pragmatic. His interest in Megan seems contrived, i.e., for her to know him well enough to believe that he is innocent. There is no chemistry, no allure and no love scene. A kiss in the shadows and a "morning after" scene quickly dismiss the sexual content of the relationship. The purpose appears metaphorical in playing out Pollack's attraction of opposites and for plot development. As a plot device, the relationship allows for emotional intimacy between the characters so that some degree of trust can be established between them.

Whether intended by the director or not, *Absence of Malice* can be read on a level beyond the theme of reality versus illusion, which is Pollack's stated purpose. The film suggests an exploration of the relationship between the press and the individual citizen. Pollack and his screenwriter present a complex story which reveals the potential danger of an irresponsible press to the freedom of the individual citizen.[5] The film asks the viewer to be concerned for balance between the individual and the common good, between a person's right to privacy and

Paul Newman in *Absence of Malice* (Columbia, 1981).

the public's right to know, between the consequences of both personal and jour-
nalistic actions and the ambiguous line that is drawn between them.

    The film can stimulate the viewer to revisit the issues of a free press, to
grapple with its boundaries and sensationalism, to try to clarify the ethos of
the media, and to re-examine its place in a democratic republic.

    Pollack's personal interest in the material was in illusion, that things are
not always as they appear. The theme of illusion began with the unscrupu-
lous investigator who merely laid a file upon his desk, giving the appearance
of an investigation which did not in fact exist.

Paul Newman confronts Sally Field in *Absence of Malice* (Columbia, 1981).

The illusion grew into "fact" through the catalytic action of Megan Carter, who created a world of truth which did not exist. Assumptions quickly become facts, and an innocent person was made "to appear" guilty. The question then arises: Can we ever know "truth"?

In the case of Gallagher, assumptions were made about him because of his connection to the mob. There is no doubt that the film supports Gallagher's loyalty to his uncle, Malderone (Luther Adler), but Gallagher's guilt by association is not truth, only the appearance of truth.

Megan makes an insightful statement toward the end of the film. One of her co-workers is about to write the story on the outcome of the Gallagher investigation. She asks Megan if it is true that she was involved with Gallagher. Megan's reply is that it is not true, but it is accurate. The truth has been qualified to mean that facts can be reported accurately. However, facts do not necessarily add up to the truth, showing Megan's growth and redemption.

Critics denounced the film's unrealistic representation of the press. The flagrant errors made by Megan Carter throughout the film, they contended, did not serve to balance the issues under examination. Though Pollack believes that he tries to balance the issues in his films, the press is in no way presented in a positive light in *Absence of Malice*. The key to Pollack's point of view may be reflected in the film's title, which in one reading might be construed to see the press as "above the law."

In a meeting with the newspaper's attorney, Megan is counseled not to worry if her story is indeed factual. The attorney states, "As a matter of law, truth is irrelevant" providing there is "absence of malice."[6] In effect, Gallagher cannot win a lawsuit against the paper and the paper is libel-free, since Megan has written the "truth" as she knows it. This philosophy is the core of the film, and the point of view the director opposes. The irony of the situation lies in the "quest for truth" that the press philosophically represents, when in fact "truth" in terms of law, hence in practice, may be "irrelevant"— and in this case, even deadly.[7]

Absence of Malice reveals a yearning for honesty, integrity and respect for the individual. Through a well-constructed plot, strong dialogue and distinctly defined characters, Pollack revealed many of the forces that can destroy the individual citizen's freedom when irresponsible journalism exists. In this way, the film supports the values of responsible journalism by demonstrating its absence. Such practices as intelligent investigation, corroboration, evaluation and sensitivity for the privacy of people, who may be innocently injured, are revealed as essential to the profession.

Absence of Malice is excellent entertainment. In light of Watergate and other press-related scandals in recent years, the film emerges as relevant in its presentation of a contemporary moral dilemma.

Chapter 15

Tootsie (1982)

About the Production

TOOTSIE WAS filmed on location in New York City. Principal photography commenced in April 1982 and was completed on August 27. It opened in the U.S. on December 17. By January 19, 1983, the picture had grossed over $69,000,000. In 1996, *Tootsie* was rated #31 on *Variety*'s list of the 50 top-grossing films with a reported $177 million.

The title of the film came from Dustin Hoffman's mother, who died before the picture was completed. Hoffman was reportedly paid $4.5 million for the role of Michael Dorsey.[1]

The Rating Board gave the picture an "R" due to the language in a scene involving Teri Garr and Dustin Hoffman (as Sandy prepares for her audition). Garr needed Hoffman's character to "enrage" her in order to play the audition successfully. The use of an expletive (twice) in this short conversation laced with light humor was the Board's reason for the rating. After Pollack appealed the decision, and since the film contained no sex, violence or nudity, *Tootsie* received a PG rating.[2]

Source of Material

The derivation of the script for *Tootsie* was complex, according to Susan Dworkin, author of *Making Tootsie*. In 1978, the script from which *Tootsie* evolved belonged to Henry Plitt of the Plitt Theater Chain. It was purchased by Charles Evans, the executive producer of the film, after he read it as a favor to Buddy Hackett, who wanted a role in the picture. The script at that time was called *Would I Lie to You?*, and it had been written by Don McGuire.

Once Evans owned the property, he retained Bob Kaufman to rewrite the script (which was destined to become a sitcom). When Dick Richards, a friend of Evans, read the script, he became involved. Together they produced a new script about an out-of-work actor who lands a job as a nurse on a soap opera.

After Kaufman departed the picture, Richards showed the script to Dustin Hoffman. Hoffman had been considering playing a female character, and he had been working on a script with Murray Schisgal about a male tennis player who passes as a woman. Hoffman wanted Hal Ashby to direct, but he was unavailable. Columbia suggested Sydney Pollack and a new writer to replace Schisgal, Larry Gelbart.

Once Pollack gained control of the picture, he, Hoffman and Gelbart spent nine days at Pollack's beach house in California developing the script which ultimately made its way into production. However, the script continued to evolve throughout the shoot. There were occasions when the crew was unable to plan setups for the day's shooting, and last-minute changes were always being made. The shooting script literally emerged from day to day on the set in New York City.[3]

Pauline Kael has noted that several other writers had their hand in the script, including Elaine May, Barry Levinson, Valerie Curtin and Robert Garland. The screenplay had to be submitted to the Writers Guild for arbitration to determine who should receive screen credit.[4]

Synopsis

Tootsie is the story of Michael Dorsey (Dustin Hoffman), whose professional integrity and assertive manner have virtually made him unemployable as an actor. Determined to raise $6000 to produce his roommate's play, Michael auditions for a woman's role on a popular soap opera.

His female impersonation is so realistic that he secures the role and at the same time learns what it is like to be a woman in a man's world. The impersonation leads to a number of conflicts and gender confusion as well as Michael falling in love with soap opera co-star Julie Nichols (Jessica Lange).

As Michael assumes the role of "Dorothy," his life becomes enormously complicated and deceptive. However, he finds himself growing fonder of the character he created, and "Dorothy" begins to assume her own traits. By the film's ending, Michael is able to cleverly unravel all the tangled webs he has created and repair most of his broken relationships. He has also made enough money to produce Jeff's play, and recognizes that he has become a better man because of his experiences as a woman.

Analysis

One of the most popular films of 1982, *Tootsie* starred Dustin Hoffman in an Oscar-nominated performance as a struggling actor who finds "himself" when he secures an acting role as a woman administrator on TV's *Southwest General*. The film is a comedy, and the balance Pollack creates between humor and serious social and interpersonal issues makes the story moving as well as consistently entertaining.

Sydney Pollack and Dustin Hoffman in _Tootsie_ (Columbia, 1982).

Hoffman's comedic timing is excellent, and Teri Garr, Dabney Coleman, Bill Murray, Charles Durning and Jessica Lange (who won an Oscar for Best Supporting Actress) are all sharply defined and accessible characters. Pollack, in his role as Michael Dorsey's agent, enjoys several well-executed comedic scenes with Hoffman.

Pollack had refused to direct _Tootsie_ as it was originally presented to him. According to Pollack, "_Tootsie_ was a silly, stupid movie ... it had no point." While working with Gelbart and Hoffman on the script, Pollack finally located "a spine" for the film, i.e., that Michael Dorsey becomes a better man for having been a woman. With the armature for the film clearly defined, Pollack and his writers were able to create a character who moves from misogyny to sensitivity and finally to a sense of balance with regard to his own manhood and his relationships with women.

The essence of _Tootsie_ is in the characterization of "Dorothy." Hoffman believed that for the film to work he needed not only to look like a real woman (in order for the characters around him to believe he was a woman and not look ridiculous for doing so), but also to act like a real woman, i.e., to literally locate the woman inside of him. The question he asked himself repeatedly was, "What if I had been born a woman? What kind of woman would I be?"[5]

Hoffman had to bury himself in "Dorothy"; disappear into her disguises. Once Hoffman "found Dorothy," he and Pollack labored to find the "look" they needed. After several makeup artists, changes of lighting and wardrobe, and a delay in shooting, the visual image was finally achieved. That "look" was the key to the film, and casting was delayed until it was mastered.[6]

The heart of *Tootsie* is Michael's gradual re-evaluation of himself as a man, based on the new perceptions he has gained in his role as Dorothy Michaels. In effect, Michael, as "Dorothy," has been faced with seeing men through a woman's eyes, and he doesn't like what he sees. While "Dorothy" is subjected to stereotypic, degrading, chauvinistic treatment, Michael recognizes the same attitudes in himself. As "Dorothy" becomes friends with the women on the set, Michael learns that he has the capacity to be with and enjoy women on this level. Consequently, Michael's role-playing begins to free him from the behavior patterns which have limited him as a man. By the end of the film, Michael is open to integrating the wisdom and sensitivity of "Dorothy" into his male personality.

Pollack noted that he and his star disagreed on two points. The first involved "how much the world cares about the life of an actor." The second issue related to the tone of the film and how bawdy it should be. Pollack was concerned with the traps that the filmmakers could fall into in a film which depicted a female impersonator. He believed that the important theme involved in the film was the issue of Michael's transformation. Pollack wanted the film to add up to a metaphorical lesson.[7]

As the story goes, Michael Dorsey is unable to find work "on either coast" due to his tenacious integrity as an actor. He has alienated directors and producers in television and theater, and his agent cannot even get him an audition for a "dog commercial." Faced with unemployment, Michael auditions for the role of a woman administrator on the television soap opera *Southwest General*. What begins as an acting challenge becomes a game of deception. In the midst of Michael's deception, he falls in love with Julie (Jessica Lange), one of the co-stars, and, as "Dorothy" becomes a role model for the women on the show due to "her" assertive yet likeable style.

Confusion over gender issues creates several subplots which eventually drive Michael to reveal his identity. Two men are attracted to "Dorothy" believing she is a woman. John Van Horn (George Gaines) is a sleazy doctor on *Southwest General*. He finds "Dorothy's" assertiveness attractive and makes sexual advances toward "her." Julie's father (Charles Durning), a widower, is taken by "Dorothy's" homespun, Southern belle persona and asks "Dorothy" to marry him.

Julie, of course, believes "Dorothy" is a woman and the intimacies they share draw Michael into a desire for Julie, which eventually plays out as "Dorothy" initiating a lesbian encounter. Julie is repelled by the advance, and "Dorothy" tries to explain, but cannot disclose "her" real identity at this point, thus leaving the relationship shattered.

Michael has also initiated a relationship with Sandy (Teri Garr), a long-time friend and fellow actor. Sandy is not terribly stable, and Michael finds himself both supporting her as a friend and becoming sexually involved with her to hide his duplicity.

The villain in the film is Ron (Dabney Coleman), the soap opera director. Ron uses women at will and patronizes them on the set. Ron is Julie's boyfriend when Michael appears on the scene, and Michael's identification with Ron's traits, i.e., the way he treats women, is essential to Michael's redemption. As "Dorothy," Michael is on the receiving end of Ron's demeaning remarks and chauvinistic behavior. And more times than not, "Dorothy" finds a way to stand up to the director and reverse the submissiveness of the female characters as they appear in the script. "Dorothy" becomes a heroine and feminist role model, as the public responds to her strength and independence, and the show's ratings begin to rise.

While there are many humorous scenes in the film, one stands out among viewers as the most memorable, and at the same time sets the stage for the impersonation. It is a motivation scene, and without it, Michael would not have been driven to "put on a dress." The "tomato scene" forces Michael to the edge and to the most challenging role of his acting career.

Michael has just learned that his agent, George Fields (Pollack), has failed to secure a role for him on Broadway in *The Iceman Cometh*. Angered, Michael races over to his agent's office. The witty dialogue that ensues in Fields' office reveals Michael's idiosyncratic behavior as an actor. He played the part of a tomato for a commercial, and the production went a half a day over schedule because Michael would not sit down. The banter which continues between the two characters is filled with humor as well as revelation. The agent declares to Michael, "No one will hire you!" Michael replies, "Oh, yeah!" and walks out, determined to prove that his agent is wrong. Michael then becomes "Dorothy Michaels" and auditions for the role of Emily Kimberly on *Southwest General*.

Tootsie is a valid film, and it offers its audience a depth not often found in commercial comedies. Touching upon topics such as maturity, friendship as the basis of love, self-worth and self-perception, Pollack and his writers transformed the initial storyline into a sensitive, honest, relevant film that encourages personal growth and respect between the sexes.

"Dorothy" and Julie build a strong friendship based on trust, generosity, sharing and nurturing, which allows a special bonding to take place, a bonding only females share. As "Dorothy" experiences that bonding, the man inside of her responds with a sexual gesture — rather than an affectionate one. The gesture is misunderstood as a lesbian advance, and "Dorothy" loses Julie's trust.

"Dorothy" also serves as a role model for the women in the film who are "without power" or afraid to be assertive. Through "Dorothy," they begin to gain strength and self-respect, following "her" lead to make more constructive choices in their lives. An important change of character occurs in Julie, who ends her romantic involvement with her director boyfriend, a man who has continually been unfaithful and taken her for granted.

Pollack's use of a love story as a metaphor for opposing values is unique in *Tootsie*. While the literal love story is established between Julie and Michael, the metaphorical love story is between "Dorothy" and Michael, representing opposing points of view, fully developed characters living and loving within the same physical body.

Pollack's circular structure is apparent in the film as Michael finds himself still unemployed at the end of the picture. However, he has met his goal: to make enough money to produce his roommate's play. Michael's future as an actor and his relationship with Julie remain ambiguous. However, Julie begins to soften toward Michael as the film closes, and there is some indication that at least they might remain friends.

As Janet Lorenz remarked about the film, "*Tootsie* becomes a dazzlingly executed comedy that manages, if only for a moment, to cross the line that separates men and women."[8]

Chapter 16

Out of Africa (1985)

About the Production

OUT OF AFRICA was shot on location in Kenya, East Africa, with an estimated budget of $30 million. Principal photography was completed in approximately 112 days. Pollack made 11 trips to Nairobi the year before shooting commenced.

Out of Africa is to date Pollack's most critically acclaimed motion picture. The production won seven Academy Awards including Best Picture, Best Director, Best Screenplay, Sound, Cinematography, Art/Set Direction and Original Score. In addition, the film garnered numerous national and international acknowledgments from the National Board of Review, New York Critics, Los Angeles Critics, Golden Globes, Italian Silver Ribbon, David Di Donatello, United Kingdom BAFTA and United Kingdom Critics.

With *Out of Africa*, Pollack abandoned the wide-screen format.

Source of Material

The film is based on the book *Out of Africa* and other writings by Isak Dinesen, *Isak Dinesen: The Life of a Storyteller* by Judith Thurman and *Silence Will Speak* by Errol Trzebinski.

The project was around for many years, with such notable directors as Orson Welles and David Lean attempting to develop a screenplay that would capture the lyricism of Dinesen's writings. Kurt Luedtke, the Pulitzer Prize–winning journalist, was finally successful, and the film version of *Out of Africa* was born with Pollack at the helm.

According to her writings, from 1913 to 1931 Karen Blixen (Christentze Dinesen) lived in British East Africa (Kenya), where she ran a coffee plantation. She left Denmark and came to Africa to marry Baron Bror Blixen, the twin brother of the man she really loved. They were married on January 14, 1914, and divorced in 1921. During her time in Kenya, Karen developed a powerful emotional attachment to Denys Finch Hatton, an English earl's son.

Karen Blixen published in Danish under her married name, but used the male pseudonym Isak Dinesen in her English publications, reportedly "out of loyalty to her dead lover's language."[1] She died in 1962.

Synopsis

In Denmark, an elderly Baroness Blixen writes about her experiences in Africa. Through the use of flashback, her story unfolds. A youthful Karen joins Bror in Africa after he has secured a farm in the Ngong Hills. Instead of buying a dairy farm with Karen's mother's money, Bror has decided to plant coffee. Karen arrives in time for the wedding, then travels to her home where she is met by the natives who live near her farm and the native servants who will care for her and her household.

Karen and Bror's relationship is rocky and he stays away to hunt, leaving her to work the farm alone. In his absence, Karen develops a friendship with hunters Berkeley Cole and Denys Finch Hatton, who occasionally stop to visit her and share her fineries and her stories.

Karen contracts syphilis from Bror and returns to Denmark to be cured. When she comes back to Africa, she discovers Bror's continued infidelity and asks him to move into town. Once Karen is alone on the farm, Denys Finch Hatton initiates a liaison, taking Karen on safari. Their love affair becomes the central issue in the story.

After a time, Karen and Denys experience discord and finally separate. At the conclusion of the film, Bror has asked for a divorce, Denys has been killed and Karen's coffee crop has been destroyed. Financially devastated, Karen returns to Denmark.

Analysis

Pollack described the text of Dinesen's book, *Out of Africa*, as "an elegy. It's a piece of music as a book. It's not a story at all. Yet it's very powerful in terms of how it makes you feel when you read it and how you feel when it ends. You are just under a spell."

By employing the beautiful yet haunting language of the author as narration throughout the film, Pollack unified as well as mystified *Out of Africa* for his audience. Meryl Streep, in her role as Karen, captured the lyric quality of Dinesen's prose along with the courage, humor, vanity, vulnerability and elegance beneath it to help create the spell that Pollack was seeking. Streep presents "a full-bodied, thinking heroine we come to know and care about deeply."[2]

The original score, composed by John Barry, elicits the same spellbinding response, especially in the theme, which combines beauty with a melancholy that leaves the viewer with a mixed sense of gratitude and loss.

Pollack operates the smoke machine during a scene in *Out of Africa* (Universal, 1985).

The episodic script for *Out of Africa* engaged more of the art of Dinesen's life than its literal events. An epic romance, the film explores the fragile and transient nature of materialism and human relationships.

In *Out of Africa*, which Pollack described as a difficult shoot both physically and aesthetically, the relationship between Denys Finch Hatton and Karen Blixen is the core of the film, and their differing views of life provide the "argument." Using the love affair as a metaphor against the social and political domination of East Africa by the British in the early part of the twentieth century, Pollack explores the dialectic between freedom and possession. Who will "own" and dominate this country is the literal thread running through the film, while Denys and Karen personally play out the tension between freedom and ownership as the film progresses to its devastating ending.

The theme of freedom is cinematically captured in the landscape of Africa and mirrors the world view of Finch Hatton, the personification of personal freedom and self-realization. Behind the cinematic characterization of Finch Hatton is Pollack's interpretation of the man based on biographical sources. According to Pollack, there were a limited number of reasons why Finch Hatton would go to Africa: either he was a misfit (as a second son he was not going to inherit) or he was uncomfortable with the restrictions of a social order, its laws and norms. Pollack believed Finch Hatton came to Africa in

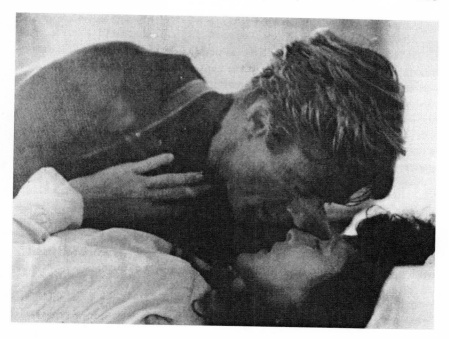

Top and Bottom: Robert Redford and Meryl Streep in *Out of Africa* (Universal, 1985).

order to be master of his own fate and to try "to live a life in which he paid no price, personally."

Ultimately, from the director's point of view, Finch Hatton's characterization allowed for the evolution of the central moral question of the film: Do you or do you not live your life knowing that the greater need is the collective one? As Pollack stated, "The minute you throw in your lot with one other person, you can't just think of yourself and your own needs."

Though Dinesen idealized him in her writings, Finch Hatton was known to be a dashing charmer whom everyone adored. It was also known that his charm was a coverup for his intense fear of emotional attachment.[3] In *Out of Africa*, Pollack and his writers created the arena for the exposition of Finch Hatton's fear of commitment by pitting him against Karen's possessiveness.

In the film, Finch Hatton lives in harmony with his environment, i.e., the land and the natives, due to his instinctive respect for the essence of life, which for him is based on freedom. This trait is dramatized when he allows a lioness to go unharmed rather than kill her as she approaches Karen in the wild, because he understands the habits and responses of the animal and wishes to preserve nature rather than destroy it. Ambiguity does arise in the character of Finch Hatton, however, since he also hunts for money. He walks a line between respecting nature and exploiting it, which adds complexity to his characterization.

In contrast, Karen's possessive and controlling instincts are dramatized in her attempts to stop the flow of the river with a dam, restrict the growth of the natural vegetation, conform the servants to her lifestyle (symbolized by forcing a servant to wear white gloves) and force schooling on the native children. Karen's possessions (her china and her crystal) are concrete representations of her materialistic orientation and her need to "own."

In addition, her possessive instincts blind Karen to the significance of Denys' love. She fears his absence from her, questions his intentions when Felicity wants to accompany him on a safari, and tells him that she hopes they will marry someday because "she wants to be worth something." Karen's European conventions of love and marriage contradict Denys' philosophy of freedom.

Denys balks at Karen's wifely instinct to mend his shirt and her jealousy over Felicity, which cause him to retreat. Yet his genuine love for her is unmistakable. Karen, however, cannot be satisfied with that love because of who she is.

Modern psychologist M. Scott Peck describes genuine love as that quality that "not only respects the individuality of the other but actually seeks to cultivate it, even at the risk of separation or loss."[4] In *Out of Africa*, Denys consistently validates Karen's personal worth and seeks to cultivate her individuality by contributing to her experiences and growth. Rather than stop her from traveling to see her husband, Denys gives her a compass to help her find her way, thus respecting her initiative and bravery. Appreciating her talent as a storyteller, he offers her a pen and encourages her to write down her stories. Denys shares with her a view of Africa from an airplane which teaches her that the human spirit, like the land, is meant to be free. He takes her on a safari, knowing that she will instinctively understand the grace and beauty of the land and its natural inhabitants before it is gone. He brings her a gramophone on which she can enjoy Mozart. He offers her romantic and sexual love. In reality, Denys helps free Karen's spirit and imagination, her emotions and her sexuality.

Impressed by the courage of Karen Blixen, whom he described as an "extraordinary woman" who turned "every tragedy into wisdom," Pollack and his screenwriters created a multi-faceted protagonist of strength and sensitivity, completely human and believable.

In the process of dimensionalizing the character, however, the writers did not deny Karen her imperfections. While she is truly a courageous woman, loveable and vulnerable, her aristocratic upbringing has made her arrogant, snobbish, demanding and materialistic. With no outlet for her intelligence and sensibilities in Denmark and her failure to marry, her life with Bror in Africa was an escape into a world of adventure and the challenges of a country dominated by men and under foreign rule.

Karen's creative mind and artistic sensibilities are what draw her to Denys, whose love of literature provides them with common ground. Through the relationship of these kindred spirits, both Karen and Denys find intimacy and spiritual and emotional happiness for a time. However, according to Pollack, while Finch Hatton is able to "learn from a strong, wise woman, he doesn't learn enough, and isn't finally able to overcome the last hurdle that it would take to be together."[5]

This incongruence is dramatized at the end of the film. Before their final parting, Karen and Denys discuss how each of them has changed. Karen has learned to let go of her possessions and Denys has "begun to like her things." Moreover, Denys admits that he is no longer happy living alone. As Karen leaves a political reception where she has begged the new governor to provide land for the natives, Karen tells Denys of her losses. For a brief moment she hopes that he will overcome his fear of commitment as he faces the realization that she is leaving Africa. But he cannot. When Karen asks Denys, "Would you keep me then?", he does not reply.

As in most of Pollack's films, there is no happy ending for the protagonists. Symbols of consumption bring the film to its unhappy conclusion, paralleling the consumption of the land and its natives by colonizers and hunters. Karen's fertility has been destroyed by syphilis, her coffee plantation burns to the ground, and Denys is killed in a fiery plane crash.

Having lost all that she valued, Karen is ready to accept the needlessness of ownership, finally understanding Denys' admonition that "we are not owners here."[6] As the director returns the protagonist to a state both physically and psychologically similar to where she began, Karen ends her journey as she initiated it in Denmark: an unmarried, childless woman with seemingly no future.

Top and Bottom: Two shots of Meryl Streep as Karen in *Out of Africa* (Universal, 1985).

Pollack at the 58th Academy Award Ceremony with his two Oscars—Best Picture and Best Director—for *Out of Africa* **(Universal, 1985).**

As the film ends, Karen has sold or given away all that remains of her possessions, including the compass which Denys gave her. Preparing to leave her farm for the last time, Karen's thoughts are of Africa, and in one of the film's most moving voiceovers, Pollack relates her relationship with this country which gave her life even as it consumed it:

> If I know a song of Africa, of the giraffe and the African new moon ... of the plows in the fields and the sweaty faces of the coffee pickers, does Africa know a song of me? Will the air over the plain

quiver with a color that I have had on, or the children invent a game
in which my name is, or the full moon throw a shadow over the
gravel of the drive that was like me, or will the eagles of the Ngong
Hills look out for me?[7]

Danish aristocrat, wife, businesswoman, farmer, nurse, adventurer, storyteller, writer and lover, Karen Blixen in Pollack's version of *Out of Africa*
experienced all that life could offer except motherhood, which she chose to live
vicariously through the school she started for the native children. A completely
human character with the strengths, frailties and moments of heroism common to the human condition, Karen Blixen is Sydney Pollack's most fully
developed female protagonist.

Havana (1990)

About the Production

UNABLE TO shoot the film in Cuba, Pollack began principal photography in Santo Domingo, Dominican Republic, on November 22, 1989. Shooting was completed on April 28, 1990. *Havana* was introduced at the International Festival of New Latin American Cinema from December 4–17, 1990, and at the Brussels International Film Festival, January 9–19, 1991.

Source of Material

Havana was based on an original screenplay first read as character sketches in 1976 by the director. The story was created by Judith Roscoe. Credit for the screenplay is shared by Roscoe and David Rayfiel.

Synopsis

Havana recreates an era in the style of *Casablanca*, this time exploring political turmoil in Cuba during the end of the Batista regime (circa 1958). Lena Olin in her role as Bobby Duran plays a principled foreigner — a Swede — married to Arturo, a Cuban aristocrat and revolutionary (Raul Julia, uncredited). Dedicated to her husband's cause, i.e., the overthrow of Batista and the imposition of Fidel Castro as the leader of a liberated Cuba, Bobby enlists the services of American gambler Jack Weil (Robert Redford), whom she meets on a ferry to Havana. Through Weil, Bobby is able to smuggle radios onto the island. Weil, who is in Cuba to set up a high-stakes poker game, becomes intrigued with the woman and is awakened by her principles. The film successfully compares the two Cubas which exist side-by-side in the late 1950s: the hedonistic culture represented by Weil and his constituents versus the oppressed citizenry represented by Bobby and Arturo.

After Weil drives Bobby's car off the ferry and into Havana and the police fail to locate the contraband, Weil propositions her. Uninterested, she turns him down and Weil heads for the casinos to set up a poker game. The viewer is introduced to the glamour and decadence of Havana through Weil's associations with casino managers, high rollers and female American tourists on the make.

When Bobby and Arturo are arrested and the husband is presumed dead, Weil becomes interested in Bobby's whereabouts. Fortunately, he plays poker with the police officials, which gives him an advantage in locating and securing Bobby's release.

After being tortured and interrogated, Bobby leaves the prison and Weil takes her to his apartment to recuperate from her traumatic experience. Believing that Arturo is dead, Weil pursues Bobby as she returns to the country to join the rebels in the midst of the revolution. After a plea for her to save him from his empty life, Weil brings Bobby back to Havana to arrange her safe escape from Cuba.

When Weil learns that Arturo is still alive, he devises a scheme to secure his release. Bobby returns to her husband, the coup is successful, the casinos are trashed by the revolutionaries, and Weil returns to Florida alone.

Analysis

Havana was a long-awaited love story, promising the exotic locations and lyricism of *Out of Africa*. A commercial failure, the film discussed some important themes against a political backdrop that could have delivered on its promises. However, neither the love story nor the characterization of Bobby Duran worked beyond a superficial level. Since it followed on the heels of *Out of Africa*, perhaps too much was expected of the film, despite the love the director had for the characters of Bobby Duran and Jack Weil.

Filmed on location in the Dominican Republic, *Havana* was something of a dream to Pollack. He first read the characters of Jack and Bobby as sketches in 1976. Their memory lingered through the years. Pollack describes *Havana* as...

> ...the same film I have been making over and over for twenty-five years, in the sense of the love story ... the argument between two people ... in the sense that it's the woman who knows the way, and it is the man who is trying to learn it. Jack Weil is very close to the other characters Redford has played. It's sort of the end of the road for the same guy. In this case it dealt with a guy too old to be doing what he is doing, a guy trying to continue a way of life that he was way past being able to be satisfied by, but didn't know what to replace it with. It had all the ache that I look for.

Jack Weil is an amoral gambler, with no ambitions or convictions outside his gambling and sexual appetites. Yet, once he meets a deeply-principled woman committed to the revolution, he begins to be transformed ethically and philosophically. As the sensual, hedonistic lifestyle of the Batista regime comes to an end with the success of the revolution, Weil's presence as witness to the historic moment mirrors his realization that something is over for him as well.

Crude language, sleazy bars and sexual situations were added to the film, albeit with some restraint, to provide the flavor of exploitation and corruption that the city of Havana epitomized in 1958, the element from which Weil could be redeemed through his association with Bobby.

The film is set in counterpoint, and through his effective use of cross-cutting, Pollack aptly creates two Havanas: one which supports corruption and decadence, the other which seeks liberation from oppression.

The corruption of Havana is represented in the hedonistic elements of the American presence in Cuba lived out through Weil and his gambling associates. Meyer Lansky's name surfaces as the mob leader who controls Havana's casinos. Further corruption is revealed in the Cuban government and the police. Everyone can be bought.

In contrast, the film dramatizes the systematic torture and murder of the citizens by government agents as well as the ardor of the revolutionaries, rich and poor, in their efforts to end their oppression and overthrow Batista. Bobby and her husband, Arturo, a Cuban aristocrat, identify with the ideals of the revolutionaries and aid the efforts of the Castroites to effect a coup, completing the opposing force in the dialectic.

One of the principal criticisms of the film involved the failure of the love story to really work. Upon reflection, the characterization of Bobby Duran may be the underlying cause of the inefficacy of the love story.

While movies ask the viewer to suspend disbelief in certain circumstances, sometimes the "truth" of the moment as experienced by a viewer will not allow the leap to be made. Such a case can be made for reading the character of Bobby Duran and her "love affair" with Jack Weil.

Bobby's characterization allows for the introduction of a love story to serve as Pollack's metaphor for opposing points of view and, concurrently, a vehicle for Weil's redemption. But it undermines the value of what could have been a remarkable and powerful character. It can be argued that the characterization of Bobby in *Havana* is inconsistent with Pollack's other films which feature a strong female protagonist (*The Way We Were, Out of Africa*), because, in this case, the female character's strength, i.e. Bobby's moral courage, is sacrificed in order for the male protagonist to be redeemed. In his other films, Pollack never devalues the woman's morality to redeem the man.

In *Havana*, the script presents us with a believable Jack Weil, whose attraction to Bobby is easy to accept. However, the reverse is not the case. Questions are quickly raised about a woman who survived torture and a war-torn countryside, but who can't say no to a man who looks like Robert Redford. Why would Bobby involve herself with Weil and succumb to a sexual liaison with a man she doesn't know and with whom she has nothing in common? Where is it established that her marriage is unfulfilling sexually, so that the motivation for her "love-in" with Weil could be due to sexual repression, as some critics have assumed? And finally, why would she abandon the cause and the people for whom she was willing to be tortured and die, because her husband is dead? Wouldn't one expect his death to motivate her to stick it out — for her husband's sake, if no one else's? What ever happened to loyalty?

The script weakens Bobby's personal virtue by linking her revolutionary commitment to loyalty to her husband rather than a sincere belief in their cause. With this choice, the filmmakers sacrifice Bobby's integrity for Weil's nobility, devaluing the character's inspirational qualities and her inherent dignity.

All of Pollack's characters are flawed, just as all human beings are flawed. One of his strengths as a filmmaker lies in developing characters who are real, human, accessible and believable. But the key to Pollack's multidimensional female characters lies in the wisdom of their choices. By allowing Bobby to agree to leave the country and succumb to Weil's advances, the director ultimately lost her to his audience.

In terms of social commentary, the film sends a dangerous message by inferring that no one — not even a seemingly committed revolutionary — can resist sexual temptation. The inference that those who love on a spiritual or idealistic plane are somehow repressed or unfulfilled as whole human beings supports dualistic thinking. It is a stereotype which devalues those who respect their commitments and obligations, who do not succumb to casual sexual liaisons at vulnerable moments in their lives, and who have the strength to sacrifice their own needs for the good of others.

Sacrifice for the greater good is a theme which runs through *Havana*, yet the picture fails to present us with a "consistently faithful" Bobby Duran whom we ultimately can respect.

The filmmakers might argue that the "humanity" of the characters (namely a physical attraction, a moment of vulnerability, a loss of direction) validates the characters' sexual involvement and tentative love story. On the contrary, the film suggests the value chosen was the extraction of Weil's nobility (so he could win her, then give her up) and the inclusion of an obligatory love scene, elevated by using it as a device to reflect Weil's ability to turn lust to romance. One wonders what might have happened if Arturo Duran had really died and Bobby had left Havana with Weil. What would the future have been like for these two radically different people?

Thus, *Havana* leaves us with a film ripe with contradictions and messages which (on the surface) seem noble and inspiring, but (at a deeper level) lower our expectations of ourselves and our society.

Critics have also commented on the absence of the character of Arturo Duran, the aristocrat and Bobby's husband. Raul Julia played the role unbilled, and his character was one which some critics believed was overlooked for

Tomas Gutierrez Alea (left), advisor for the film *Havana* (Universal, 1990), speaks with Pollack on the set.

development. In spite of his limited screen time, Duran is a powerful character; further development for the purposes of the storyline might have been intriguing. Had *Havana* integrated Arturo and his revolutionaries, it might have been better received by American audiences.

What is best about *Havana* is reflected in Pollack's film art. The director's presentation of the two Havanas, which he juxtaposes throughout the film, is powerful, effective and consistent. One cross-cutting sequence is most notable.

Jack Weil is drinking and involved in a sexual liaison with two female American tourists. During the tryst, Pollack repeatedly cuts to the revolutionaries who are being arrested and murdered by the Batista regime. Weil's pleasure-seeking is made all the more repulsive by the visualization of the revolution's brutality. Thus, as the party goes on in the casinos or in Weil's apartment, the future of the country hangs in the balance.

The film's climax, although somewhat underplayed, is noteworthy. Weil discovers that Bobby's husband is alive. Upon returning to her, he knows he must tell her the truth and lose her in the process. As Bobby leaves Weil's apartment, it is apparent that the revolution has succeeded, for the people are rejoicing in the streets. Pollack slows down the action as Bobby moves through the crowd, re-connecting emotionally with her commitment to the revolution. Pollack then cuts to Weil moving against the crowd. No longer detached from his feelings for others, Weil, though still isolated, reflects through Redford's subtle but perceptive expression and movement the pain of the loss of Bobby as well as the realization of what is happening to Havana and the lifestyle to which he has grown accustomed.

While *Havana* is disappointing in some ways and its characters never seem real, Pollack's examination of the "two Havanas" makes the picture worthwhile. The director's usual circular structure is present in the storyline as Jack returns to Florida whence he came and Bobby returns to her husband and the "people," metaphorically representing the characters' inability to change. However, as the epilogue discloses that Jack remains a gambler, it also reveals that he now reads human interest stories in the newspaper.

The melancholy so characteristic of the director's poetic nature is present in the final scene, as Weil stands on a Florida beach and looks out over the ocean toward Cuba, hopeful that Bobby may be "blown off course" and cross his path again.

Finally, *Havana* presents its audience with a moral question, which is a recurring concern for Pollack. Jack Weil is its symbol in *Havana*, just as Denys Finch Hatton is its symbol in *Out of Africa*: "Do you or do you not live your life knowing that the greater need is the collective one?"

The Firm (1993)

About the Production

PRINCIPAL PHOTOGRAPHY began on November 9, 1992, and was completed on March 20, 1993. Locations included Memphis, the Cayman Islands, Boston and Washington, D.C.

The film was released on June 30, 1993, *Variety* reported a cumulative box office total of $117.9 million on July 27, 1993. By August 26, *The Firm* had earned $144.9 million.

Robin Wright was originally cast in the role of Abby McDeere, and Meryl Streep was mentioned at one time to play a female version of Avery Tolar, the womanizing attorney and Mitch McDeere's mentor.

Paramount purchased the film rights to novelist John Grisham's *The Firm* for a reported $600,000. Tom Cruise is said to have been paid $12,000,000 to star as Mitch McDeere.[1]

Source of Material

The film was based on John Grisham's best-seller *The Firm.*

Synopsis

McDeere (Tom Cruise), a graduate of Harvard Law School, is wooed by the Memphis law firm of Bendini, Lambert and Locke. Impressed by their Southern "hospitality," the high salary and amenities, Mitch takes the job. His wife Abby (Jeanne Tripplehorn) is not charmed by the lawyers in the firm nor impressed by the promise of wealth, but she accepts her husband's choice.

As their life in Memphis begins, Abby discovers the control which the firm exerts over its employees and their families, and Mitch learns from the FBI that he has been duped by a slick group of lawyers who have ties to the mob and readily eliminate lawyers who disapprove of their shady dealings. The firm has tapped Mitch's telephone, he is followed, and he is set up and photographed in a sexual liaison with a stranger in the Cayman Islands. The photographs provide blackmail material with which to control Mitch just in case (as Tolar comments) "the usual inducements don't work."[2]

The blackmail photographs box Mitch in from one side, while the FBI threatens him from another. Wayne Tarrance (Ed Harris) is an FBI agent bent on exposing the corruption within the firm and bringing down the mob. Tarrance threatens to deny Mitch's brother's parole in an effort to force his cooperation. Meanwhile, two lawyers in the firm are killed in a boating accident, raising suspicion as to the culpability of the firm in their deaths.

Unable to keep his infidelity from his wife, Mitch confesses his liaison in the Cayman Islands, and this leads to their estrangement. Knowing that the firm has bugged their home and car and aware that Devasher (Wilford Brimley) is listening to their conversations, Abby prepares to leave Memphis under the pretext of her mother's illness.

As the pressures mount, Mitch devises an intricate plan (which only a Harvard graduate could conceive) which frees his brother, indicts the firm on mail fraud charges for overbilling their clients, neutralizes the mob, saves himself and his career from destruction and reestablishes a relationship with his wife.

Action takes place in three locations while Mitch's plan advances. Tammy and Abby are in the Cayman Islands to copy files, Ray McDeere is being released from prison in Louisiana and is on his way out of the country, and Mitch is in Memphis eluding the firm, confronting the mob and dealing with the FBI.

Unknown to Mitch, Abby becomes involved with Tammy in their scheme to copy the "files" in the Cayman Islands which the FBI need to indict the firm. Abby goes to the Caymans to sidetrack Tolar in a false romantic interlude, allowing Tammy access to the files. But the files do not offer Mitch enough information to indict the firm. He must return to the office and access Tolar's computer for information.

As Mitch is locating the missing information on Tolar's computer, Devasher discovers a FAX sent by a prison guard regarding Ray McDeere's release. Realizing that Mitch "cut a deal" with the FBI, he informs Lambert, and the partners close in on Mitch. A phone call from Tarrance alerts Mitch to the firm's knowledge of his actions, and he begins to run.

After evading the firm's henchmen, Mitch visits the Peabody Hotel and meets with the Morolto brothers. Convincing them of his silence with regard to their illegal business dealings (money laundering) under attorney-client privilege, he asks for the release of their billing records in order to indict the firm for overbilling their clients.

Tarrance and McDeere have a concluding scene in which Mitch explains how knowing and using the law actually saved him. In an ironic twist, the emphasis the firm placed on passing the bar exam served to bury them. Mail fraud was a topic on the exam.

Abby returns and Mitch discovers he has not lost his wife. The two pack and leave Memphis en route to Boston.

Analysis

The Firm is one of Pollack's more literal as well as complex films. While it belongs to the thriller genre, and the characters are not developed to the extent of his more artistic pictures, *The Firm* is significantly more dimensionalized than *Three Days of the Condor.* Since motivations are key to understanding the complex plot, Pollack and his writers added depth to the characters of Mitch McDeere, Avery Tolar and Abby McDeere in order to enlist the viewer's sympathies and understanding of the characters' choices.

Pollack liked the character of Mitch McDeere. As he stated in an interview on the *South Bank Show*, people identify with the character because he epitomizes the American Dream. Mitch McDeere is a continuation of the tradition in American films which pits the individual against a bureaucracy. The protagonist always fights against corruption, whether as the "loner cowboy," the private detective or the idealistic lawyer.

Mitch's version of the American Dream is reflected in a career which is "perfect and shiny on the outside with all the accoutrements of prestige and wealth associated with the position." Mitch has a low-interest mortgage, a Mercedes and a country club membership, and the firm will pay off his student loans. But underneath the surface, "everything is corrupt and rotten."[3]

Pollack supported this character's resonance when he stated that "we came out of the '80s with a kind of resentment ... anger ... and disillusionment. We discovered that lawmakers are as corrupt as lawbreakers."[4]

As Grisham's novel sold more and more copies, Pollack became increasingly concerned with taking on the project. He recognized that he had two obstacles to overcome in making the film: it was a best-selling novel and, as in any film adaptation, he had to make choices which would necessitate changing the storyline and the characters.

The issue of compression in adapting the book to film was a daunting enterprise in itself. As Pollack noted, it was a 500-page novel, filled with characters essential to the fabric of the piece. Pollack stated in more than one interview that he was uncomfortable changing Grisham's novel, and he was concerned with audience reaction. Nevertheless, Pollack made two important alterations: he expanded Abby McDeere's character in order to accommodate his own need for a love story, and he significantly altered the ending. Changing the ending required radical changes to the story from the middle on.

One significant change involved the infidelity. The Cayman Islands seduction scene that takes place on the beach was not confessed in the book. Due to his need to create some version of a love story, Pollack chose to have Mitch

Pollack coaches Tom Cruise for a scene in *The Firm* **(Paramount, 1993).**

confess the infidelity in order to create an estrangement. From the estrangement, a love story would develop and the opportunity for Mitch to redeem himself.

Another issue which concerned Pollack in his adaptation was the logic of the story, which he did not believe would hold up in a visual medium. Consequently, he attempted to pull away every possible piece of foundation, eliminate every "out" for the protagonist, so that the audience would believe Mitch had no choice but the one that he made. To support this approach, Pollack added a "layer of force" to Mitch's circumstances by developing the connection between Mitch's incarcerated brother Ray (David Strathairn) and private detective Eddie Lomax (Gary Busey).

The result of the adaptation was a well-executed, suspenseful drama, complex enough to keep the viewer from guessing the ending. While there was some controversy among critics over the believability of the ending and the clarity of Mitch's plan to outwit and outrun the firm and the FBI, the film was successful in its attempt to treat the original themes in the book.

As in all Pollack films, the love relationship serves as a metaphor for the opposing points of view in the story. While the theme of the film concerns legal corruption, the armature or spine of the story rests in the simply expressed question of social status and its recipe for genuine happiness, played out handsomely between Mitch and Abby.

The film is clear in its revelation about the characters' motives for making

Tom Cruise on the run in *The Firm* (Paramount, 1993).

the choices they make. Mitch McDeere is driven by a fear of inadequacy. He hails from a poor family, has a brother who is in jail for manslaughter and a mother who lives in a trailer park. In addition, his wife comes from a wealthy family, and Mitch believes she has given up her social position to marry him. Mitch is also extremely bright, finishing fifth in his class at Harvard. He is in demand as he graduates, and although he is offered many different opportunities, he chooses the one which pays the most and requires the most of him personally. A victim of his own ambition, Mitch pays a price for his decision to go to Memphis. He loses his wife's trust and nearly his career and his own life.

Abby McDeere, played by Jeanne Tripplehorn, is an elementary schoolteacher, raised in a wealthy Southern family. While supportive of her husband, Abby has the wisdom to know that wealth and the symbols of wealth given to Mitch by the firm will not fix the "hole" he has inside him.

Hal Holbrook as Oliver Lambert leads the pack of corrupt lawyers, with Gene Hackman serving as Mitch's mentor. Hackman's Avery Tolar has an eye for women, including Mitch's wife, and Pollack is able to bring depth to his character through the telephone conversations Tolar has with his estranged wife. In this way, the audience gains some sympathy for Tolar, recognizing his fundamental decency—a decency which has been corrupted by his association with the firm.

Ed Harris portrays the tough FBI investigator Wayne Tarrance, who pressures Mitch into exposing the firm. Harris' role is stereotyped, and he does not gain the viewer's sympathy. On the contrary, Tarrance epitomizes the unsavory methods of governmental agencies in their intimidation and ruthless pursuit of their own ends. Tarrance cannot be trusted and Mitch knows it. This relationship is reminiscent of Pollack's other films, such as *Absence of Malice, The Way We Were* and *Three Days of the Condor*, which illustrate the paradox of the individual's need to stand up to the bureaucracy which has been established to "serve and protect."

Holly Hunter's Tammy Hemphill is the feisty, brassy secretary of private detective Eddie Lomax. Lomax, who is also Hemphill's lover, is murdered by hitmen after they discover his association with Mitch's incarcerated brother. After witnessing the murder, Tammy becomes involved in Mitch's scheme to free his brother and indict the firm.

Since *The Firm* is a thriller, Pollack developed a monorail scene as an equivalent of the western "gunfight." Mitch is trying to escape the hitmen and he boards a tram from Mud Island. Pollack used a mini-cam and a dirt bike to effect the cross-cutting rhythm between Mitch (thinking deeply) and his pursuers (who are running to catch him). According to Pollack, no special effects or hi-tech devices were used in this sequence.

The circular structure of the film is played out with Mitch and Abby leaving Memphis in their battered old car at the end of the film, just as they arrived. At the film's conclusion, Mitch finds himself unemployed and looking for a new start in his marriage as well as his career.

An entertaining thriller, *The Firm* captures the themes of Grisham's novel while putting its own spin on the characters and their escape from a world destined to destroy them. Pollack focuses on the destructiveness of a man's choices in the character of Mitch McDeere. Reminiscent of some of Pollack's other male protagonists, Mitch joins Jeremiah Johnson, Sonny Steele (*The Electric Horseman*), Bobby Deerfield and Hubbell Gardiner (*The Way We Were*) as characters who find themselves victimized by their own choices.

Chapter 19

Sabrina (1995)

About the Production

PRINCIPAL PHOTOGRAPHY began January 30, 1995, and was completed June 21, 1995. Locations included Long Island and New York City; Paris, France; and Martha's Vineyard, Massachusetts. The summer release date was rescheduled, and *Sabrina* premiered on December 15, 1995. *Variety* reported that *Sabrina* had earned $20.8 million at the box office by December 28, 1995.[1]

The Larrabee mansion seen in the film is an estate on Long Island Sound called Salutation. Built in 1929 by Junius Spencer Morgan, a grandson of J. Pierpont, it was vacant and under renovation in 1995. The production crew added a wing onto the garage (Sabrina's childhood home) and also completed an outdoor ballroom.

High-powered lighting encircling the site was provided by a mini-power plant installed on the property. The bright lights confused the local birds as to the time of day, and they proceeded to chirp all night. However, the noise from the tree frogs was more of a problem during shooting. To alleviate the frog problem, prop men would hit the ground beneath the trees with two-by-fours to temporarily quiet the frogs before the shooting of dialogue scenes.[2]

Scott Rudin noted in an interview with *Premiere* that Pollack did not want a star to play the role of Sabrina. "[B]ecause of the whole Audrey Hepburn thing, I think he felt he'd have a better chance of being judged freshly without the baggage of a name."[3]

The three finalists for the role of Sabrina were Juliette Binoche, Darcey Bussell and Julia Ormond. Due to an ear infection, Ormond was confined to a London hospital during the filming of *First Knight*, which enabled her to audition for the role of Sabrina.

The remake of *Sabrina* alerted the fashion world although Ann Roth, the picture's costume designer, noted that "fashion in this film is a non-event."[4] Roth created clothes based on Ormond's style. Sabrina dressed the part of a high school girl on Long Island, and when she went to Paris it was important that she appear to be a misfit in that world of fashion.

Kenneth Turan of the *Los Angeles Times* was unconvinced by Ormond's dowdy clothing and glasses which he felt were overplayed in contrast to the earlier version where Audrey Hepburn "looked girlish one moment, and devastating the next."[5]

Source of Material

Pollack's *Sabrina* was based on the 1954 Billy Wilder film (adapted by Billy Wilder, Samuel Taylor and Ernest Lehman from the play *Sabrina Fair* by Samuel Taylor). The original film starred Audrey Hepburn, William Holden and Humphrey Bogart.

The genesis of the film began with a script being developed by Scott Rudin, who eventually produced the new *Sabrina*. Working on a script with screenwriter Barbara Benedek, Rudin described the love triangle by saying, "It should be like *Sabrina*." After Benedek watched the original Wilder version, she suggested that they do the remake. Paramount concurred (they produced the original) and rewrites began. Once Pollack was on board, his frequent screenwriting collaborator David Rayfiel joined Benedek to create a more realistic and contemporary picture within the confines of the fairy tale.[6]

Synopsis

A young woman, Sabrina Fairchild (Julia Ormond), is raised on the Larrabee estate on Long Island. Her father (John Wood) is a British chauffeur who works for the wealthy family. All her life, Sabrina has adored David Larrabee (Greg Kinnear), the handsome younger son of Maude Larrabee (Nancy Marchand). She is consumed by the fantasy that one day she will be noticed and loved by David. After leaving high school, Sabrina spends some time in Paris in the employ of a friend at *Vogue* magazine. Her Paris experiences help her to grow and to begin to discover her own unique gifts. Sabrina develops an interest in photography as well as a love for Paris and its romantic enchantments.

When she returns to Long Island, Sabrina has matured. Upon her arrival home, she is swept into a continuation of her fantasy with David Larrabee, only to be diverted by his engagement to a wealthy pediatrician, Elizabeth Tyson (Lauren Holly). The merger of the two wealthy families is imminent, and older brother and CEO Linus Larrabee (Harrison Ford) views the marriage as a profitable business deal, since the Tysons own the patent on an indestructible flat panel television screen.

Fearful that Sabrina may interfere with the pending marriage (and wreck the merger), Linus attempts to seduce her with a trip to Martha's Vineyard. As Sabrina's fondness for Linus grows, she discovers his plan to abandon her.

In the end, it is Linus, the heartless industrialist obsessed with making money, who falls in love with Sabrina. Leaving his business dealings in the hands of his brother, Linus follows her to Paris, and they all live happily ever after.

Analysis

Unlike any previous Pollack films, *Sabrina* is a fairy-tale with a happy ending for all major characters in the story. It is beautifully photographed and scored, and these cinematic elements create a romantic and charming world in which dreams *can* come true.

Unlike Pollack's other films, *Sabrina* does not explore an important political, social or philosophical issue. It is a simple, romantic comedy combining aspects of the Cinderella myth with that of the Ugly Duckling. While the new *Sabrina* briefly elicits some discussion about the "merging" of someone of wealth with a "servant" — a theme central to the original version — this issue is dismissed rather early in the film as irrelevant in the present day.

Pollack was not eager to do a remake of Billy Wilder's 1954 film. "People are very unforgiving about remakes, particularly of something like *Sabrina*. So many people were so charmed by it. I said no two or three times."[7]

Pollack approached the remake as a challenge. Billy Wilder's version "never told how it would be possible for this young girl and this rigid money-obsessed man to fall in love." While it was inferred, the audience did not see the process. Pollack was interested in dramatizing that part of the love story.

The director also wanted to see if he could make the film more contemporary. He tried to combine disparate elements, to tell a fairy-tale in an age of cynicism and conglomerates. Pollack set a love story in the middle of the world of high finance with a character who is obsessed with making money. The merging of a woman who believes in romance with the entrepreneur established the spine of the picture for Pollack, satisfying his requirement for the interplay of opposing forces.

Pollack's view of the world of high finance, the multinational conglomerate and vertical integration influenced his cinematic choices:

> Nothing is fragmented any more.... If you make entertainment, you need to own all the delivery systems. There is a kind of warfare that exists in this type of doing business. There is nothing sentimental or romantic about it.

To bring the picture into the 1990s, the writers had to transform the characters. For example, the female characters were dimensionalized. Audrey Hepburn in the 1954 *Sabrina* was a kitchen servant — a "graduate" of the Cordon Bleu cooking school. In 1995, Julie Ormond's character spends some time working for *Vogue* magazine in France and discovers a talent for photography. In addition, David's fiancée, Elizabeth Tyson is a successful pediatrician. Pollack also eliminated the father figure in the Larrabee household and developed Maude Larrabee as the tough and outspoken matriarch of the Larrabee dynasty.

Additional script changes called for Linus Larrabee to inhabit the world of hi-tech communications rather than sugar cane and plastics. According to Scott Rudin, Pollack related to the character of Linus through his own associations with archetypal corporate executives, individuals "whose ferociousness in [their] work was electrifying to be around."[8]

The character of David Larrabee, Sabrina's object of desire, is that of the quintessential romantic. He is obsessed with women, leisure and entertainment. David never goes to the office. In the role of the playboy, Greg Kinnear (host of NBC's late-night talk show *Later*) is charming and warm, characteristics to which Sabrina is attracted. When David is reintroduced to Sabrina after her return from Paris, he is drawn to her beauty and the idea of romance. Caught up in the moment, he is willing to forget his commitment to his fiancée to woo Sabrina.

David appears irresponsible. However, due to his brother's entrepreneurial fanaticism, David has assumed the only role available, i.e. Linus' alter ego. David lives off the family fortune and romances the ladies until Linus is swept away by his love for Sabrina.

Pollack attempted to ground his film in more realistic terms than the 1954 version, but the transformation of Sabrina from schoolgirl to mature womanhood was not clearly motivated for a 1990s audience. Sabrina begins to relinquish her childish fantasies during her time in Paris. Her new experiences add breadth and depth to her emerging sense of identity, and also offer her a larger world through which to view her infatuation with David. She learns from the strong women she meets in Europe as well as from the photographer with whom she attempts an affair. However, the audience is asked to suspend disbelief when Sabrina arrives in New York dressed and coiffed as if she is a woman in her thirties. Here is where the fairy-tale re-emerges.

The film also takes on mythic overtones. Linus and Sabrina discuss the derivation of her name while flying in his private jet to Martha's Vineyard. She explains that her name came from a poem. In the poem, Sabrina is a saviour, one who saves a virgin from a fate worse than death.

The symbolism of the poem refers to the role Sabrina will play in saving Linus from his destructive lifestyle. He is uninitiated in his experience of personal relationships, having dealt only with business affairs. Sabrina has been initiated into the larger world by living in Paris and experiencing romance. It is she who will offer that experience to Linus. Linus acknowledges Sabrina's place in his redemption as he says in mythical language, "Save me, Sabrina-fair. You are the only one who can."

There is a de-romanticization or de-mythologizing which takes place in *Sabrina*. In literary criticism, the breaking of the concrete symbol representing a character's psyche accompanies the process of de-mythology. The champagne flutes accompanying the ritual seduction of women in the solarium are David's concrete symbol of his psyche. The breaking of the glasses symbolizes the end of David's pattern and the end of his lifestyle.

Illusion plays a major role in the characterization of Sabrina. Sabrina's romantic nature is demonstrated as she moves from one illusion to another. First there is David, with whom she is obsessed; then there is Paris, which she views through rose-colored glasses; then there is Linus, whom she believes she has changed.

The emerging relationship between Sabrina and Linus Larrabee reveals some Freudian overtones, according to film critic Roger Ebert. He noted in his review of *Sabrina* that Linus would presumably be much older than Sabrina, and her interest in him would mirror her need to find a replacement figure for her chauffeur father.[9]

Strong women inhabit the world of *Sabrina*. Maude Larrabee, Elizabeth Tyson and Sabrina's Paris mentor are independent, decisive and wise women. Sabrina as the force that initiates Linus' transformation maintains Pollack's vision of a wise woman who must show the man the error of his ways. Unlike the women in Pollack's other films, Sabrina is not particularly strong, yet Ormond's portrayal reveals a potentiality for strength amid the naiveté, sensitivity and vulnerability so organic to the character.

What is most evocative about Pollack's *Sabrina* is the production design, especially the environment created at the Larrabee mansion in the party sequences. These scenes are incredibly romantic; one has the sense of being in the midst of the party, the atmosphere is so well-defined.

Pollack's circular structure is not engaged in *Sabrina*, as the fairy tale and its happy ending require that all characters change rather than return to their former psychological states. Linus is redeemed by coming into touch with things of the heart, which is the transformation required by the conventions of the story. The other characters simply fall into place around him.

Sabrina combines light-hearted, high-quality entertainment with constructive values in a modern context, making the picture suitable for all members of the family. Highlights of the production include John Williams' enchanting score, exquisite cinematography, production design and fine performances by Harrison Ford, Julia Ormond, Greg Kinnear and an admirable supporting cast.

Filmography

Acting Credits

1. *War Hunt* (1962)
   Produced by United Artists and T.D. Enterprises. Released through United Artists. Genre: War/drama. Running time: 81 minutes.

   Credits: Producer: Terry Sanders. Director: Denis Sanders. Screenplay: Stanford Whitmore. Director of Photography: Ted McCord. Music: Bud Shank. Editors: John Hoffman, Edward Dutko. Art Director: Edgar Lansbury. Assistant Director: Jack Bohrer. Sound: Roy Meadows. Picture Vehicle Driver: Francis Ford Coppola. Electrics Grip: Noel Black.

   Cast: John Saxon (Private Raymond Endore), Robert Redford (Private Roy Loomis), Charles Aidman (Cpt. Wallace Pratt), Sydney Pollack (Sgt. Van Horn), Gavin MacLeod (Private Crotty), Tommy Matsuda (Charlie), Tom Skerritt (Cpl. Showalter), Tony Ray (Private Fresno)

2. *Tootsie* (1982) See **Directing Credits**.

3. *The Player* (1992)
   Avenue Pictures in association with Spelling Entertainment. A David Brown/Addis-Weschler Production. Genre: Comedy. Running time: 123 minutes. Rating: R.

   Credits: Producer: David Brown, Michael Tolkin, Nick Wechsler. Co-producer: Scott Bushnell. Co-Executive Producer: William S. Gilmore. Executive Producer: Cary Brokaw. Director: Robert Altman. Screenwriter: Michael Tolkin (from his novel *The Player*). Director of Photography: Jean Lepine. Editors: Geraldine Peroni. Music: Thomas Newman. Production Design: Stephen Altman. Art Director: Jerry Fleming. Set Decorator: Susan Emshwiller. Wardrobe Designer: Alexander Julian. Associate Producer: David Levy. Unit Production Manager: Tom Udell. 1st Assistant Director: Allan Nichols. 2nd Assistant Director: C.C. Barnes. Apprentice Editor: Dylan Tichenor. Supervising Sound Editor: Michael Redbourn. Film Editor: Maysie Hoy. Production Executives: Claudia Lewis, Pamela Hedley. Production Supervisor: Jim Chesney. Leadman: Peter Borck. Location Manager: Jack Kney. 1st Assistant Camera: Robert Reed Altman. 2nd Assistant Camera: Cary McKrystal. 3rd Assistant Camera: Craig Finetti. Karaoke Videos:

Larry "Doc" Karman. Assistant Editor: A. Michelle Page. 2nd Assistant Editor: Alisa Hale. Dialogue Editors: Joseph Holsen, Ed Lachmann. Sound Effects Editor: Ken Burton. Assistant Sound Editor: Bill Ward. Music Editor: Bill Bernstein. Music Scoring Mixer: John Vigran. Orchestration by: Thomas Pasatieri. Re-Recording Mixers: Matthew Iadarola, Stanley Kastner. Recordist: Rich Gooch. Foley Artists: John Post, Paul Holtzborn. Foley Mixer: Bob Deschaine. Foley Recordist: David Jose. Production Sound Mixer: John Pritchett. Boom Operator: Joel Shryack. Cable Puller: Emily Smith-Baker. Gaffer: Don Muchow. Best Boy Electric: Andrew Day. Electricians: Robert Bruce, Val De Salvo, Tom McGrath, Chris Reddish. Key Grip: Anthony T. Marra II. Best Boy Grip: Michael J. Fahey. Dolly Grip: Wayne Stroud. Grips: Kevin Fahey, Scott "El Gato" Hollander, Tim Nash. Wardrobe Supervisor: Lydia Tanji. Wardrobe Assistants: Angela Billows, Vicki Brinklord. Makeup Artist: Deborah Lassen. Hairdresser: Scott Williams. June's Artwork: Sydney Cooper. Property Master: James Monroe. Assistant Property Master: Julie Heuer. Set Dressers: Matthew Altman, John Bucklin, David Ronan, Jim Samson. Swing Gang: Daniel Rothenberg, Mario Perez. Assistant Location Manager: Paul Boydston. Scenic Painter: John Beauvas. Painter: Ricky Riggs. Construction Coordinator Loren Corney. Construction Foreman: Pat Maurer. Carpenters: Chris Harneus, Darryl Lee, Kenneth Funk, Thomas Calloway, John Evans, Justin Kritzer. Art Department Coordinator: Michele Guastello. Production Coordinator: Cynthia Hill. Assistant Coordinator: Betsy Chase. Production Secretary: Stacy Cohen. Production Accountant: Kimberly Edwards Shapiro. Assistant Accountant: Cheryl Kurk. Avenue Financial Representative: Sheri Halfon. Additional Accounting Services: Judy Geletko. Post Production Accounting: Catherine Webb. Assistant to Robert Altman: Jim McLindon. Assistant to Cary Brokaw: Robin Hage, Danielle Knight. Assistant to Nick Wechsler: Alison Balian. Sandcastle 5 Representative: Celia Converse. Production Assistants: Angie Bonner, John Brown III, Signe Corriere, Steve Day, Kelly Householder. Script Supervisor: Carole Starkes. Stunt Coordinator: Greg Walker. Special Effects: John Hartigan. Animal Trainer: Jim Brockett. Photographer: Lorey Sebastian. Set Medic: Tom Moore. Transportation Coordinator: Derek Raser. Transportation Captain: J.T. Thayer. Drivers: Christopher Armstrong, Ron Chesney, Steve Earle, Don Feeney, D.J. Gardiner, Greg Willis. Caterer: Rick Branin Catering. Craft Service: Stuart McCauley, Andrea Berty. Extras Casting: Magic Casting. Location Security: Artis Security. Negative Cutter: Bob Hart. Color by Deluxe. Color Timer: Michael Stanwick Titles and Opticals by: Mercer Title and Optical. Title Design: Dan Perri. Legal Services: Sinclair Tennenbaum and Co, Wyman and Isaacs. Financing provided by: The Daiwa Bank Ltd. Completion Bond: Film Finances Inc. Promotion arranged by: Andrew Varela. Publicity by: Clein + White Inc. Title Painting by: Charles Bragg. Re-recording Facilities: Skywalker Sound — A Division of LucasArts Entertainment Company.

Cast: Tim Robbins (Griffin Mill), Greta Scacchi (June Gudmundsdottir), Fred Ward (Walter Stuckel), Whoopi Goldberg (Detective Avery), Peter Gallagher (Larry Levy), Brian James (Joel Levison), Cynthia Stevenson (Bonnie Sherow), Vincent D'Onofrio (David Kahane), Dean Stockwell (Andy Civella), Richard E. Grant (Tom Oakley), Sydney Pollack (Dick Mellen), Lyle Lovett (Detective DeLongpre), Dina Merrill (Celia), Angela Hall (Jan), Leah Ayres (Sandy), Paul

Hewitt (Jimmy Chase), Randall Batinkoff (Reg Goldman), Jeremy Piven (Steve Reeves), Gina Gershon (Whitney Gersh), Frank Barhydt (Frank Murphy), Mike E. Kaplan (Marty Grossman), Kevin Scannell (Gar Girard), Margery Bond (Witness), Susan Emshwiller (Detective Broom), Brian Brophy (Phil), Michael Tolkin (Eric Schecter), Stephen Tolkin (Carl Schecter), Natalie Strong (Natalie), Pete Koch (Walter), Pamela Bowen (Trixie), Jeff Weston (Rocco); Steve Allen, Richard Anderson, Rene Auberjonois, Harry Belafonte, Shari Belafonte, Karen Black, Michael Bowen, Gary Busey, Robert Carradine, Charles Champlin, Cher, James Coburn, Cathy Lee Crosby, John Cusack, Brad Davis, Paul Dooley, Thereza Ellis, Peter Falk, Felicia Farr, Kasia Figura, Louise Fletcher, Dennis Franz, Teri Garr, Leeza Gibbons, Scott Glenn, Jeff Goldblum, Elliott Gould, Joel Grey, David Alan Grier, Buck Henry, Anjelica Huston, Kathy Ireland, Steve James, Maxine John-James, Sally Kellerman, Sally Kirkland, Jack Lemmon, Marlee Matlin, Andie MacDowell, Malcolm McDowell, Jayne Meadows, Martin Mull, Jennifer Nash, Nick Nolte, Alexandra Powers, Bert Remsen, Guy Remsen, Patricia Resnick, Burt Reynolds, Jack Riley, Julia Roberts, Mimi Rogers, Annie Ross, Alan Rudolph, Jill St. John, Susan Sarandon, Adam Simon, Rod Steiger, Joan Tewkesbury, Brian Tochi, Lily Tomlin, Robert Wagner, Ray Walston, Bruce Willis, Marvin Young

Music Credits: "Snake and Drums of Kyoto"—Written and performed by Kurt Neumann; Liz Mann Music. "Precious"—Written by Les Hooper; Chesford Music Publications; *Entertainment Tonight* Theme by Michael Mark; Published by Addax Music Company. "Tema Para Jobim"—Music by Gerry Mulligan; Lyrics by Joyce; Performed by Joyce, Milton Nascimento; Courtesy of Estudio Pointer Ltd. and RCA Electronica Ltd. Mulligan Publishing Company.

4. *Husbands and Wives* (1992)

Tri Star Pictures. Genre: Drama. Running time: 107 minutes. Rated: R. Released: September 1992.

Credits: Producer: Robert Greenhut. Executive Producers: John Rollins, Charles H. Joffe. Director: Woody Allen. Screenplay: Woody Allen. Associate Producer: Thomas Reilly. Co-producers: Helen Robin, Joseph Hartwick. Director of Photography: Carlo Di Palma. Editing: Susan E. Morse. Production Designer: Santo Loquasto. Art Director: Speed Hopkins. Set Decorator: Susan Bode. Costume Designer: Jeffrey Kurland. Casting: Juliet Taylor. Production Manager: Joseph Hartwick. 1st Assistant Director: Thomas Reilly. 2nd Assistant Director: Richard Patrick. Location Manager: Dana Robin. Production Coordinator Helen Robin. Script Supervisor: Kay Chapin. Production Auditor: Peter Lombard. Casting Associate: Laura Rosenthal. Art Department Coordinator: Glen Lloyd. Camera Operator: Dick Mingalone. Assistant Cameraperson: Michael Green, Michael Carocciolo. 2nd Assistant Cameraperson: Liz Dobelman. Camera Trainee: John Fortunato. Still Photographer: Brian Hamill. Video: Joe Trammell. Set Dresser: Dave Weinman. Property Master: James Mazzola. Key Grip: Bob Ward. Best Boy Grip: Ronald Burke. Gaffer: Ray Quinlan. Best Boy Electric: Jim Manzione. Construction Coordinator: Ron Petagna. Standby Carpenter: Joe Alfieri. Chief Construction Grip: Vincent Guarriello. Master Scenic Artist: James Sorice. Standby Scenic Artist: Cosmo Sorice. Production Sound Mixer: James Sabat. Boom Operator: Louis

Sabat. Sound Recorder: Frank Graziadei. Re-recording Mixer: Lee Dichter. Projectionist: Carl Turnquest, Jr. Makeup: Fern Buchner. Hairstylist: Romaine Greene. Assistant Costume Designer: Eric Mendelsohn. Costume Assistant: Lauren Gibson. Men's Wardrobe Supervisor: Bill Christians. Women's Wardrobe Supervisor: Patricia Eiben. Assistant Film Editors: William Kruzykowski, Kent Blocher. Sound Editor: Bob Hein. Assistant Sound Editors: Gina Alfano, Tom Foligno. Assistant Production Coordinator Lois Nalepka. Production Associate: Scott Kordish. Assistant Production Auditor: Michael Jackman. Assistant to Mr. Greenhut: Ilyse Reulinger. Assistant to Mr. Allen: Julie Sriro. Location Scouts: Megan Monaghan, Antoine Douaihy, Drew Dillard. Studio Manager: Brain Mannain. Additional Casting: Todd Thaler Casting. Transportation Captains: Harold "Whitey" McEvoy, Peter Tavis. 2nd 2nd Assistant Director: Justin Moritt. DGA Trainee: David Hamby. Production Assistants: Tom Amos, Tracy Bonbrest, Tristan Bourne, Tony Fleming, Dave Hummel, Sam Hutchins, Leslie Loftis, Tina Stauffer, Gilbert S. Williams, Jr., Nicholas Wolfert, Tom Yeager. Color by DuArt Film Laboratories. Prints by Technicolor. Titles by The Effect House Corp. Negative Matching: J.G. Films, Inc. Publicity: PMK Public Relations. Lenses and Panaflex Cameras by Panavision.

Cast: Woody Allen (Gabe Roth), Mia Farrow (Judy Roth), Judy Davis (Sally), Juliette Lewis (Rain), Liam Neeson (Michael), Sydney Pollack (Jack), Lysette Anthony (Sam), Nick Metropolis (TV Scientist), Cristi Conaway (Shawn Grainger), Timothy Jerome (Paul), Rebecca Glenn (Gail), Galaxy Craze (Harriet), Hampton's Party Guest (John Doumanian), Gordon Rigsby (Hampton's Party Guest), Ron Rifkin (Rain's Analyst), Ilene Blackman (Receptionist), Blythe Danner (Rain's Mother), Brian McConnachie (Rain's Father), Bruce Jay Friedman (Peter Styles), Benno Schmidt (Judy's Ex-Husband), Jeffrey Kurland (Interviewer/Narrator), Ron August (Rain's Ex-Lover), John Bucher (Rain's Ex-Lover), Matthew Flint (Rain's Boyfriend). Jerry Zaks, Caroline Aaron, Jack Richardson, Nora Ephron, Ira Wheeler (Dinner Party Guests). Kenneth Edelson, Michelle Turley, Victor Truro, Kenny Vance, Lisa Gustin, Anthony Nocerino (Gabe's Novel Montage). Philip Levy (Taxi Dispatcher), Connie Picard (Banducci Family Member), Steve Randazzo (Banducci Family Member), Tony Turco (Banducci Family Member), Adelaide Mestre (Banducci Family Member), Jessica Frankston (Birthday Party Guest), Merv Bloch (Birthday Party Guest)

Music Credits: "What Is This Thing Called Love"— By Cole Porter; Performed by Leo Reisman and his Orchestra; Courtesy of Academy Sound and Vista Limited. "West Coast Blues"— By John L. (Wes) Montgomery; Performed by Wes Montgomery; Courtesy of Fantasy, Inc. "Symphony No. 9 in D"—(Andante Comodo) by Gustav Mahler; Performed by Sir John Barbirelli and the Berlin Philharmonic Orchestra; Courtesy of Angel EMI Classics by arrangement with CEMA Special Markets. "That Old Feeling"— By Lew Brown and Sammy Fain; Performed by Stan Getz and Gerry Mulligan; Courtesy of Polygram Special Products; A Division of Polygram Group Distribution, Inc. "Top Hat, White Tie and Tails"— by Irving Berlin; Performed by Bernie Leighton. "Makin' Whoopee"— By Walter Donaldson and Gus Kahn; Performed by Bernie Leighton. "The Song Is You"— By Jerome Kern and Oscar Hammerstein II; Performed by Bernie Leighton.

5. *Death Becomes Her* (1992)

Universal Pictures. Genre: Comedy. Running time: 104 minutes. Rating: PG-13. Released: July 1992.

Credits: Producers: Robert Zemeckis, Steve Starkey. Co-producer: Joan Bradshaw. Director: Robert Zemeckis. Screenwriters: Martin Donovan, David Koepp. Director of Photography: Dean Cundey. Editing: Arthur Schmidt. Music: Alan Silvestri. Production Designer: Rick Carter. Art Director: Jim Teegarden. Set Director: Jackie Carr. Costume Designer: Joanna Johnston. Casting: Karen Rea. Unit Production Manager: Joan Bradshaw. 1st Assistant Director: Marty Ewing. 2nd Assistant Director: Cherylanne Martin. 2nd 2nd Assistant Director: Dana Kuznetzkoff. Visual Effects Supervisor: Ken Ralston. Makeup Design: Dick Smith. Prosthetics Makeup Supervisor: Kevin Haney. Special Body Effects Designed and Created by: Tom Woodruff, Jr., and Alec Gillis. Assistant Art Directors: Erin Cummins, Lauren Cory, Paul Sonski, Linda Berger. Leadman: Tim Donelan. Drapery Foreman: John Slatsky. Set Dressers: Max Brehme, Steven Jarrard, Scott Leslie, Bruce Fuslier, William Wright. Production Illustrators: Thomas Cranham, David Lowery, Marty Kline. Set Designers: Lauren Polizza, Elizabeth Lapp, Masako Masuda, John Berger. Art Department Coordinator: Caroline Quinn. Location Manager: Karleen Gallegly. Assistant Location Manager: Richard Delabio. Property Master: John Zemansky. Assistant Property Masters: Lee Drygas, Dan Bentley. 1st Assistant Editor: Carin-Anne Strohmater. Assistant Editor: Stephen Meek. Apprentice Editor: Jeremiah O'Driscoll. Script Supervisor: Ann Rapp. Production Coordinator: Jacqueline A. Shea. Production Assistant: Kevin Landry. Camera Operator: Raymond N. Stella. 1st Assistant Camera: Clyde Bryan. 2nd Assistant Camera: Jolanda Wiffli. Camera Loader: Hason Garcia. Still Photographer: Deana Newcomb. Production Sound Mixer: William B. Kaplan. Boom Operator: Earl E. Sampson. Cableperson: D.G. Fisher. Video Engineer: Ian Kelly. Assistant Costume Designer: Barcie Waite. Costume Supervisor: Pam Wise. Costumers: Linda Redmon, Diana Wilson, Gilbert Hernandez, Deborah Hopper, Paul St. John, Patricia Bersci. Seamstress: Nicole Tapp. Sketch Artist: Kevin Carrigan. Chief Lighting Technician: Mark D. Walthour. Assistant Chief Lighting Technician: Steve Chandler. Lighting Technician: Anthony Wong, Keith Roverud, Mark Soucie, Edward Thompson, Jr., Gary Sneed, Ben Graham, John Zirbel, O'Shana Walker. Theatrical Lighting Coordinator: Dan Flannery. Key Grip: Ron Cardarelli. Best Boy Grip: Sid Lucero. Dolly Grip: Dave Wachtman. Grips: Marty Dobkousky, Steve Cardarelli, John O'Grady, Michael Heath, Robert Hernandez. Special Effects Supervisor: Michael Lantieri. Special Effects Foreman: Don Elliot. Special Effects: Brian Tipton, Tom Pahk, John Porter, Gregory Tippie, Wayne Radouin, Dan Ossello. Ms. Hawn's Prosthetics: Lance Anderson. Assisted by David Anderson. Mr. Willis' Makeup: Michael Mills. Ms. Streep's Makeup: Roy Helland. Ms. Hawn's Makeup: Tom Case. Additional Makeup: Greg Nelson. Body Makeup: Nadege Schoenfeld. Key Hairstylist: Susan Germaine. Ms. Streep's Hairstylist: Roy Helen. Ms. Hawn's Hairstylist: Kathy Blondell. Hairstylist: Shirley Crawford. Greensmen: Craig Ayers, Jeff Thomas, Steve Miller. Standby Painters: William Solomon. Construction Coordinator: Jerry Fitzpatrick. Construction Foreman: Richard Bruns. Foremen: Robert

Simpson. Elliot Jennings, Todd Young, Warren Williams, Dwight Lowell. Paint Foreman: Thomas Bartholomew. Labor Foreman: Rick Ross. Plaster Foreman: Dave Robbie. Rigging Gaffer: Pat Marshall. Best Boy: Kurt Marshall. Rigging Lighting Technicians: Robert Fillis, John Antunovich. Key Rigging Grip: Bud Heller. Best Boy: Jeffrey Katelman. Rigging Grip: Raymond Michels. Assistant Production Coordinator: Janine Cavoto. Production Secretary: Melissa Wiechmann. Unit Publicist: Patti Hawn. Assistant Accountants: Joanie Spates, Edward Poveda, Sandy Kraft. Construction Accountant: Teri Rentaria. DGA Trainee: Mark Tobey. Production Associate: Rick Porras. Production Assistants: Carol Bawer, Roby Marshall, Adam Beason, Julia Martholomew, Christine Norton. Josh Lusby, Sharon Felder, Steven Boyd. Assistant to Mr. Zemeckis: Deborah Cain. Assistant to Mr. Starkey: Hayley B. Miller. Assistant to Mr. Donovan: Jesse Stills. Assistant to Mr. Koepp: Arlene Trainoff. Assistant to Ms. Streep: Maggie Earle. Assistant to Ms. Hawn: Michael Birzniers. Assistants to Mr. Willis: Marina Massaro, Nita Willis, Stephen Eads. Dialect Coach: Timothy Monich. Casting Associate: Donna M. Ekholdt. Extras Casting: Central Casting. Musical Sequences Designed and Choreographed by Brad Jeffries. Assistant Choreographer: Leslie Cook, Darrel Wright. Stunt Coordinator: Walter Scott. Physical Training: Body by Jake. Meryl Streep's Stand-In: Pauline Arthur Loomis. Bruce Willis' Stand-In: Johnny Johnson. Goldie Hawn's Stand-In: Melody McCord. Dog Trainer: Gary Gero. Craft Service: Tim Gonzales. Catering: Tony's Food Service. First Aid: Thomas Foster. Location Projectionist: Lisa Hackler. Underwater Director of Photography: Jack Cooperman. Transportation Coordinator: Rob Neilson. Transportation Captain: Snook Houston. Co-Captain: Ron Kelley. Supervising Sound Editors: Charles L. Campbell, Ronald Malouf. Sound Editors: Larry Carow, Jeff Clark, Albert Gasser, Nils Jensen, Howard Nieman. Assistant Sound Editors: Angie Luckey, Jerry Edeman. Assistant Film Editor: Lorraine Salk. Foley: Taj Soundworks. Foley Artists: Kevin Bartnof, Hilda Hodges. Foley Mixed by: Carolyn Tapp. Foley Recordist: Marilyn Graf, Sandra Garcia. ADR Supervisor: Larry Singer. ADR Editors: Tom Whiting, Corrine Sessarego. ADR Assistant Editor: Rod Rogers. ADR Mixer: Doc Kane. Recordist: Mike Boudry. Re-recording Mixers: Nick Alexander, Jim Bolt, Andy D'Addario. Recordist: Albert Romero. Orchestrations: William Ross. Music Editor: Ken Karman. Assistant Music Editor: Jacqueline Tager. Music Recording Mixer: Dennis Sands. Music Programmer: David Bifano. Music Contractor: Sandy DeCrescent. Featured Violin Soloist: Stuart Canin. Music Services: Joann Kane. Process Composition by: Hansard. Main and End Titles Designed and Produced by R. Greenberg Associates, Inc., New York City. Opticals by: Cinema Research. Negative Cutting: Gary Burritt. Color Tinting: David Orr.

Second Unit: 2nd Unit Directors: Max Kleven, Ken Ralston. 1st Assistant Director: Bruce Moriarty. 2nd Assistant Director: Carla McCloskey. 2nd 2nd Assistant Director: David Povidio. Director of Photography: Don Burgess. Camera Operator: Chris Squires. 1st Assistant Camera: Josh Bleibtreu. Sound Mixer: John Patchett. Script Supervisor: Sandy Mazzola. Property Master: Melissa Feinberg. Chief Lighting Technician: Peter Clarson. Key Grip: Tommy May. Special Effects: John Grey. Special Visual Effects by Industrial Light and Magic, a division of LucasArts Entertainment, Marin County, California. Visual Effects Producer: Debbie Denise. Visual

Effects Art Director: Doug Change. Optical Photo Supervisor: Bruce Vecchitto, Brade Kuehn. Visual Effects Editors: Timothy Eaton, Michael McGovern. Computer Graphics Super: Doug Smythe. Supervising Mold Maker: Steve Garley. Effects Camera Supervisor: Bruce Walters. Animation Supervisor: Wes Takahasu. Rotoscope Supervisor: Tom Bertino. Executive Post Production: Ed L. Jones. General Manager: Jim Morris. Visual Effects Coordinators: Anne Calanchini, Sandra Almond Williams. Camera Operators: Patrick Turner, Peter Daulton, Selwyn Eddie III. Camera Assistants: Vance Piper, Robert Hill, Kate O'Neill. Optical Line Up: Tom Rosseter, Jennifer Lee, Debra Wolff, Kristen Tratina, John Whisnant, Peg Hunter. Optical Camera Operators: Keith Johnson, Kenneth Smith, Don Clark, Jon Alexander, Jeff Doran, James Lim. Optical Processing: Tim Geidman, Mike Ellis, Rob Fernley. Computer Graphics Production Supervisor: Judith Weaver. Co-Supervisor: Lincoln Hu. Artists: Barbara Brennan, Richard L. Cohen, Carol N. Frederick, Sandy Houston, Geoff Campbell, Rachel Falk, John Horn, Sandra Fold Karpman, Laurel Klick, Greg Maloney, Ron Morland, Patrick Myers, Carolyn Engle Rendu, Stephen Rosebaum, Andrew Schmidt, Thomas J. Smith, Jeffrey R. Light, Jim Mitchell, George Murphy, Joseph Pasquall, Stuart Robertson, John Schlag, Alex Seiden, Robert Weaver. Film Scanner Supervisor: Josh Pines. Senior Scanning Operator: Randall K. Bean. Scanning Operator: George Gambetta. Assistant Effects Editors: Jon Pode, Roberto McGrath. Effects Camera Operators: Charlie Clavadetscher, Steve Reding, Colin Campbell, Jim Hagedorn. Animators: Gordon Baker, Scott Bonnenfant. Rotoscopers: Jack Mongovan, Terry Molatore, Joanne Hafner, Lisa Drostova, Leslie Arvig, Debra Mainum. Matte Painting: Mark Sullivan. Modelmakers: Mike Cummins, Mike Lynch, Richard Miller, Mark Siegal, Brian Gernand, Margie McMahon, Alan Peterson, Chuck Wiley. Miniature Electronics Design: Jon Roteman, Jack Haye. Gaffer: Robert Finley III. Stagehands: Robert Doherty, Michael Olague. Engineer: Mike MacKenzie. Plate Photography Coordinator: Penny Runge. Post Production Coordinators: Susan Adele Colletta, Shari Malyn, Lisa Vaughn. Negative cutters: Louis Rivera, Preston Richard. Still Photographer: David Owen. Production Assistant: Tina Matthies.

Cast: Meryl Streep (Madeline Ashton), Bruce Willis (Ernest Menville), Goldie Hawn (Helen Sharp), Isabella Rossellini (Lisle Von Rhumans), Sydney Pollack (Doctor), Ian Ogilvy (Chagall), Adam Storke (Dakota), Nancy Fish (Rose), Alaina Reed Hall (Psychologist), Michelle Johnson (Anna), Mary Ellen Trainor (Vivian Adams), William Frankfather (Mr. Franklin), John Ingel (Eulogist), Clement Von Franckenstein (Opening Man), Petrea Burchard (Opening Woman), Jim Jansen (Second Man), Mimi Kennedy (Second Woman), Paula Tocha (Landlord), Mark Davenport (Eviction Cop), Thomas Murphy (Eviction Cop), Michael Mills (Police Officer), Psychiatric Patients: Sonia Jackson, Jill C. Klein, Jean Pflieger, Debra Jo Rupp, Carol Ann Susi, Kay Yamamoto. Jacquelyn K. Koch (Messenger Girl), Anya Longwell (Chagall Receptionist), Stuart Mabray (Chagall Security), Louise Rapport (Older Woman at Party), Colleen Morris (Starlet), Jonathan Silverman (Jay Norman), Meg Witner (Woman at Book Party), Carrie Yazel (Girl at Dakota's), Michael A. Nickles, John Enos, Dan Clark, Fabio, Joel Beeson (Lisle's Body Guards), Ron Stein (Elvis), Bonnie Cahoon (Greta Garbo), Stephanie Anderson (Marilyn Monroe), Bob Swain (Andy Warhol), Eric Clark (James Dean), Dave

Brock (Jim Morrison), Lydia Peterkoch (Blonde with Jim Morrison), Phillip Cooper (Coroner), Ernest Harada (Coroner), Susan Kellermann (Second Doctor), Kevin Caldwell (Medical Technician), Alex P. Hernandez (Medical Technician), Donna Ekholdt (Sobbing Nun), Tammy Gantz (Sobbing Nun), Melissa Martin (Sobbing Nun), Jeff Adkins, Cheryl Baxter, Cameron English, Ed Forsyth, Bob Gaynor, Don Hesser, Michael Higgins, Kenneth Hughes, Kenneth Knaff, Glean Lewis, Keith McDaniel, Charles McGowan, Regan Patno, Lacy Darryl Phillips, Matt Sergott, Paul Thorpe, Sergio Trujillo (Dancers), Randy Crenshaw, Jon Joyce, Jerry Whitman (Singers), Ken Johnston (Bruce Willis' Stunt Double), Denise Lynne Roberts (Meryl Streep's Stunt Double), Barbara Klein, Debby Lynne Ross, Denise Lynne Roberts (Goldie Hawn's Stunt Doubles), Gino Acevedo, Norman Cabrera, Guy Himber, David Nelson, Christoper Hunt, Wayne Toth, N. Brock Winkless, IV (Puppeteers), Mickie T. McGowan, Laurie Faso, Joe Baker, Efrain Figueroa, Jennifer Darling, Louisa Leschun, June Kyoko, Sherry Lynn, Lawrence Steffan, Bill Faruer, Burr De Benning (ADR Loop Group)

Music Credits: "Me"—Written by Jeffrey Aymes; Lyrics: Martin Donovan and Donald Knapp; Arranged by William Ross.

6. *Eyes Wide Shut* (No release date set; limited credits available) Warner Bros.

   Credits: Directed by: Stanley Kubrick.
   Cast: Tom Cruise, Nicole Kidman, Sydney Pollack.

Directing Credits

1. *The Slender Thread* (1965)
   Paramount Pictures. An Athene Production. Genre: Drama. Running time: 98 minutes. Black-and-White. Premiered: New York, December 23, 1965. Released on videocassette in U.S. June 24, 1992.

   Credits: Producers: Stirling Silliphant and Stephen Alexander. Director: Sydney Pollack. Screenplay: Stirling Silliphant. Suggested by the *Life Magazine* article by Shana Alexander and based on an actual incident. Music: Quincy Jones (composer and director). Director of Photography: Loyal Griggs. Art Directors: Jack Poplin, Hal Pereira. Set Decoration: Robert Benton, Joseph Kish. Makeup Supervision: Wally Westmore. Hair Style Supervision: Nellie Manley. Aerial Photography: Nelson Tyler. Editing: Tom Stanford. Costumes: Edith Head. Sound: John Carter and Charles Grenzbach. Assistant Director: Don Roberts. Dialogue Coach: Frank London. Process Photography: Farciot Edouart. Unit Production Manager: William C. Davidson.

   Cast: Sidney Poitier (Alan Newell), Anne Bancroft (Inga Dyson), Telly Savalas (Dr. Coburn), Steven Hill (Mark Dyson), Edward Asner (Detective Ridley), Indus Arthur (Marion), Paul Newlan (Sgt. Ward), Dabney Coleman (Charlie), H.M. Wynant (Doctor), Robert Hoy (Patrolman S. Peters), John Benson (Patrolman Bert

Enyard), Kay Doubleday (Jinny), Archie Smith (Janitor), Lou Clark (1st Night Watchman), David Harris (2nd Night Watchman), Phillip Browne (Office Boy), Joseph R. Denini (Aid Vehicle Dispatcher), Ardis K. Erikson (Elevator Operator), Nicolas Prebezac (Boy on Beach—10 years), Mike Circh (Lover), Edie Kirchhoff (Lover), Thomas Hill (Liquor Salesman), Greg Jarvis (Chris), Dr. O. L. Haavik (Pastor), Richard Doorish (Pete—11 yrs), Marjorie Nelson (Mrs. Thomas), Melody Greer (Zipper Girl), Bernard Frawley (Poker Player), Howard Hall (Drunk), Geraldine Lucks (Convention Wife), Marylin Ward (Convention Wife), Glen Diehl (Conventioneer), Peter Donnelly (Conventioneer), Charles C. Andrews (Motel Manager), Stephen Pellegrini (Police Cadet), William R. Rhodes (Police Dispatcher), Jerome R. Brand (Police Cadet), Karen Morris (Mrs. Hillman), John Napier (Dr. Alden Van), Jo Helton (Nurse), Jan Bradley (New Nurse), Jason Wingreen (Technician), Janet Dudley (Edna), Daryle Ann Lindley (Dancer), Raymond B. Ochoa (Dancer), Marly Been (Dancer), Steve Ciro (Dancer), Walter Mazlow (1st Newsman), Allen Emerson (2nd Newsman), Lane Bradford (Al McCardle), Viola Harris (Telephone Supervisor), Charlotte Stewart (Telephone Operator), Steven Marlo (Arthur Foss), George Savalas (Pool Player), Karen Parker (Girl), Nicholas Prebezac, Drew Eskenazi, Erin Almond, Pam Bagby (Children at Beach), Sons of Adam (Discotheque Band)

2. *This Property Is Condemned*. (1966)

Paramount Pictures. A Seven Arts and Ray Stark Production. Genre: Drama. Running time: 110 minutes. Premiered: New York, August 3, 1966. Released on laserdisc and videocassette.

Credits: Producers: John Houseman and Ray Stark. Executive Producer: Milton Feldman. Director: Sydney Pollack. Screenplay: Francis Ford Coppola, Fred Coe, Edith Sommer (and David Rayfiel non-credited). Based on a one-act play by Tennessee Williams. Music: Kenyon Hopkins. Director of Photography: James Wong Howe. Production Design: Stephen Grimes. Art Director: Phil Jeffries. Set Director: William Kiernan. Editing: Adrienne Fazan. Makeup: Garrett Morris and Edwin Butterworth. Production Manager: Clarence Eurist. Costumes: Edith Head. Sound: Harry Lindgren and Charles Grenzbach. Assistant Director: Eddie Saeta. Aerial Photography: Nelson Tyler. Special Photographic Effects: Paul Lerpae. Process Photography: Farciot Edouart. Miss Wood's Hair Style Design and Execution: Maryce Bates. Miss Wood's Costumer: Ann Landers.

Cast: Natalie Wood (Alva Starr), Robert Redford (Owen Legate), Charles Bronson (J.J. Nichols), Kate Reid (Hazel Starr), Mary Badham (Willie Starr), Alan Baxter (Knopke), Robert Blake (Sidney), John Harding (Johnson), Dabney Coleman (Salesman), Ray Hemphill (Jimmy Bell), Brett Pearson (Charlie Steinkamp), Jon Provost (Tom), Bob Random (Tiny), Quentin Sondergaard (Hank), Michael Steen (Max), Bruce Watson (Linsay Tate), Nick Stuart (Railroad Conductor)

Music Credits: "Li'l Liza Jane"—Traditional. "Sing You Sinners"—By Sam Coslow and W. Franke Harling. "Wish Me a Rainbow"—By Jay Livingston and Ray Evans; Sung by Natalie Wood and Mary Badham. "Just One More Chance"—By Sam Coslow and Arthur Johnston. "Happy Birthday to You"—By Mildred Hill and Patty S. Hill.

3. *The Scalphunters* (1968)
   United Artists. A Levy-Gardner-Laven Production/Norlan Productions. Genre: Western/comedy. Running time: 103 minutes. Premiered: New York, April 2, 1968. Released on videocassette.

   Credits: Producers: Jules Levy, Arthur Gardner, Arnold Laven. Director: Sydney Pollack. Screenplay: William Norton. Production Managers: Henry Spitz, Jack Corrick. Music: Elmer Bernstein. Director of Photography: Duke Callaghan, Richard Moore. Art Director: Frank Arrigo. Film Editing: John Woodcock. Wardrobe Supervisor: Joe Drury. Sound: Jesus Gonzalez Gancy. Makeup: Gary Liddiard. Script Supervisor: Charlsie Bryant. Property Master: Donald B. Nunley. Equestrian Supervisor: Kenneth Lee. Casting: Lynn Stalmaster. Assistant Director: Charles R. Scott, Jr. Music Editing: Richard Carruth. Sound Effects Editing: Frank Warner. Stunt Coordinator: Tony Epper. Choreographer: Alex Ruiz. Special Effects: Herman Townsley. Title Design: Phill Norman. Production Assistants: Michael Scheff, Marilyn Fiebelkorn. Color by Deluxe. Cameras and lenses by Panavision.
   Cast: Burt Lancaster (Joe Bass), Shelley Winters (Kate), Telly Savalas (Jim Howie), Ossie Davis (Joseph Lee), Dabney Coleman (Jed), Paul Picerni (Frank), Dan Vadis (Yuma), Armando Silvestre (Two Crows), Nick Cravat (Ramon), Tony Epper, Chuck Roberson, John Epper, Jack Williams (Scalphunters), Amelia Rivero, Alicia Del Lago (Scalphunters' Women), Nestor Dominguez, Francisco Oliva, Benjamin Ramos, Enrique Tello, Raul Martinez, Jose Martinez, Rodolfo Toledo, Jose Salas, Cuco Velazquez, Alejandro Lopez, Raul "Pin" Hernandez, Pedro Aguilar (Kiowas)

4. *Castle Keep* (1969)
   Columbia. A Filmways Picture. Genre: War. Running time: 106 minutes. Rating: R. Color. Premiered: New York, July 23, 1969.

   Credits: Producers: Martin Ransohoff and John Calley. Associate Producer: Edward L. Rissien. Director: Sydney Pollack. Screenplay: Daniel Taradash and David Rayfiel based on the novel *Castle Keep* by William Eastlake. Production Manager: Ludmilla Goulian. Unit Manager: Suzanne Wiesenfeld. Executive Producer: Ben Kadish. Music composed and conducted: Michel Legrand. Director of Photography: Henri Decae. Aerial Photography: Nelson Tyler. Art Designer: Rino Mondellini. Art Directors: Max Douy, Jacques Douy, Morton Rabinowitz. Editing: Malcolm Cooke. Assistant Film Editor: Michele Robert. Costume Design: Jacques Ponteray. Sound Engineer: Antoine Petitjean. Assistant Sound Engineer: Yves Dacquay. Special Effects: Lee Zavits. Assistant Director: Marc Maurette, Stevo Petrovic. Casting: Lyn Stalmaster. Camera Operator: Charles H. Montel. Makeup: Robert J. Schiffer. 2nd Unit Director: Ray Kellogg. Set Dresser: Charles Merangel. Wardrobe: Jack Martel. Choreography: Dirk Sanders. Title Design and Opticals: Phill Norman-Cinefx. Color by Technicolor. Cameras and lenses by Panavision.
   Cast: Burt Lancaster (Major Falconer), Patrick O'Neal (Cpt. Beckman), Jean-Pierre Aumont (The Comte de Maldorais), Peter Falk (Sgt. Rossi), Astrid Hereen

(Therese), Scott Wilson (Cpl. Clearboy), Tony Bill (Lt. Amberjack), Al Freeman, Jr. (Private Benjamin), James Patterson (Elk), Bruce Dern (Billy Bix), Michael Conrad (Sgt. DeVaca), Caterina Boratto (Red Queen), Bisera (Baker's Wife), Elizabeth Teissier, Anne Marie Moskovenko, Marja Allanen, Eya Tuli, Elizabeth Darius, Karen Blanguernon, Maria Danube (Red Queen Girls), Ernest Clark, David Jones

5. *They Shoot Horses, Don't They?* (1969)

Cinerama Release. A Palomar Picture. A Chartoff-Winkler/Pollack Production. Genre: Existential melodrama. Running time: 120 minutes. Rating: PG. World Premiere: December 11, 1969. West Coast Premiere: December 17, 1969 at Picwood Theater, Los Angeles. Released on videocassette/released in limited edition letterbox laserdisc. 25th Anniversary of release celebrated November 18, 1994 at Samuel Goldwyn Theater in Los Angeles. Screened newly restored master print in stereo with original release running time: 123 minutes. 25th anniversary restoration produced and supervised by: Michael Arick. Laboratory services provided by YCM Labs. Sound engineering services provided by Chace Productions. Distributor: ABC/Capital Cities.

Credits: Producers: Irwin Winkler, Robert Chartoff. Executive Producer: Theodore B. Sills. Associate Producer: John Green. Director: Sydney Pollack. Screenplay: James Poe and Robert E. Thompson based on a novel by Horace McCoy. Production Manager: Edward Woehler. Music: John Green and Albert Woodbury. Lyrics: Edward Heyman. Music Editing: Harry King. Music Coordinator: Randy Rayburn. Director of Photography: Philip H. Lathrop. Production Designer: Harry Horner. Marathon Dancers Supervisor: Tom Panko. Set Director: Frank McKelvy. Camera: Duke Callaghan. Editing: Fredric Steinkamp. Costumes: Donfeld. Sound: Tom Overton. Assistant Director: Al Jennings. Assistant Film Editor: Don Guidice. Men's Costumer: Mike Harte. Script Supervisor: Joyce Webb. Unit Publicity: Emily Torchia. Ms. Fonda's Hairstyles: Sydney Guilaroff. Makeup: Frank McCoy. Production Illustrator: Mort Rabinowitz. Sound Effects Editor: Norval Crutcher. Women's Costumer: Mina Mittleman. Dialogue Director: Herb Dufine. Property Master: Ben L. Goldman. Casting: Lynn Stalmaster. Color by Deluxe. Cameras and lenses by Panavision.

Cast: Jane Fonda (Gloria), Michael Sarrazin (Robert), Susannah York (Alice), Gig Young (Rocky), Red Buttons (The Sailor), Bonnie Bedelia (Ruby), Michael Conrad (Rollo), Bruce Dern (James), Allyn Ann McLerie (Shirl), Michael Conrad (Rollo), Al Lewis (Turkey), Robert Fields (Joel), Marge Kennedy (Mrs. Layden), Lynn Willis (Coley James), Severn Darden (Cecil), Jacquelyn Hyde (Jackie), Felice Orlandi (Marlo), Art Metrano (Max), Gail Billings (Lillian), Maxine Greene (Agnes), Mary Gregory (Nurse), Robert Dunlap (College Boy), Paul Mantee (Jiggs), Tim Herbert (Doctor), Tom McFadden (Second Trainer), Noble "Kid" Chissell (First Trainer)

Music Credits: Song "Easy Come, Easy Go."

6. *Jeremiah Johnson* (1972)

Warner Bros. A Wizan/Sanford Production. Genre: Western/adventure. Running time: 108 minutes. Rating: PG. Premiered: Cannes Film Festival,

May 9, 1972. Released in U.S.: December 21, 1972. Released on laserdisc and videocassette.

Credits: Producers: Joe Wizan and Sydney Pollack. Associate Producers: John R. Coonan, Mike Moder. Director: Sydney Pollack. Screenplay: John Milius and Edward Anhalt (and David Rayfiel, non-credited) based on the novel *The Mountain Man* by Vardis Fisher and the story *Crow Killer* by Raymond W. Thorp and Robert Bunker. Production Manager: John R. Coonan. Music: John Rubenstein, Tim McIntire. Director of Photography: Duke Callaghan. Art Director: Ted Haworth. Set Decorator: Raymond Molyneaux. Film Editor: Thomas Stanford. Sound: Charles Wilborn. Costumes: Bernie Pollack. Assistant Director: Mike Moder. Makeup: Gary Liddiard, Ken Chase. Hairstyles by: Lynn Del Kail. Property Master: Allan Levine. Gaffer: Joe Adessa. Sound Editors: Josef von Stroheim, Mike Colgan. Assistant Editors: Don Guidice, Carol Jackson. Technical Advisor: John Arlee. Casting: Lynn Stalmaster. Livestock Supervisor: Kenneth Lee. Locations by Cinemobile Systems. Opticals by Opticals West-NSS. Titles by Phill Norman. Color by Technicolor. Cameras and Lenses by Panavision.

Cast: Robert Redford (Jeremiah Johnson), Will Geer (Bear Claw), Stefan Gierasch (Del Gue), Josh Albee (Caleb), Delle Bolton (Swan), Joaquim Martinez (Paints His Shirt Red), Allyn Ann McClerie (Crazy Woman), Richard Angarola (Chief Two Tongues Lebeaux), Paul Benedict (Reverend), Charles Tyner (Robideaux), Jack Colvin (Lieut. Mulvy), Matt Clark (Qualen)

Filmed in Uinta National Forest, Wasatch National Forest, Ashley National Forest, Zion National Park and Snow Canyon State Park.

7. *The Way We Were* (1973)

Columbia Pictures. A Ray Stark/Sydney Pollack Production. Genre: Romance. Running time: 118 minutes. Rating: PG. Premiered: New York, October 17, 1973. Released on laserdisc and videocassette.

Credits: Producers: Ray Stark and Sydney Pollack. Director: Sydney Pollack. Screenplay: Arthur Laurents (and David Rayfiel and Alvin Sargent, non-credited). Production Director: Russ Saunders. Associate Producer: Richard Roth. Director of Photography: Harry Stradling, Jr. Music: Marvin Hamlisch. Production Design: Stephen Grimes. Editing: Margaret Booth, John Burnett. Costumes: Dorothy Jeakins, Moss Mabry. Sound: Jack Solomon. Assistant Director: Howard Koch, Jr. Script Supervisor: Betty Crosby. Titles: Phill Norman. Set Decorator: William Kiernan. Properties: Richard Rubin. Music Editor: Ken Runyon. 2nd Assistant Director: Jerry Zeismer. Makeup: Donald Cash, Jr., Gary Liddiard. Hairstyles: Kay Pownall. Sound Effects: Kay Rose. Re-recording: Richard Portman. Unit Publicist: Carol Shapiro.

Cast: Barbra Streisand (Katie Morosky), Robert Redford (Hubbell Gardiner), Bradford Dillman (J.J.), Patrick O'Neal (George Bissinger), Lois Chiles (Carol Ann), Viveca Lindfors (Paula Resiner), Allyn Ann McLerie (Rhea Edwards), Murray Hamilton (Brooks Carpenter), Herb Edelman (Bill), Diana Ewing (Vicki Bissinger), Sally Kirkland (Pony Dunbar), Don Keefer (Actor), Marcia Mae Jones (Peggy Vanderbilt), George Gaynes (El Morocco Cpt.), Eric Boles (Army Cpl.), Barbara Peterson (Ashe

Blonde), Brendan Kelly (Rally), Roy Jenson (Army Cpt.), James Woods (Frankie), Connie Forslund (Jenny), Robert Gerringer (Dr. Short), Susie Blakely (Judianne), Ed Power (Airforce), Suzanne Zenor (Dumb Blonde), Dan Seymour (Guest)

Music Credits: "The Way We Were"— Composed by Marvin Hamlisch; Lyrics by Marilyn and Alan Bergman; Sung by Barbra Streisand.

8. *The Yakuza* (1975)

A.k.a. *Brotherhood of the Yakuza.* Warner Bros. A Sydney Pollack Production. Genre: Crime/action/romance. Running time: 112 minutes (original cut: 123 min). Rating: R. Premiered: New York, March 19, 1975. Released on laserdisc and videocassette.

Credits: Produced and directed by Sydney Pollack. Screenplay: Paul Schrader and Robert Towne, based on a story by Leonard Schrader. Co-Producer: Michael Hamilburg. Unit Production Manager: John R. Coonan. Executive Producer: Shundo Koji. Music: Dave Grusin. Directors of Photography: Okazaki Kozo, Duke Callaghan (American sequences). Production Design and 2nd Unit Director: Stephen Grimes. Art Director: Ishida Yoshiyuki. Editing: Fredric Steinkamp. Film Editors: Thomas Stanford, Don Guidice. Costume Designer: Dorothy Jeakins. Sound Mixer: Basil Fenton-Smith. Special Effects: Richard Parker, Kasai Tomoo. Assistant Directors: D. Michael Moore, Mike Abe. Assistant Production Manager: William Ross. Production Coordinator: Gaylin Schultz. Production Secretary: Michie Ross. Titles Designed: Phill Norman. Re-Recording Mixer: Arthur Piantadosi. Sound Effects: Edwin Scheid. Music Editor: Ted Whitfield. Makeup: Gary Morris. Script Supervisor: Hope Williams. Camera Operator: Robert Byrne. Assistant Camera Operator: Clifford Ralke. Assistant Editors: Carol Ann Jackson and Ralph Sandler. Assistant to Mr. Pollack: Sheila Barnes. Location Auditor: Ken Ryan. Costumer: Bucky Rous. Color by Technicolor. Cameras and lenses by Panavision.

Production Personnel: Kuroki Masami, Yada Seiji, Sugimoto Takeshi. Assistant to Executive Producer: Sato Masao. Unit Production Managers: Nagaoka Isao, Yamamoto Yoshio. Script Girl: Tsushima Keiko. Gaffer: Masuda Yoshaki. Tattoo Artist: Mohri Seija. Assistant Camerman: Matsuo Tamio. Props: Miyagawa Toshio. Grip: Murase Haruhisa. Wardrobe: Mori Mamoru.

Cast: Robert Mitchum (Harry Kilmer), Takakura Ken (Tanaka Ken), Brian Keith (George Tanner), Herb Edelman (Oliver Wheat), Richard Jordan (Dusty), Kishi Keiko (Eiko), James Shigeta (Goro), Okada Eiji (Tono), Christina Kokubo (Hanako), Kyosuke Machida (Kato), Go Eiji (Spider), Lee Chirillo (Louise), M. Hisaka (Boyfriend), William Ross (Tanner's Guard — American), Shirakawa (Tanner's Guard — Japanese), Akiyama (Tono's Guard), Harada (Goro's Doorman), Robert Ito (Voices)

Music Credits: "Only the Wind"—Japanese Lyrics: Aku Yu; Composed by Dave Grusin.

9. *Three Days of the Condor* (1976)

Paramount Pictures. A Dino De Laurentis Presentation. Genre: Thriller. Running time: 118 minutes. Rating: R. Premiered: New York, September 24, 1975. Released on laserdisc and videocassette.

Credits: Producer: Stanley Schneider. Co-produced by Wildwood Enterprises, Inc. Director: Sydney Pollack. Screenplay: Lorenzo Semple, Jr., and David Rayfiel, based on the novel *Six Days of the Condor* by James Grady. Production Director: Paul Granapoler. Assistant to Producer: Frederico de Laurentis. Music: Dave Grusin. Director of Photography: Owen Roizman. Production Design: Stephen Grimes. Art Director: Gene Rudolf. Supervising Editor: Fredric Steinkamp. Film Editor: Don Guidice. Ms. Dunaway's Costume: Theoni V. Aldridge. Wardrobe: Bernie Pollack, Joseph W. Dehn. Production Sound: Dennis Maitland. 1st Assistant Director: Pete Scopa. 2nd Assistant Directors: Mike Haley, Ralph Singleton, Kim Kuramada. Casting: Shirley Rich. Set Decorator: George de Titta. Property Manager: Allan Levine. Special Effects: Augie Lohman. Master Scenic: Bruno Robotti. Gaffer: Dusty Wallace. Key Grip: Robert Ward. Location Coordinator: Michael Britton. Re-recording: Arthur Piantadosi. Camera Operator: Enrique Bravo. Script Supervisor: Maggie James. Office Coordinator: Adeline Leonard. Production Accountant: Sam Goldrich. Title Design: Phill Norman. Costume Design: Joseph C. Aulisi. Makeup: Gary Liddiard, Bob O'Bradovich. Ms. Dunaway's Makeup: Lee Harmon. Hairdresser: Susan Germaine. Sound Editor: Joseph E. Von Stroheim. Music Editor: Ted Whitfield. Optical Effects: Creative Film Arts. Technicolor/Panavision.

Cast: Robert Redford (Joe Turner), Faye Dunaway (Kathy Hale), Cliff Robertson (Higgins), Max Von Sydow (Joubert), John Houseman (Wabash), Addison Powell (Atwood), Walter McGinn (Barber), Tina Chen (Janice), Michael Kane (Wicks), Don McHenry (Dr. Lappe), Michael Miller (Fowler), Jess Osuna (Major), Dino Narizzano (Harold), Helen Stenbure (Mrs. Russell), Patrick Gorman (Martin), Hansford H. Rowe, Jr.(Jennings), Carlin Glynn (Mae Barber), Hank Garrett (Mailman), Arthur French (Messenger), Jay Devlin (Tall Thin Man), Frank Savino (Jimmy), Robert Phalen (Newberry), John Randolph Jones (Beefy Man), Garrison Phillips (Hutton), Lee Steele (Heidegger), Ed Crowley (Ordinance Man), John Connell (TV Reporter), Ed Setrakian (Customer), Norman Bush (Alice Lieut.), James Keane (Store Clerk), Myron Natwick, Michael Prince (Civilians), Carol Gustafson (Land Lady), Sal Schillizzi (Locksmith), Harmon William (CIA Agent), David Bowman (Telephone Worker), Eileen Gordon (CIA Receptionist), Robert Dahdah (Santa Claus), Steve Bonino, Jennifer Rose, David Allen, Glenn Ferguson, Paul Dwyer (Kids), Marian Swan, Dorothi Fox (Nurses), Ernest Hardin, Jr. (Teenager)

10. *Bobby Deerfield* (1977)
    Columbia/Warner Bros. A Sydney Pollack Production. Genre:
    Drama/sports. Running time: 124 minutes (cut to 99 minutes for cable
    television). Rating: PG. Premiered: New York, September 29, 1977.
    Released on videocassette.

Credits: Produced and directed by Sydney Pollack. Screenplay: Alvin Sargent based on the novel *Heaven Has No Favorites* by Erich Maria Remarque. Production Executive: William Finnegan. Production Manager (France): Philippe Modave, (Italy) Guy Luongo. Executive Producer: John Foreman. Music: Dave Grusin. Director of Photography: Henri Decae. Art Director: Mark Frederix. Production Design: Stephen Grimes. Editing: Fredric Steinkamp. Men's Wardrobe: Bernie Pollack. Women's Wardrobe: Annalisa Nasalli Rocca. Sound: Basil Fenton-Smith. Assistant

Director: Paul Feyder. 2nd Assistant Director: Meyer Berreby. Script Supervisor: Catherine Prevert. Set Decorator: Gabriel Bechir. Makeup: Brad Wilder, Jacky Boubon. Hairstylist: Alex Archambault. 2nd Unit Director: Stephen Grimes. Camera Operator: Yves Rodallec. Assistant Editor: William Steinkamp. Assistant Editor (France): Catherine Kelber. Music Editor: Ted Whitfield. Sound Editors: Josef Von Stroheim, Marvin I. Kosberg. Casting Coordinator: Boaty Boatwright. Casting: Margot Capelier. Production Sound: Basil Fenton Smith. Music Scoring Mixer: Dan Wallin. Re-Recording: Arthur Piantadosi, Les Fresholtz, Mike Minkler. Auditor (United States): Kenneth Ryan. Auditor (France): Jose Lichtig. Titles: Phill Norman. Special Effects: Augie Lohman. Gaffer: Georges Ferriere. Dolly Grip: Jean Gimello. Location Coordinator: Antoine Compin. Stunt Coordinator: Remy Julienne. Color by Metrocolor. Cameras and lenses by Panavision. Formula 1 Cars Driven by: Carlos Pace, Tom Price, James Hunt, Patrick Depaillier, Mario Andretti. Martini Racing Division, Alfa, Brabham Formula 1 Racing Team and Bernie Ecclestone (Technical Assistants).

　　Cast: Al Pacino (Bobby Deerfield), Marthe Keller (Lillian Morelli), Anny Duperey (Lydia Picard), Walter McGinn (Leonard Deerfield), Stephan Meldegg (Karl Holtzman), Romolo Valli (Uncle Luigi), Jaime Sanchez (Delvecchio), Norm Nielsen (The Magician). Tourists: Mickey Knox, Dorothy James. Guido Alberti (Priest in Garden), Monique Lejeune (Catherine Modave), Steve Gadler (Bertrand Modave), Van Doude (The Flutist), Aurora Maris (Woman at Gas Station), Gerard Hernandez (Carlos Del Montanaro), Maurice Vallier (Priest), Antonio Faàdi Bruno (Vincenzo), Andre Vallardy (Autograph Hound), Feodor Atkine (Tommy), Patrick Floersheim (Mario), Bernie Pollack (Head Mechanic), Al Silvani (Mechanic), Isabelle De Blonay (Nurse), Franco Ressel (Man with Dog), Dominique Briand (Reporter). Brigitte Hult, Alane Persson (Magician's Attendants), Brian Pinero (Second Young Man), Sylvio Valente (Tap Dancer), Ermelinda De Felice

11. *The Electric Horseman* (1979)

Columbia. A Ray Stark/Wildwood Enterprises Production. Genre: Western. Running time: 121 minutes. Rating: PG. Premiered: New York, December 21, 1979. Released on videocassette and laserdisc.

　　Credits: Producer: Ray Stark. Director: Sydney Pollack. Screenplay: Robert Garland (and David Rayfiel and Alvin Sargent, non-credited). Screen story by Paul Gaer and Robert Garland, based on an original idea by Shelly Burton. Associate Producer/Production Manager: Ronald Schwary. Music: Dave Grusin. Director of Photography: Owen Roizman. Production Design: Stephen Grimes. Art Director: J. Dennis Washington. Set Decorator: Mary Swanson. Editing: Sheldon Kahn. Costume Designer: Bernie Pollack. Sound: Al Overton, Jr., Arthur Piantadosi, Les Fresholtz, Michael Minkler. Assistant Director: M. Michael Moore. 2nd Assistant Director: Bart Roe. Casting: Jennifer Shull. Choreographer and Assistant to Mr. Pollack: Bernardine Kent. Titles: Wayne Fitzgerald. Men's Costumes: Art Martinez, Richard LaMotte. Women's Costumes: Rita Salazar, Francine Jamison. Production Coordinator: Mary Gay Hollander. Script Supervisor: Julie Pitkanen. Production Associate: Michael Britton. Transportation Coordinator: Gary Paulsen. Location Manager: Don Kruger. Unit Publicist: Jack Hirschberg. Property Master: Eddie

Aiona. Gaffer: Ted Holt. Key Grip: R. Reinholt Rose. Special Effects: Augie Lohman. Makeup: Gary Liddiard. Ms. Fonda's Makeup: Bernadine Anderson. Hairstylist: Marine Pedraza. Livestock Supervisor: Kenny Lee. Supervising Sound Editor: Gordon Davidson. Assistant Editor: Marilyn Madderon. Music Editor: Else Blangsted, La Da Productions. Stills by: Howard Bingham. Camera Operator: James Glennon. Camera Assistants: John Jensen, Rob Hahn. Sound Editors: William Sawyer, Kurt Schulkey, Robert A. Reich, Ross Taylor. Sound Assistants: John E. Davis, Neil Burrow. Re-recording Mixers: Alan Piantadosi, Les Fresholtz, Michael Minkler. Music Scoring Mixer: Dan Walin. Filmed at Caesar's Palace, Las Vegas, Nevada. Songs sung by Willie Nelson.

Cast: Robert Redford (Sonny Steele), Jane Fonda (Hallie Martin), Valerie Perrine (Charlotta Steele), Willie Nelson (Wendell), John Saxon (Hunt Sears), Nicholas Coster (Fitzgerald), Alan Arbus (Danny), Wilford Brimley (Farmer), Will Hare (Gus), Basil Hoffman (Tolland), Timothy Scott (Leroy), James B. Sikking (Dietrich), James Kline (Tommy), Frank Speiser (Bernie), Quinn Redeker (Bud), Lois Areno (Joanna), Sarah Harris (Lucinda), Tasha Zemrus (Louise), James Novak (Dennis), Debra Maxwell (Convention Hostess), Michele Heyden (Sonny Angel), Robin Timm (Model Narrator), Patricia Blair (Fashion Narrator), Gary M. Fox (Bell Man), Richard Perlmutter (Desk Clerk), Carol Eileen Montgomery (Carol), Theresa Ann Dent (Ranch Breakfast Model), Perry Sheehan Adiar (Mrs. George Phillips), Sarge Allen (Mr. Phillips), Sylvie Strauss (Matron), Richard Knoll (Dealer), Angelo Giouzelis (Matre'D), Mark Jamison (Major Domo), Brendan Kelly (Grocer), Sheila B. Wakely (Store Clerk), X.V. Kelly (Sheriff), Gary Shermaine (Trucker), Gary Liddiard (Townsman), Jerry Kurland, J. Carlton Adair, Charles J. Monahan, George W. Etter, Raymond G. Maupin, Bob C. Barrett (AMPCO Personnel), Red McIlvaine, Frank Nicholas, Johnny Magnus, Vic Vallaro, Bob Bailey, Roger Lowe (Reporters), Molly McCall, Mickey Gilbert (Stunt People), Bruce Paul Barboar, Corky Behrle, Ken Endoso, Ralph Garrett, Conrad Palmisano, Mary K. Peters, Rick Seaman, Sonny Shields, Rock Walker (Stunts Chase Sequences)

12. *Absence of Malice* (1981)
     Columbia. A Mirage Enterprises Production. Genre: Drama. Running time: 116 minutes. Rating: PG. Released: November 19, 1981. Released on videocassette.

Credits: Produced and directed by Sydney Pollack. Screenplay: Kurt Luedtke. Executive Producer: Ronald L. Schwary. Music: Dave Grusin. Director of Photography: Owen Roizman. Production Designer: Terence Marsh. Production Manager: Ronald Schwary. Editing: Sheldon Kahn. Assistant Director: David McGiffert. Costume Designer: Bernie Pollack. Casting: Lynn Stalmaster and Associates. 2nd Assistant Director: Rafael Elortegui. Set Decorator: John Franco, Jr. Men's Costumer: Bob Moore. Women's Costumer: Rita Salazar. Hairstylist: Terri Cannon. Makeup Artist: Don L. Cash. Ms. Field's Makeup: Dorothy Pearl. Publicity: Beverly Walker. Property Master: Edward A. Aiona. Transportation Coordinator: Gerald R. Molen. Camera Operator: James Glennon. Camera Assistant: Rob Hahn. Script Supervisor: Wilma Garscadden-Garrett. Gaffer: Gary Holt. Key Grip: Bob Rose. Construction Coordinator: Chuck Stein. Construction

Foreman: Willie Marceau. Sound Mixer: Bert Hallberg. Boom Man: Ralph Babcock. Supervising Sound Editor: Gordon Davidson. Associate Editor: Lois Freeman. Assistant Editor: Joe Mosca. Music Editor: Else Blangsted. Sound Editors: Chester L. Slomka, Robert A. Reich, Meil Burrow. Re-recording Mixers: Arthur Piantadosi, Les Fresholtz, Tom Dahl. Music Scoring Mixer: Dan Wallin. Assistant Property Master: Robert Boettcher. Leadmen: William S. Maxwell, III, John A. Scott, III. Location Manager: Ned McLeod. Local Casting: Beverly McDermott Casting. Auditor: Ken Ryan. Assistant Auditor: Penny McCarthy. Transportation Captain: Mike McDuffee. Transportation Captain (Miami): Hank Scelza. Production Coordinator: Patricia Matzdorff. Lenses and Panaflex Camera by Panavision. Color by Deluxe, Opticals by Pacific Title.

Cast: Paul Newman (Michael Gallagher), Sally Field (Megan Carter), Bob Balaban (Elliot Rosen), Melinda Dillon (Teresa Perrone), Barry Primus (Waddell), Luther Adler (Malderone), Josef Sommer (McAdam), Wilford Brimley (Wells), Don Hood (Quinn), John Harkins (Davidek), Arnie Ross (Eddie Frost), Anna Marie Napoles (Nickie), Shelley Spurlock (Sarah Wylie), Shawn McAllister (Hood 1), Joe Petrullo (Hood 2), Rooney Kerwin (Walker), Oswaldo Calvo (John), Clardy Malugen (Donna), Sharon Anderson (Secretary), Jody Wilson (Raggedy Lady), Ilse Earl (Nun), Alfredo Alvarez Calderon (Rodriguez), Pat Sullivan (Meersma), Bill Hindman (Priest). FBI Agents: John Archie, Timothy Hawkins, Ricardo Marquez. Patrick Matzdorff (Susan), Reporters: Diane Zolten, Kathy Suergiu, Jeff Gillen. Ted Bartsch (Beverage Manager), Sugar Ray Mann (Copy Boy), Richard O'Feldman (Driver), Chuck Lupo (Dock Boy), John Di Santi (Longshoreman), Laurie V. Logan (McAdam's Assistant), Jack McDermott, Mark Harris, Bobbie-Ellyne Kosstrin, Lynn Parraga, Lee Sandman, Barry Hober (News Staff), Gary Van Auken (Marshall)

13. *Tootsie* (1982)

Columbia. A Mirage/Punch Production. Genre: Comedy/romance. Running time: 116 minutes. Rating: Originally, R; Appealed, PG. Released: December 17, 1982. Released on videocassette.

Credits: Producers: Sydney Pollack and Dick Richards. Executive Producer: Charles Evans. Director: Sydney Pollack. Story: Don McGuire and Larry Gelbart. Screenplay: Larry Gelbart, Murray Schisgal. Music: Dave Grusin. Director of Photography: Owen Roizman. Production Designer: Peter Larkin. Editing: Fredric Steinkamp and William Steinkamp. Costume Designer: Roth Morley. Casting: Lynn Stalmaster, Toni Howard and Associates. Unit Production Manager: Gerald R. Molen. Assistant Director: David McGiffert. 2nd Assistant Director: Joseph Reidy. Mr. Hoffman's Makeup Created and Designed by: Dorothy Pearl and George Masters. Costume Supervisor: Bernie Pollack. Auditor: Ken Ryan. Men's Costumes: Franke Piazza. Women's Costumer: Jennifer Nichols. Makeup Artist: C. Romaina Ford. Mr. Hoffman's Makeup: Allen Weisinger. Hair Stylists: Joe Cosca, Tony Marrero. Ms. Lange's Makeup: Dorothy Pearl. Ms. Lange's Hair Stylist: Toni Walker. Set Decorator: Tom Tonery. Camera Operator: Bill Steiner. Camera 1st Assistant: Michael Green. Camera 2nd Assistant: Scott Rathner. Unit Still Photographer: Brian Hamill. Unit Publicist: Ann Guerin. Sound Mixer: Les Lazarowitz. Boom Man: Tod Maitland. Gaffer: Dick Quinlan. Key Grips: Bob Rose and Michael

Miller. Scenic Artist: William Lucek. Property Master: Jimmy Rait. Extras Casting: Sylvia Fay. Script Supervisor: Renee Bodner. Assistant Editors: Nancy Weizer, Don Brochu, Jill Savitt. Music Editor: Else Blangsted. Assistant Auditor: Pete Lombardi. Transportation Captain: Whitey McEvoy. Sound Effects: Effective Sound Unlimited, Tom McCarthy, Jr., Don Walden. Re-recording Mixers: Arthur Piantadosi, Les Fresholtz, Dick Alexander. Location Mgrs: Ezra Swerdlow, Jonathan Filley. DGA Trainee: Ann Egbert. Production Office Coordinator: Bruce Patterson. Assistant Production Office Coordinator: Harriette Kanew. Assistant to Dustin Hoffman: Lee Gottsegen. Assistant to Sydney Pollack: Crin Connolly. Production Assistants: Tom Burns, Justine Cooke, David Sardi, Carey Bozanich, Stephanie Brooks, Gary Vermillion, Karl Steinkamp, Toni Lani. Lenses and Paniflex Camera by Panavision. Color by Technicolor. Titles and Opticals by Pacific Title.

    Cast: Dustin Hoffman (Michael Dorsey/Dorothy Michaels), Jessica Lange (Julie), Teri Garr (Sandy), Dabney Coleman (Ron), Charles Durning (Les), Sydney Pollack (George Fields), George Gaynes (John Van Horn), Geena Davis (April), Doris Belack (Rita), Bill Murray (Jeff) unbilled, Ellen Foley (Jacqui), Peter Gatto (Rick), Lynn Thigpin (Jo), Ron Schwary (Phil Weintraub), Debra Mooney (Mrs. Mallory), Amy Lawrence (Amy), Kenny Sinclair (Boy), Susan Merson (Page), Michael Ryan (Middle-Aged Man), Robert D. Wilson, (Stage Hand), James Carruthers (Middle-Aged Man), Estelle Getty (Middle-Aged Woman), Christine Ebersole (Linda), Bernie Pollack (Actor #1), Sam Stoneburner (Actor #2), Marjorie Lovett (Salesgirl), Willy Switkes (Man at Cab), Gregory Camillucci (Maître d'), Barbara Spiegel (Billie), Tony Craig (Spencer), Walter Cline (Bartender), Suzanne Von Schaack (Party Girl), Anne Shropshire (Mrs. Crawley), Pamela Lincoln (Secretary), Mary Donnet (Receptionist), Bernie Passeltiner (Mac), Mallory Jones (Girl #1), Patti Cohane (Girl #2), Murray Schisgal (Party Guest), Greg Gorman (Photographer), Anne Prager (Acting Student), John Carpenter (First Actor), Bob Levine (Second Actor), Richard Whiting (Priest), Jim Jansen (Stage Manager #2), Susan Egbert (Diane), Kay Self (Acting Student), Tom Mardirosian (Stage Manager), Richard Wirth (Mel — Technical Director), Gavin Reed (Director), Annie Korzen, Ibbits Warriner, Lois DeBanzie, Stephen C. Prutting, Carole Holland (Autograph Hounds)

    Music Credits: Original Songs — Lyrics by Alan and Marilyn Bergman; music by Dave Grusin. "Tootsie" and "It Might Be You" — Sung by Stephen Bishop.

14. *Out of Africa* (1985).
    Universal Pictures. A Mirage Enterprises Production. Genre: Epic romance/adaptation. Running time: 161 minutes. Rating: PG. Shot in 70mm and 35mm. Released: December 13, 1985. Released on videocassette in U.S., April 7, 1988; laserdisc, December 1988.

    Credits: Produced and directed by Sydney Pollack. Co-Producer: Terry Clegg. Executive Producer: Kim Jorgensen. Associate Producers: Judith Thurman and Anna Cataldi. Screenplay: Kurt Luedtke (and David Rayfiel, non-credited), based on the books *Out of Africa, Letters from Africa, Shadows on the Grass* by Isak Dinesen, *Isak Dinesen: The Life of a Storyteller* by Judith Thurman, and *Silence Will Speak* by Errol Trzebinski. Production Manager: Gerry Levy. Production Designer: Stephen Grimes. Music: John Barry. Director of Photography:

David Watkin. Art Directors: Herbert Westbrook, Colin Grimes, Cliff Robinson. Set Director: Josie MacAvin. Editing: Fredric Steinkamp, William Steinkamp, Pembroke Herring, Sheldon Kahn. Costume Designer: Milena Canonero. Sound Mixer: Peter Handford. Casting: Mary Selway. 1st Assistant Director: David Tomblin. Camera Operator: Freddie Cooper. 2nd Unit Directors: Simon Trevor, Jack Couffer. Aerial Photography: Peter Allwork. Location and Field Consultant: John Sutton. Location Managers: Grania O'Shannon, Allan James. 2nd Assistant Director: Roy Button. Assistant Directors: George Menoe, Patrick Kinney, Meja Mwangi, Tom Mwangi. Production Consultant: Monty Ruben. Script Supervisors: Nikki Clapp, Lissa Ruben. Production Coordinator: Margaret Adams. Steadicam Operator: Steve St. John. Gaffer: Maurice Gillett. Grips: Ray Hall, Ibrahim Jibril, Mahmud Sheikh Omar, Ricky Hall, Ali Matata, Mohamed Ngela, Mohamed Wafula. Best Boy: Alan Barry. Boom Operator: John Stevenson. Construction Manager: Geoff Langley. Property Master: Bert Hearn. Assistant Costume Designer: Joanna Johnston. Wardrobe: Kenny Crouch, Jennie Hawkins, Andres Fernandez Sotillos, Stephen Cornish, Elizabeth Ryrie, Pat McEvan. Costume Maker: David Garrett. Miss Streep's Hair and Makeup: J. Roy Helland. Mr. Redford's Makeup Artist: Gary Liddiard. Chief Makeup Artist: Mary Hillman. Makeup Artist: Norma Hill. Chief Hairdresser: Vera Mitchell. Hairdresser: Joyce James. Post Production Supervisor: Robin Forman. Associate Editor: Claudio Cutry. Assistant Editors: Don Brochu, Jeffrey Bell, Karl Steinkamp, Craig Herring, Saul Saladow, Joseph Mosca, Rick Meyer. Supervising Sound Editor: Tom McCarthy, Jr. Music Editor: Clif Kohlweck. ADR Editor: William Manger. Re-recording Mixers: Chris Jenkins, Gary Alexander, Larry Stensvold. Music Scoring Mixer: Dan Wallin. Negative Cutter: Donah Bassett. Local Casting (Kenya): Sarah Withey. Production Accountant: Brian Gibbs. Publicist: Patricia Johnson. Still Photographer: Frank Connor. Special Effects Supervisor: David Harris. 2nd Unit Camera Operator: Rodrigo Gutierrez. Production Assistants: David Hilton, Thomas Thanangadan. Production Secretary: Christine Buuri. Voice Casting: Barbara Harris. Chief Animal Trainer: Hubert Wells. Kikuyu Advisor: Nelson Chege. Music Research: Alan Smyth. African Music Advisor: George W. Senoga-Zake. Location Camps and Safari Services Provided by Ker and Downey Safaris, Kenya. Filmed in Technovision. Color by Rank Film Laboratories. Prints by Technicolor. Photographed on AFTA XT Color Negative. Main Title Design by Phill Norman. Titles by Pacific Title. Opticals by Universal Title. Soundtrack available on MCA.

Cast: Meryl Streep (Karen Blixen), Robert Redford (Denys Finch Hatton), Klaus Maria Brandauer (Bror Blixen), Michael Kitchen (Berkeley Cole), Malick Bowens (Farah), Joseph Thiaka (Kamante), Michael Gough (Delamere), Suzanna Hamilton (Felicity), Stephen Kinyanjui (Kinyanjui), Rachel Kempson (Lady Belfield), Graham Crowden (Lord Belfield), Leslie Phillips (Sir Joseph), Shane Rimmer (Belknap), Mike Bugara (Juma), Job Seda (Kanuthia), Mohammed Umar (Ismail), Donal McCann (Doctor), Kenneth Mason (Banker), Tristram Jellinek (First Commissioner), Stephen Grimes (2nd Commissioner), Annabel Maule (Lady Byrne), Benny Young (Minister), Sbish Trzebinski (Beefy Drunk), Allaudin Qureshi (Regiv), Niven Boyd (Young Officer), Iman (Mariammo), Peter Strong (Huge Man), Abdullah Sunado (Esa), Amanda Parkin (Victoria), Muriel Gross (Lady Delamere), Ann Palmer (Dowager), Keith Pearson (Missionary Teacher)

Music Credits: "Concerto for Clarinet and Orchestra in A"—Written by Wolfgang Amadeus Mozart; Performed by Jack Brymer, Clarinet, The Academy of St. Martin-in-the-Fields; Directed by Neville Marriner; Courtesy of Phillips Classic Productions, The Netherlands. "Sonata in A Major-Rondo Alla Turca"—Written by Wolfgang Amadeus Mozart; Performed by Andras Schiff; Courtesy of London Records, A Division of Polygram Classics, Inc. "Sinfonia Concertante in E Flat Major for Violin and Viola"—Written by Wolfgang Amadeus Mozart; Performed by Alan Loveday, Violin; Stephen Shingles, Viola, The Academy of St. Martin-in-the-Fields; Directed by Neville Marriner; Courtesy of London Records, A Division of Polygram Classics, Inc. "Three Divertimenti"—Written by Wolfgang Amadeus Mozart; Performed by The Academy of St. Martin-in-the-Fields; Directed by Neville Marriner; Courtesy of London Records, A Division of Polygram Classics, Inc.

15. *Havana* (1990)

Universal Pictures. A Mirage Enterprises Production. Genre: Drama. Running time: 145 minutes. Rating: R. Released: December 9, 1990. Released on videocassette in U.S., May 9, 1991; laserdisc, May 16, 1991.

Credits: Producers: Sydney Pollack and Richard Roth. Executive Producer: Ronald L. Schwary. Director: Sydney Pollack. Story: Judith Rascoe. Screenplay: Judith Rascoe and David Rayfiel. Music: Dave Grusin. Director of Photography: Owen Roizman. Production Designer: Terence Marsh. Art Director: George Richardson. Editing: Fredric Steinkamp and William Steinkamp. Costume Designer: Bernie Pollack. Sound Mixer: Peter Handford. 1st Assistant Director: David Tomblin. Unit Production Manager: Ronald L. Schwary. Production Accountant: Ken Ryan. Production Supervisor: Mark Allan. Transportation Coordinator: Steve Molen. 2nd Assistant Directors: Jose Luis Escolar, Lee Cleary. Assistant Art Directors: Peter Childs, Dianne Wager. Draftsmen: Martin Hitchcock, Dave Allday. Camera Operator: Rob Hahn. 1st Assistant Cameraman: Dennis J. Laine. 2nd Assistant Cameramen: John Ellingwood, Robert Keslow. Continuity Supervisor: Anne Rapp. Boom Operator: Martin Trevis. Sound Engineer: Don Brown. 2nd Unit Director of Photography: Richard Bowen. Set Decorator: Michael Sierton. Assistant Set Decorator: Charles Steward. Swing: Steven H. George. Choreographer: Vincent Paterson. Location Manager: Robin Citrin. Chief Lighting Technician: Gary H. Holt. Best Boy: Robert Kratiger. Rigging Gaffer: William L. Peets. Rigging Best Boy: Rick Benedetto. Electricians: Tom Cantrell, Lonnie Gatlin, Jim Kratiger. Key Grip: Tim Ryan. Best Boy Grip: Carl Gibson, Jr. Rigging Key Grip: Frank J. Keever. Dolly Grip: David L. Merrill. Grips: William Kenney, Mitch Lookabaugh, Richard C. Lewis. Standby Painter: Dave Wescott. Craftserviceman: Tim Gonzalez. Special Effects: Tony Vandenecker. Assistant Special Effects: William E. Dawson. Property Master: Steven Levine. Assistant Property: Glenn Forbes. Supervising Makeup Artist: Gary Liddiard. Makeup Artists: Thomas Hoerber, Dennis Liddiard. Supervising Hairstylist: Susan Carol-Schwary. Hairstylist: Kathe Swanson. Men's Wardrobe: Hugo Pena, Darryl M. Athons, Eric H. Sanders. Women's Wardrobe: Kathy O'Rear, Sue Moore, Cha Blevins, Kelly Porter. Assistant Production Accountant: Mayda Renizzi-Holt.

Assistant Accountant: Kay Jordan. Production Office Coordinator: Nanette A. Siegert. Production Secretaries: Patricia Salazar, Mary Escoto. 3rd Assistant Director: Felipe Vicini. Unit Publicist: Beverly Walker. Still Photographer: Elliott Marks. Projectionist: Billy R. Brashier. Illustrator: Nikita Knatz. Assistants to Mr. Pollack: Donna Ostroff, David Kohan. Assistants to Mr. Schwary: Teresa A. Ekwall. Assistant to Mr. Redford: Robbie Miller. Shipping Coordinator: William A. Johnson. Transportation Captain: Maxwell Robert Johnson. Drivers: Al J. Hersh, Gary Hardman, Gary Duncan, William A. Esparsa, Jonny Johnson, Bob Johnson, Richard A. Lee, Rick Padgett, Jr., David Teasley, Jose Benito Cantu. Construction Coordinator: Ray Barrett. Construction Buyer: Michael King. Assistant Construction Manager: Michael Nugent. Supervising Carpenter: Steve Allaway. Supervising Rigger: Nobby Clarke. Supervising Stagehand: Jack Dyer. Supervising Plasterer: Paul Tappin. Supervising Painter: Paul Wescott. Scenic Artist: Jose Duarte. Post Production Supervisor: Karen Marmer Allen. Assistant Film Editors: Karl Steinkamp, Michael Wilson. Apprentice Film Editor: Susan Alexander. Production Assistants: D. Clayton Miller, Kevin H. Lillestol, Bryan Constans, Les Knight. Supervising Sound Editor: J. Paul Huntsman. Music Editorial Consultant: Else Blangsted. Music Editor: Bunny Andrews. Assistant Music Editor: Lise Richardson. Music Clearance: Jill Meyers. Supervising ADR Editor: Jessica Galavan. ADR Editor: Thomas Whiting. Foley Editors: Lucy Coldsnow, Butch Wolf. Foley Artists: Robin Harlan, Sarah Monat. Music Scoring Mixers: Don Murray, John Richards. Re-Recording Mixers: Chris Jenkins, D.M. Hemphill, Mark Smith. Sound Effects Editor: Joel Valentine. Dialogue Editors: Robert Mackston, Matthew Sawelson. Assistant Sound Editors: Carolann Sanchez Shapiro, Desmond Cannon. Voice Casting: Barbara Harris. Negative Cutter: Gary Burritt. Negative Timer: Reid Burns. Music Consultant: Joel Sill. Cameras and lenses by Panavision. Titles Designed by Phill Norman. Titles and Opticals by Pacific Title. Cranes and Dollys by Chapman. Rerecorded by Todd AO/Glen Glenn Studios. Color by Deluxe. Dolby Stereo.

Cast: Robert Redford (Jack Weil), Lena Olin (Bobby Duran), Alan Arkin (Joe Volpi), Tomas Milian (Menocal), Raul Julia (Duran [unbilled]), Daniel Davis (Marion Chigwell), Tony Plana (Julia Ramos), Richard Farnsworth (Professor), Mark Rydell (Myer Lansky), Vasek Simac (Willy), Fred Asparagus (Baby Hernandez), Richard Portnow (Mike), Betsy Brantley (Diane), Lise Cutter (Patty), Dion Anderson (Roy Forbes), Carmine Carridy (Cpt. Potts), James Medina (Cpl.), Joe Lala (Cuban Businessman), Salvadore Levy (Menocal's Lieut.), Bernie Pollack (Hotel Man), Owen Roizman (Santos), Dion Anderson (Roy Forbes), Segundo Tarrau (Ricardo), Felix German (Tomas), Giovanna Bonnelly (Monica), Pepito Guerra (Manager), Anthony Bayarri (Modest Casino Cuban), Alfredo Vorshirm (Modest Casino Tuxedo), Hugh Kelly (Carlos), Franklin Rodriguez (Jose), David Jose Rodriguez (Bufano), Victor Rivers (Young Cuban #1), Alex Ganster (Young Cuban #2), Rene Monclova (SIM #1), Miguel Angel Suarez (SIM #2), Terri Hendrickson (Dancer #1), Karen Russell (Dancer #2), David Gibson (Sailor), Adriano Gonzalez (Rebel Cpt.), Raul Rosado (Roadblock Sgt.), Mildred Ventura (Woman at Burning Villa), Bonita Marco (Stripper #1), Sharon Velez (Stripper #2), Darlene Wynn (Stripper #3), Miguel Bucarelly (Gomez), Carlos Miranda (Inspector #1), Enrique Chao Barros (Inspector #2), Daniel Vasquez (Kid), Carmen De Franco (Monica's Grandmother).

Music Credits: "Round and Round"—Written by Lou Stallman and Joe Shapiro; Performed by Perry Como; Courtesy of RCA Records. "Mambo # 5"—Written by Perez Prado. "One Night"—Written by Dave Bartholomew and Pearl King; Performed by Fats Domino; Courtesy of EMI, A Division of Capital Records, Inc; By arrangement with CEMA Special Markets. "I Think of You"—Written by Jack Elliott and Don Marcotte; Performed by Frank Sinatra; Courtesy of Capitol Records, Inc; By arrangement with CEMA Special Markets. "The Christmas Song"—Written by Mel Torme and Robert Welles. "La Gloria Eres Tu"—Written by Jose Antonio Mendes. "Grusero Sal Sero"—Written by George Hernandez. "Have Yourself a Merry Little Christmas"—Written by Ralph Blane and Hugh Martin; Performed by Doris Day; Courtesy of CBS Records, Music Licensing Department. "Cuban's Nightmare"—Written and performed by Tito Puente; Courtesy of RCA Records. "Moonglow"—Written by Will Hudson, Eddie Delange, Irving Mills. "Me Voy Pal Pueblo"—Written by Mercedes Valdez. "Olvido"—Written by Miguel Matamoros. "Too Late Now"—Written by Alan Jay Lerner and Burton Lane. "Rum and Coca-Cola"—Written by Morey Amsterdam and Paul Baron and Jeri Sullavan; Performed by the Andrews Sisters; Courtesy of MCA Records. "Los Tamalitos De Olga"—Written by Jose Fajardo. "Damisela Encantadora"—Written by Ernesto Lecuona. "Let's Get Away From It All"—Written by Tom Adair and Matt Dennis. Performed by Frank Sinatra. Courtesy of Capitol Records, Inc.; By arrangement with CEMA Special Markets. "A Los Rumberos de Belen"—Written by Roberto Nunez; Performed by Grupo Serra Maestra; Courtesy of EGREM Records. "C.C. Rider"—Written by Chuck Willis. "Defiendeme Santa Barbara"—Written by Dagoberto Acosta; Performed by Linda Leida, Javier Vasquez y Su Conjunto; Courtesy of Caiman Records. "Why Do Fools Fall in Love"—Written by Frankie Lymon and Morris Levy; Performed by Frankie Lymon and the Teenagers; Courtesy of Rhino Records, Inc. "Beyond the Sea"—Written by Charles Trenet and Jack Lawrence; Performed by Bobby Darin; Courtesy of Altantic Recording Corp; By arrangement with Warner Special Products. "Rico Vacillon"—Written by Rosendo Ruiz, Jr. "Mi Habana"—Written by George Hernandez. "Memories Are Made of This"—Written by Terry Gilkyson, Frank Miller and Richard Dehr; Performed by Dean Martin; Courtesy of Capitol Records, Inc.; By arrangement with CEMA Special Markets. "London by Night"—Written by Carroll Coates; Performed by Frank Sinatra; Courtesy of Capitol Records, Inc.; By arrangement with CEMA Special Markets. "Me Voy Pal Pueblo"—Written by Mercedes Valdes. "Ochun"—Written by Johnny Richards.

16. *The Firm* (1993)
   Paramount Pictures (US); United International Pictures (worldwide). A Mirage Enterprises Production. Genre: Thriller. Running time: 154 minutes. Rating: R. Shooting schedule: November 9, 1992–March 20, 1993. Theatrical release in U.S.: June 30, 1993; Released on videocassette in U.S. by Paramount Home Video, December 16, 1993, and re-released on video October 19, 1994, and May 21, 1996 (Tom Cruise Collection). Reviews: *Variety,* 6/28/93; *LA Times,* 6/30/93; *New York Times,* 6/30/93.

Credits: Producers: Sydney Pollack, Scott Rudin and John Davis. Executive Producers: Lindsay Doran and Michael Hausman. Director: Sydney Pollack. Screenplay: David Rabe, Robert Towne and David Rayfiel. Based on the novel by John Grisham. Music: Dave Grusin. Director of Photography: John Seale. Production Designer: Richard MacDonald. Set Decorator: Casey Hallenbeck. Art Director: John Willett. Editing: William Steinkamp and Fredric Steinkamp. Costumes: Ruth Myers. Unit Production Manager: Michael Hausman. 1st Assistant Director: David McGiffert. 2nd Assistant Director: Carla Corwin. Unit Manager: Scott Ferguson. Steadicam Operator: Mark Van Loon. Sound Mixer: David MacMillan. Chief Lighting Technician: Mo Flam. 1st Company Grip: Robin Knight. Property Master: Robin Miller. Costume Supervisor: Bruce Ericksen. Mr. Cruise's Costumer: David Page. Key Hairstylist: Bill Farley. Mr. Cruise's Hairstylist: Lyndell Quitou. Makeup Supervisor: Ben Nye, Jr. Mr. Cruise's Makeup: Richard Dean. Production Coordinator: Nanette Siegert. Script Supervisor: Anne Rapp. Location Manager: Michael Dellheim. Production Accountant: Elton MacPherson. Construction Coordinator: Bill Bradford. Print Supervisor: Tom Ivanjack. Stunt Coordinator: Andy Armstrong. Special Effects: Ken Estes. Transportation Coordinator: Jerry Jackson. Publicist: Lauren Beth Strogoff. Post Production Supervisor: Karen Marmer. 1st Assistant Camera: Brian Armstrong. 2nd Assistant Camera: Bob Mancuso. Steadicam Camera Assistant: Douglas Schwartz. Camera Loader: David Brink. Still Photographer: François Duhamel. Boom Operator: Steve Bowerman. Cableperson: Kevin E. Patterson. Video Artist: Paul Murphy. Assistant Art Director: James Feng. Art Department Coordinator: Yael Haffner. Assistant Set Decorator: Steven Husch. Set Dressers: Lisa Miller, David Weathers, Joseph McAfee Jr., Spencer Register. Greensperson: Thomas Gilbert. Draperies: Mary Kate Edmonstone. Assistant Chief Lighting Technician: Andy Day. Electricians: Robert Bruce, Tom Clark, Darryl Wilson, Steve Spallone. Rigging Electrician: John Velez. 2nd Company Grip: Riko Schatke. Dolly Grip: Charles Brown. Grips: Tommy "Mooky" Walker, Lee McLemore. Rigging Grip: Sunny Johnson. Assistant Property Master: Michael Gastaldo. Property Assistant: Chris Ubick. Assistant Costume Designer: Marjorie McCown. Costumer: Luke Reichle. Set Supervisor and Wardrobe: Robin Borman. Wardrobe Assistant: Rachel Heilpenn. Assistant Production Coordinator: Debbie Charboneau. 2nd 2nd Assistant Director: Scott Harris. Location Coordinator: Alonzo Woods. Casting Associate: Debra Zane. Casting Assistant: Amy Taksen. Location Casting Consultant: Jo Doster. Assistant Film Editors: Michael T. Wilson, Karl Steinkamp, Joyce Arrastia. Apprentice Film Editors: Robert Steinkamp, Randy Bricker. Music Editor: Ted Whitfield. Music Recorded by: Don Murray. Piano Consultant: David L. Abell. Supervising Sound Editor: J. Paul Huntsman. Sound Effects Editors: John Haeny, Myron Nettinga. Supervising ADR Editor: Jessica Gallavan. ADR Editor: J. Christopher Jargo. Dialogue Editors: Matthew Sawelson, Adam Sawelson, Gary Lewis, David Beadle. Foley Editors: Lucy Coldsnow-Smith, Jeff Rosen, Jonathon Klein. Assistant Sound Editors: Carolann Sanchez-Shapiro, Carmen Flores, Jennifer Portman. Voice Casting: Barbara Harris. Re-recording Mixers: Chris Jenkins, Mark Smith, Doug Hemphill. Re-recorded by Todd-AO/Glen Glenn Studios. Assistant Production Accountants: Jeanine Wilson, Lisa Knudson. Payroll Accountant: John "J.R." Craigmile. Accounting Assistant: Marjorie Chodorov.

Construction Forepersons: Jerry Henry, Mark Favert. Construction Manager: Gerry Byrne. Production Painters: Claudia Gilligan-Ivanjack, Sharleen Bright. Additional Special Effects: Steve Wolf. Aerial Camera: David Butler. Aerial 1st Assistant Camera: Steve Jackman. Helicopter Pilot: David Jones. Underwater Photography: Pete Romano. Transportation Captain: Richard David. Transportation Dispatcher: Vicki Lybrand. Picture Car Coordinator: Dennis Milliken. Transportation Assistant: A. McRae Hilliard. Animal Trainer: Mathilde DeCagny. Computer Graphics and Engineering: John Monsour. Production Assistants: Darin Rivetti, Derek Johansen, John Saunders, Sam Velasco, Jennifer Blair, Doug Sims, Leo McDaniel, Tom Ludwig. Assistant to Mr. Pollack: Donna Ostroff. Assistant to Mr. Cruise: Michael Doven. Assistant to Mr. Rudin: Mike Thompson. Assistant to Mr. Davis: Brooke Brooks. Assistants to Mr. Hausman: Jenny Evans, Lauren Buckley. Assistant to Ms. Doran: Carol King. Catering: Frank Woodward For Stars Catering, Inc. Craft Service: Drew Clarke. Craft Service Assistant: Wende Martin. Police Coordinator: Larry Leggett. Color Timer: Philip Hetos. Negative Cutter: Theresa Repola Mohammed. Title Design by Phill Norman. Titles and Opticals by Pacific Title. Color by Deluxe. Dailies by Technicolor. Panavision Cameras and Lenses. Music consultant: Joel Sill. Re-recorded by Todd-AO/Glen Glenn Studios. Soundtrack available on MCA.

Grand Cayman Islands Unit: Location Managers: Daniel Stroh, Randolph Ostrow. Assistant Location Manager: Ian Stone. Extras Casting: Kim Davis. Art Dept. Coordinator: Ann Cockerton. Aerial Photography Pilot: Ed Connelly.

Washington, D.C. Unit: Assistant Production Coordinator: Cathleen Clarke. Location Manager: Peggy Pridemore. Location Assistant: Stephanie Antosca.

Boston Unit: Location Managers: Michael Dick, Eric Davidson.

Cast: Tom Cruise (Mitch McDeere), Jeanne Tripplehorn (Abby McDeere), Gene Hackman (Avery Tolar), Ed Harris (Wayne Tarrance), Holly Hunter (Tammy Hemphill), Hal Holbrook (Oliver Lambert), Terry Kinney (Lamar Quinn), Wilford Brimley (William Devasher), David Strathairn (Ray McDeere), Gary Busey (Eddie Lomax), Steven Hill (Voyles), Tobin Bell (Nordic Man), Barbara Garrick (Kay Quinn), Jerry Hardin (McKnight), Paul Sorvino (Morolto [uncredited]), Paul Calderon (Richie), Jerry Weintraub (Capps), Sullivan Walker (Abanks), Karina Lombard (Woman on the Beach), Margo Martindale (Nina Huff), John Beal (Locke), Dean Norris (Squat Man), Lou Walker (Mulholland), Debbie Turner (Rental Agent), Tommy Cresswell (Wally Hudson), David Kimball (Randall Dunbar), Don Jones (Attorney), Michael D. Allen (Attorney), Levi Frazier, Jr. (Restaurant Waiter), Brian Casey (Telephone Installer), Rev. William J. Parham (Minister), Victor Nelson (Cafe Waiter), Richard Ranta (Congressman Billings), Janie Paris (Madge), Frank Crawford (Judge), Bart Whiteman (Dutch), David Dwyer (Prison Guard), Jerry Chipman (FBI Agent), Mark Johnson (FBI Agent), Jimmy Lackie (Technician), Afemo Omilami, Clinton Smith (Cotton Truck Drivers), Susan Elliott, Erin Branham (River Museum Guides), Ed Connelly (Pilot), Joey Anderson (Ruth), Deborah Thomas (Maid), Tommy Matthews (Elvis Hemphill), Chris Schadrack, Jeffrey Ford, Jonathan Kaplan (Lawyer Recruiters), Rebecca Glenn (Young Woman in Bar), Terri Welles (Woman Dancing with Avery), Gregory Goossen (Vietnam Veteran), Jeane Aufdenberg (Car Rental

Agent), William R. Booth (Seaplane Pilot), The Lannie McMillan Quartet (Peabody Musicians), Ollie Nightingale (Restaurant Singer), Teenie Hodges (Restaurant Lead Guitarist), Little Jimmy King (Memphis Street Musician), James White (Singer at Hyatt)

Music Credits: "Start It Up"— By Robin Ford; Performed by Robin Ford; and The Blue Line; Courtesy of GRP Records, Inc. "The Firm Shuffle"; "Another Cup of Coffee"; "Sweet Memphis"— By Lannie McMillan, Scott Reed, Richard Cesani and Gregory McIntire; Performed by the Lannie McMillan Quartet. "Save the Best for Last"— By Wendy Waldman, John Lind and Phil Galdston; Performed by Claire Marlo Orchestra. "Don't Put No Headstone on My Grave"— Written and Performed by Charlie Rich; Courtesy of Sire Records by arrangement with Warner Special Products. "Out of the Blue"; "Down De Road"— Written and Performed by Andy Narell; Courtesy of Windham Hill Jazz. "Maple Drive"— Written and Performed by Jack Allocco. "Stormy Monday"— Written and Performed by T-Bone Walker; Courtesy of Gregmark Records. "Money, Money, Money"— By George Novak; Performed by George Novak, Henry Leslie, Mark McTaggard, and Harry Johnston. "M-o-n-e-y"— Written and Performed by Lyle Lovett; Courtesy of MCA Curb Records. "I Sho Do"— By Mason Hodges and Billy Always; Performed by Ollie Nightingale; Courtesy of Goldwax Records Company, Inc. "Guitar Blues"— Written and Performed by Little Jimmy King; Courtesy of Rounder Records. "Dance Class"— By Andy Narell; Performed by Dave Samuels; Courtesy of GRP Records, Inc. "Blame It on the Rum"— Written and performed by James White. "Stars on the Water"— By Rodney Crowell: Performed by Jimmy Buffett; Courtesy of MCA Records. "Oboe Concerto in D Minor," "Adagio"— By A. Marcello; Perfomed by Philharmonia Orchestra; Oboe: John Anderson; Conductor: Simon Wright; Courtesy of Nimbus Records. "Never Mind"— By Harlan Howard; Performed by Nanci Griffith; Courtesy of MCA Records.

17. *Sabrina* (1995)

Alternate title: *Sabrina Fair*. Distributor: Paramount Pictures (U.S.); United International Pictures (worldwide, except Germany); Neue Constantin (Germany). In association with Constellation Films and Alcor Film. A Mirage/Scott Rudin/Sandollar Production. Genre: Fairytale/romance/comedy. Running time: 127 minutes. Rating: PG. Initial theatrical release: December 15, 1995. Released on videocassette in U.S. by Paramount Home Video, June 11, 1996. Reviews: *Daily Variety, Variety* and *Hollywood Reporter*, 12/11/95; *New York Times*, 12/15/95.

Credits: Producers: Sydney Pollack and Scott Rudin. Executive Producers: Ron Schwary and Lindsay Doran. Director: Sydney Pollack. Screenplay: David Rayfiel and Barbara Benedek. Based on the screenplay by Billy Wilder, Ernest Lehman and Samuel Taylor. Based on the play *Sabrina Fair* by Samuel Taylor. Production Manager: Ron Schwary. Assistants to Sydney Pollack: Donna Ostroff, Julia Franz. Assistants to Scott Rudin: Raul Gutierrez, Noah Ackerman, Derek Evans, Gary Goodman. Assistant to Ron Schwary: Gina Edmond-Feldman. Assistant to Harrison Ford: Jennifer Wachtell. Consultant to Harrison Ford: Peter Weireter.

Assistant to Julia Ormond: Jane Emanuel. Julia Ormond's Dialect Coach: Lilene Mansell. Assistant to Greg Kinnear: Allison McLeod. Music: John Williams. Original Songs-Music: John Williams. Lyrics: Alan and Marilyn Bergman. Director of Photography: Guiseppe Rotunno. Camera Operator: Giovanni Fiore-Col Tellacci. Production Design: Brian Morris. Art Director: John Kasarda. Assistant Art Director: Jeffrey McDonald. Storyboard Artist: Brick Mason. Art Department Coordinator: Miriam Shapiro. Set Decorator: George De Titta, Jr., Amy Marshall. Production Supervisor: Thomas A. Imperator. Production Coordinator: Katherine Kennedy Caruso. Assistant Production Coordinator: Ray Angelic. Production Secretary: Cheryl E. Compton. Office Production Assistants: George Henfling, Roxanne Ziegler. 1st Assistant Director: Tom Reilly. 2nd Assistant Director: Richard Patrick. DGA Trainee: Michael Reichman. Script Supervisor: Mary A. Kelly. Production Associate: David B. Leener. Production Assistants: Nancy Lefkowitz, Shawn Griffith, Chap Taylor, Peter Soldo, Mary Jo McGrath, Clarence B. Douglas, III, Alexander Cohen, Bac Delorme, Skip Henfling. Chief Lighting Technician: Eugene Engels. Assistant Chief Lighting Technician: John E. Smith. Rigging Electrician: Francis McBride. Electricians: Raymond Fortune, Timothy Gunners, Robert Stocklin, Steve Comesky, William Hines, Fred Muller, Jack Coffen. Production Auditor: Susan Towner. Assistant Auditors: Anamarie C. Gonzaga, Marcus Canty. Payroll Accountant: Antonia Proscia. Accounting Assistants: Matthew Demier, Sam Bruskin. Lead Person: Christopher De Titta. Set Dressers: Gilbert Gertsen, John Oates, Anthony diMeo, Gordon Gertzen, Joseph Proscia, Gerald DeTitta, Dennis Causey, Gary Levitsky. Supervising Greensperson: Ron Von Blomberg. Floral Designer: Wendy Goidell. Stage Coordinator: Brian Mannain. Master Scenic Artist: Peter Hackman. Scenic Artist: Joyce Liepertz. 2nd Scenic Artist: Greg Sullivan. Production Scenic Artist: Rochelle Edelson. Scenic Shopman: Darius Menard. Scenics: Hallie Coletta, Stephen Shellooe, Ellen Doak, Eva Davy. Art Department Production Assistant: Eric Zoback. 1st Assistant Photographer: Jay Levy. 2nd Assistant Photographer: Chris Norr. Camera Trainee: Raymond Collins. Still Photographer: Brain Hamill, Myles Aronowitz. 2nd Unit Director of Photography: Rob Hahn. 2nd Unit Camera Operator: Patrick Capone. 2nd Unit 1st Assistant: Ralph Brandofino. 2nd Unit 2nd Assistant: Paul Coleangelo. Casting Director: David Rubin. Casting Associate: Ronna Kress. Casting Assistant: Bill Kaufman. Extras Casting: Sylvia Fay Casting. Craft Service: Cecil B. de Meals. Construction Coordinator: Ronald Petagna. Construction Key Grip: Vincent Guarriello. Construction Foreman: Frank Didio. Production Carpenter: Wayne Moss. Dialect Coach: Lilene Mansell. Transportation Captain: Steven R. Hammond. Transportation Co-Captain: Thomas J. Keilig. Editors: Fredric Steinkamp, William Steinkamp. 1st Assistant Film Editor: Karl Steinkamp. Assistant Film Editors: Robert Steinkamp, Liza Sullivan. Avid Assistant Editor: Charis Maybach. Music Editor: Ken Wannberg. Post Production Mixing and Sound Editorial by Todd/AO Studios. Re-recording Mixers: Chris Jenkins, Scott Millian, Adam Jenkins. Supervising Sound Editor: J. Paul Huntsman. Supervising Sound Effects Editor: Myron Nettinga. Sound Effects Editors: Mitch Gettleman, Joe Earle. Supervising Dialogue Editor: Adam Sawelson. Dialogue Editors: Barbara Issak, Benjamin Beardwood. Supervising ADR Editor: Mary Andrews. ADR Editor: Laura Graham. Foley Editors: Jeff Rosen, Trevor Jolly. Assistant Sound Editors:

Jeanine Payne, Meredith Gold, Rebecca Nicolaou. Foley Mixer: Dean Drabin. Foley Recordist: Ann Hadsell. Foley Walkers: Robin Harlan, Sarah Monat. Assistant Editors-NY Dailies: Ann McCabe, Amanda Pollack. Voice Casting: Barbara Harris. Orchestra conducted by John Williams. Orchestrations by John Neufeld. Music Preparation: Jo Ann Kane Music Services. Orchestra Contractor: Sandy De Crescent. Music Scoring Mixer: Shawn Murphy. Music Production Set Supervisor: John E. Oliver. Larrabee Commercial by Gordon Driver. Color Timer: Denny McNeill. Negative Cutter: Theresa Repola Mohammed. Titles and Opticals by Pacific Title. Title Design: Phill Norman. Gaffer: Eugene Engels. Best Boy: John E. Smith. 1st Company Grip: Dennis Gamiello. 2nd Company Grip: Brian Fitzsimmons. Dolly Grip: Ed Lowry. Grips: Michael Finnerty, Donald Glenn, Victor Huey, Martin Lowry, Richard Montgomery. Makeup: Bernadette Mazur. Hair: Stephen Bishop. Harrison Ford's Makeup: Peter Robb-King. Harrison Ford's Hair: Lynda Gurasich. Julia Ormond's Makeup: Joe Campayno. Location Manager: Joseph Iberti. Assistant Location Managers: Heidi Topper, Kathleen Corgan. Location Assistant: Jonathan Schwartz. Location Liaison (Martha's Vineyard): Michael Wild. Property Master: Thomas C. Allen. Assistant Property Master: Diana Burton. Property Person: Ann Edgeworth. Projectionist: Ed Nardone. Publicist: Eric Myers. Sound Mixer: Danny Michael. Boom Operator: Andrew Schmetterling. Cableman: O.J. Connell III. Video Assistant: Peter A Mian. Computer Graphics Playback: Gordon Driver. Transportation Captain: Steve Hammond. Co-Captain: Thomas Kelig. Costume Designer: Ann Roth and Gary Jones. Harrison Ford's Costume Designer: Bernie Pollack. Assistant Costume Designers: Michelle Matland, Juliet Polcsa. Women's Wardrobe Supervisor: Donna Maloney. Men's Wardrobe Supervisor: Tim Alberts. Wardrobe Production Assistants: Joseph Zolfo, Carl Turpeinen. Still Photographers: Brian Hamill, Myles Aronowitz. Color by Deluxe. Dailies (NY) by Technicolor. Panavision equipment (spherical). Dolby sound.

Paris Unit: Production Manager: Jean Pierre Avice. Assistant Directors: Pascal Salafa, Jerome Borenstein. Production Coordinator: Joanny Carpentier. Art Director: Jean Michel Hugon. Casting Director: Kate Dowd. Set Dresser: Philippe Turlure. 1st Company Grip: Charlie Freess. Location Manager: Sandrine Ageorges. Transportation Manager: Isabelle Gautier. Production Auditor: Christine Bodelot. Property Person: Marc Pinquier. Extras Casting: Alberte Garo.

Cast: Harrison Ford (Linus Larrabee), Julia Ormond (Sabrina Fairchild), Greg Kinnear (David Larrabee), Nancy Marchand (Maude Larrabee), John Wood (Fairchild), Miriam Colon (Rosa), Elizabeth Franz (Joanna), Paul Giamatti (Scott), Becky Ann Baker (Linda), Dana Ivey (Mack), Lauren Holly (Elizabeth Tyson), Richard Crenna (Patrick Tyson), Angie Dickinson (Ingrid Tyson), John C. Vennema (Ron), Greg Chase (Ron), Denis Holmes (Butler), Kate Johnson (Wonderbra), Jo-Jo Lowe (Red Head), Mark J. Foley (Handsome Man), Ira Wheeler (Bartender), Margo Martindale (Nurse), J. Smith Cameron (Carol), Fanny Ardant (Irene), Valeria Lemercier (Martine), Patrick Bruel (Louis), Françoise Genty (Makeup Assistant), Ayako (India), Phillipa Cooper (Kelly), Guillame Gallienne (Assistant), Andrea Behalekova (Supermodel #1), Phina (Supermodel #2), Helena (Supermodel #3), Ines Sastre (Supermodel #4), J.B. Benn (Magician), Peter McKernan (Helicopter Pilot), Ed Connelly (Gulf Stream Pilot), Kenneth A. MacDonald (Beggar), Christine Luneau-Lipton (Ticket Taker), Alvin

Lum (Tyson Bultler), Siching Song (Mother in Hospital), Phil Nee (Father in Hospital), Randy Becker (Trainer), Susan Browning (Secretary), Saigat Mondal (Moroccan Waiter), Michael Dees (Singer at Larrabee Party), Peter L. Parks (The Senator), Thom Edmundson, Maria Edmundson, Peder Hansen, Annette Marie Hillary (David's Friends), Ron Schwary, Danny Michael (Sheiks at Larrabee Party), Dale A. Resteghini, Otto Krause, Matt Cerro, Fred Goehner, Tara Leigh, Carina Rush, William Thourlby (Linus' Friends), Robert C. Lee (Business Man), Patrick Byrnes (Friend), La Compagnie Jolie Mome (Street Singers)

   Music Credits: "Moonlight"— Music by John Williams; Lyrics by Alan and Marilyn Bergman; Performed by Michael Dees; Produced by John Williams. "Call Me Irresponsible"— By Sammy Cahn and James Van Heusen. "How Can I Remember"— Music by John Williams; Lyrics by Alan and Marilyn Bergman; Performed by Michael Dees; Produced by John Williams. "Stella by Starlight"— By Ned Washington and Victor Young. "Protection"— By Andrew Vowles, Robert Del Naja, Grantley Marshall and Tracey Thorn; Performed by Massive Attack; Courtesy of Circa Records Ltd. Virgin Records America, Inc. "Love's in Need of Love Today"— By Stevie Wonder; Performed by Blackstreet; Courtesy of Interscope Records by arrangement with Warner Special Productions. "L'Amour Est Une Etoile"— By Rene Sarvil and Vincent Scotto; Performed by Tino Rossi; Courtesy of EMI-France under license from CEMA Special Markets. "Les Petites Notes"— By Liane Foly, Philippe Viennet and André Manoukian; Performed by Liane Foly; Courtesy of Virgin France S.A. Virgin Records America, Inc. "Closer, Together, Now"— By Gordon Driver and Jeff Lams. "Rapsodie on a Theme of Paganini, 18th Variation"— By Sergey Rachmaninoff; Performed by the London Promenade Orchestra under license from Sony Music Special Products. "Dedicace"— By Michel Roger; Performed by La Compagnie Jolie Mome. "La Vie en Rose"— By E. Louiguy & Edith Piaf. "I Wish I Were in Love Again"— By Richard Rodgers and Lorenz Hart. "Love Letters"— By Edward Heyman and Victor Young. "Moonlight Becomes You"— By Johnny Burke and James Van Heusen. "My Old Flame"— By Arthur Johnston and Sam Coslow. "High Hopes"— By Sammy Cahn and James Van Heusen. "The Shadow of Your Smile"— By Johnny Mandel and Paul Francis Webster. "For All We Know"— By Sam Lewis and J. Fred Coots. "I Remember You"— By Johnny Mercer and Victor Schertzinger. "Maude's Fanfare"— By John E. Oliver. "Happy Birthday to You"— By Mildred J. Hill and Patty S. Hill. "When Joanna Loved Me"— By Jack Segal and Robert Wells. "Ruf a Dabel Le'Yan"— By Sidi Kaddour Al-Alami; Performed by El Hadj Houcine Toulali; Courtesy of Blue Silver/Institut du Monde Arabe. "Bei mir bist du schon (Means That You're Grand)"— by Sheldon Secunda, Jacob Jacobs, Sammy Cahn and Saul Chaplin. "Moonlight"— Music by John Williams; Lyric by Alan and Marilyn Bergman; Performed by Sting; Produced by Kim Turner and Sting; Courtesy of A&M Records, Inc.

18. *Random Hearts* (Projected September 1998 start)
   Sony Pictures. Producer: Sydney Pollack in association with Rastar Productions. Directed by: Sydney Pollack. Adaptation of the 1983 Warren Adler novel. Screenplay by: Kurt Luedtke and Davis Rayfiel.

   Cast : Harrison Ford.

Producing Credits

1. *Honeysuckle Rose* (1980)
Warner Bros. Genre: Drama. Running time: 119 minutes. Rating: PG.
Color. Released: July 18, 1980. Available on videocassette and laserdisc.
Also titled *On the Road Again* for TV and cassette.

Credits: Producers: Sydney Pollack and Gene Taft. Screenplay: Carol Sobieski,
William D. Wittliff and John Binder. Director: Jerry Schatzberg. Songs composed
by Willie Nelson. Performed by: Willie Nelson and Family. Music Supervision:
Richard Baskin. Unit Production Manager: Wally Samson. 1st Assistant Direc-
tor: David McGiffert. 2nd Assistant Director: Nick Marck. Script Supervisor: Joe
Gannon. Camera Operator: Jim Lucas. 1st Assistant Cameraman: Doyle Smith.
2nd Assistant Cameraman: Sal Camacho. 2nd Assistant Camera/Loader: William
Coe. Stillman: Jim Coe. Production Sound Mixer: Arthur Rochester. Music Con-
sultant: Bradley Hartman. Boomman: Rick Thornton. Cableman: Kenneth Nunn.
Concert Recordings: Enactron Truck. Re-Recording Mixers: Tom Fleischman,
Richard Portman. 1st Assistant Film Editors: Nicholas Smith, Ursala-Denine
Rowan. Assistant Film Editors: Gail Showalter, Gareth Karr, Glenn D. Cun-
ningham. Apprentice Film Editors: Don Schatzberg, Richard King, Judith Blume.
Supervising Sound Editor: Stan Bochner. Supervising Music Editor: Lou Cer-
borino. Dialogue Editor: Harvey J. Rosenstock. Key Grip: Hank Briere. 2nd Grip:
Hugh Langtry. Dolly Grip: Chuck Morgan. Concert Lighting Designer: Tim
Phelps. Gaffer: Tim Griggith. Best Boy: Terry Neville. Studio Best Boy: Don
Zobel. Rigging Gaffer: Bill Krattiger. Set Decorator: Jeff Haley. Lead Man: Del
Diener. Property Master: Rich Valesko. Assistant Property: Fred Krajewski. Con-
struction Coordinator: Stanley Karas. Propmakers: Edward Karas, John Riperti.
Painter: Dave Margolin. Painter/Paperhanger: Robert Kerns. Wardrobe Woman:
Cynthia Bales. Wardrobe Man: Darryl Athons. Makeup: Lee Harlman, Leo
Lotito, Jr. Hairstylists: Kate Pownall, Carolyn Ferguson. Casting: Dianne Crit-
tenden, Karen Rea. Casting (Texas): Liz Kegley. Casting Assistant (Texas): Pat
Orseth. Extras Casting (Texas): Barbara Lambertson. Location Manager: Bob
Elkins. Director's Secretary: Marilyn Kabani. Publicist: Jack Casey. Transporta-
tion Coordinator: Ernie Molina. Transportation Captain: Ric Belyeu. Sound Edi-
tors: Peter Frank, Michael Jacobi, Neil L. Kaufman, Dan Lieberstein, Al Nah-
mias, Jeffrey Wolf. Music Editor: Robert Q. Lovett. Assistant Sound Editors:
Harry Peck Bolles, Ernie Davidson, Andy Federman, Joan Franklin, Leslie Troy
Gaulin, Lou Graf, Dorian Harris, Marty Levenstein, Yvette Nabel, Peter
Odabashian, Karen Stern. Color Consultant for Technicolor: Otto Paoloni. Title
Design: Gino Garlanda. Titles and Opticals: Computer Opticals, Inc. Post Pro-
duction Facilities: Sound One Corporation. Color by Technicolor. Filmed in
Panavision.

Cast: Willie Nelson (Buck), Dyan Cannon (Viv), Amy Irving (Lily), Slim
Pickens (Garland), Joey Floyd (Jamie), Charles Levin (Sid), Priscilla Pointer (Ros-
alie), Mickey Rooney, Jr. (Cotton), Pepe Serna (Rooster), Lane Smith (Brag),
Diana Scarwid (Jeanne), Emmylou Harris (Emmylou), Rex Ludwick (Tex),

Mickey Raphael (Kelly), Bee Spears (Bo), Chris Ethridge (Easter), Paul English (Paul), Bobby Nelson (Bonnie), Jody Payne (Jonas), Randy "Poodie" Locke (Poodie), T. Snake (Snake), Johnny Gimble (Fiddler), Kenneth Threadgill (Yodler), Grady Martin (Grady), Hank Cochran (Hank), Jeannie Seely (Jeannie), Dick Gimble, Maurice Anderson, Ray D. Hollingsworth, Bill Mounce, Kenny Frazier (Reunion Swing Band), Gene Rader (Owen), Frank Stewart (Dorsey Lee), Lu Belle Camp (Grandma Bonham), A. L. Camp (Grandpa Bonham), Bernedette Whitehead (Jessie), Jackie Ezzell (Country Girl), Harvey Christiansen (Mr. Eubanks), Hackberry Johnson (Hackberry), Kenneth Erik Hamilton (Boy #1), Nelson Fowler (Boy #2), Guy Houston Garrett (Boy #3), Genta Boyd, Cara Kanak, (Women at Party), Augie Meyers (Stage Manager), Robert Gotschall (Store Clerk), Emilio Gonzales (Cab Driver), Mary Jane Valle (Airline Clerk), Randy Arlyn Fletcher (Police Officer), Ray Liberto (Jim), Sam Allred (Contractor), Boy Baty, John Meadows (Carpenters), Cody Hubach (Cody).

2. *Songwriter* (1984)

Tri Star. Genre: Musical. Running time: 94 minutes. Rating: R. Color. Released: October 12, 1984.

Credits: Producer: Sydney Pollack. Executive Producer: Mike Moder. Screenplay: Bud Shrake. Director: Alan Rudolph. Director of Photography: Matthew Leonetti. Production Design: Joel Schiller. Original Songs: Willie Nelson and Kris Kristofferson. Additional Music: Larry Cansler. Casting: Lyn Stalmaster. Film Editor: Stuart Pappe. Unit Production Manager: Mike Moder. 1st Assistant Director: David McGiffert. 2nd Assistant Director: Pamela Eilerson. Editors: Stephen Lovejoy, George A. Martin. Songs Produced by: Booker T. Jones, Danny Lawson. Sound Mixer: Arthur Rochester. Set Decorator: Barbara Krieger. Sound Boom: Don Coufal. Camera Operator: Michael St. Hilaire. 1st Assistant Camera: John R. Leonetti. 2nd Assistant Camera: Kevin Boyle. Music Editor: George A. Martin. Assistant Editors: James C. Johnson, Sherri Gallaway, Austin Texas. Apprentice Editors: Paula K. McKee Pappe, Tim Alverson, Gaspar. Sound Editing: Robert Grieve, Patrick Drummond, Dennis Drummond, George Anderson, Dody Dorn, John Hoeren, Reid Paul Martin. Re-Recording Mixers: Arthur Piantadosi, Chris Jenkins, Gary Alexander, Joel Fein. ADR Supervisor: Norman B. Schwartz. ADR Editor: Stephen Purvis. ADR Assistant: Linda Whittlesey. Foley Walker: Terry Burke. Production Coordinator: Janis Benjamin. Production Secretary: Anne Jordan. Production Auditor: Rusty Warren. Assistant Auditor: Ellen Adolph. DGA Intern: Cara Giallanza. Unit Publicist: Michael Klastorin. Script Supervisor: Joyce King. Makeup Artists: Edward Ternes, Greg LaCava. Hair Stylist: Ginger Blymyer. Costume Supervisor: Ernest Misko, Kathleen Gore-Misko. Property Master: Tom Tomlinson. Construction Coordinator: Tom Bartholomew. Transportation Coordinator: Jerry McKnight. Transportation Co-Captain: Jay Fuller, John East. Location Manager: Elisabeth Bennett. Gaffer: Patrick Blymyer. Best Boy: Robert A. Fillis. Key Grip: John Linder. 2nd Grip: Mark Averill. Leadman: Glen Dunn. Still Photographers: Van Redin, Joyce Rudolph. Extra Casting: Austin Actor's Clearinghouse. Color Timer: Bill Pine. 2nd Unit Cameraman: Richard Kooris. Sound Cable: Pete Stauber. Assistant Props: Mike Long. Caterers:

Michaelson's. Craft Service: Mike Garvey. Bad TV: Buddy Prewitt. First Aid: Carol Schmidt. Electricians: Terry Neville, Joel Stout, Joe Gallian, Bob Lewallen, Jeff Zucker. Grips: Lloyd Barcroft, James Maloy, Jon Maloy. Swing Gang: Tom Hawkins, Dusty Hudgins, George Bedard, Jimmy Putnam. Production Assistants: David Anderson, Suzanne Rothbaum. Construction: Dwight "Curly" Cary, Tad Smalley and Spot, Michael Palmer, Bob Sturtevant.

Cast: Willie Nelson (Doc Jenkins), Kris Kristofferson (Blackie Buck), Melinda Dillon (Honey Carder), Rip Torn (Dino McLeish), Leslie Ann Warren (Gilda), Richard C. Sarafian (Rocky Rodeo), Rhonda Dotson (Corkie), Shannon Wilcox (Anita), Jeff MacKay (Hogan), Michey Raphael (Arty), Robert Gould (Ralph), Sage Parker (Pattie McLeish), Gailard Sartain (Muireaux), Stephen Bruton (Sam), Glen Clark (Paul), Cleve Dupin (Road Manager), B.C. Cooper (Cooper), Poodie Locke (Purvis), Joe Keyes (Eddie), Amanda Bishop (Daughter #1), Kristen Renfro (Daughter #2), Sammy Allred (Disc Jockey), Bill Boyd (Blind Tommy's Brother), Steve Fromholtz (Engineer), Johnny Gimble (Fiddle Player), Eloise Schmitt (Girl on Bus), Kate Cadenhead (Groupie), Christi Carafano (Girl in Bed), Joe Gallien (Electronics Engineer), Gates Moore (First Concert Hall Manager), Larry Gorham (Concert Hall Manager), Jackie King (Guitar Player), Catherine Molloy (Doc's Girlfriend), Bobby Rambo (Party Guest), Michael Reesberg (Roarer Roadie), John Shaw (Cashier), Pete Stauber (Vacuum Cleaner Salesman), Larry Trader (Golf Roadie), Priscilla Dougherty (Incredulous Woman), Bobbie Nelson, Piano; Paul English, Drums; Bee Spears, Bass; Jody Payne, Guitar; Grady Martin, Guitar; Booker T. Jones, Keyboard; Mickey Raphael, Harmonica (Gilda's Band), Billy Swan, Donnie Fritts, Sammy Creason, Tommy McClure, Glen Clark, Stephen Bruton (Roarers Band)

Music Credits: "How Do You Feel About Fooling Around." "Forever in Your Love"—Written by Kris Kristofferson, Stephen Bruton and Mike Utley. "Night to Remember." "Who Am I." "Under the Gun"—Written by Kris Kristofferson and Glen Clark. "Cajun Hideaway"—Written by Kris Kristofferson, Glen Clark, Billy Swan and Steve Bruton. "Nobody Said It Was Gonna Be Easy"—Written by Willie Nelson and Mickey Raphael; Concerts produced by Me and Paul Concert Productions of Texas; Concert Lighting: Dusty Hudgins and David Anderson; Concert Sound by Shubert Systems; Post Production Supervision: Acme Film Editing; Titles and Opticals by Modern Film Effects; Title Design by E. Mario Cibelli, Patty Ryan.

3. *Bright Lights, Big City* (1988)

MGM/United Artists. A Mirage Production. Genre: Drama. Running time: 110 minutes. Rating: R. Color. Released: April 1, 1988. Available on videocassette and laserdisc.

Credits: Producers: Sydney Pollack and Mark Rosenberg. Screenplay: Jay McInerney. Based on the novel by Jay McInerney. Director: James Bridges. Director of Photography: Gordon Willis. Music: Donald Fagen. Casting: Mary Colquhoun. Associate Producer: Jack Larson. Costume Designer: Bernie Pollack. Executive Music Producer: Joel Sill. Music: Donal Fagan. Additional Music: Rob Modunsky. Edited: John Bloom and George Berndt. Production Design: Santo Loquasto. Director of Photography: Gordon Willis. Executive Producer: Gerald R.

Molen. Unit Production Manager: Gerald R. Molen. 1st Assistant Director: David McGiffert. 2nd Assistant Director: Stephen Wertimer. Assistant to Producers: Julie Berman. Auditor: Ken Ryan. Assistant Auditor: John A. Machone. Assistant Unit Production Manager: Ted Kuroyla. 2nd 2nd Assistant Director: Barbara Rains. Location Staff: Dennis Benatar, Nicholas Bernstein, James Davis. Production Coordinator: Harriette G. Kanew. Assistant Production Coordinator: Cynthia "C.C." Cox. Camera Operator: Don Sweeney. 1st Assistant Cameraman: Doug Hart. 2nd Assistant Cameraman: Chaim Kantor. Chief Lighting Technician: Dick Quinlan Best Boy: Bob Connors. Key Grip: Ed Quinn. Grip: Tom Gilligan. Property Master: Jim Mazzola. Assistant Property: Mike Badawood. Production Sound Mixer: Les Lazarowitz. Boom Operator: Linda Murphy. Sound Recordist: Mike Bedard. Script Supervisor: Barbara E. Stoia. Art Director: Thomas C. Warren. Set Decorator: George DeTitta. Assistant Art Director: Jefferson Sage. Assistant to Production Designer: Gil Williams. Art Department Coordinator: Glenn Lloyd. Set Dresser: Dave Weinman. Master Scenic Artist: Jim Sorice. Scenic Artist: Thomas Southern. Standby Scenic Artist: Cosmo Sorice. Construction Coordinator: Ronald Petagna. Construction Grip: Arne Olsen. Makeup Artist: Bernadette Mazur. Hair Stylist: Romaine Green. Assistant Costume Designer: Hope Hanafin. Men's Costumes: William A. Campbell. Women's Costumer: Melissa Adzima-Stanton. Transportation Captain: Jim Giblin. Co-Captain: Tom Buckman. Assistant Casting: Michael Colberg. Additional Casting: Todd Thaler. Casting: Julie Rixler. Publicity: Peggy Siegal Company. Still Photographer: Louis Goldman. Post Production Supervisor: Robin Forman. Assistant Film Editor: Maryann Brandon. Apprentice Film Editor: Peter Ellis. Sound Supervisor: Skip Lievsay. ADR Editor: George Berndt. Dialogue Editors: Teri Dorman, Susan Dudeck. Sound Effects Editors: Jim Matheny, Martin Maryska, Pamela Bentowski. Foley Editor: John Duvall. Music Editor: Curt Sobel. Playback Music Editor: Joe De Beasi. Sound Assistants: Ralph Stuart, Ann Ducommun, Peter Sullivan, Spike Allison-Hooper. Sound Apprentices: Brian Chic, Laura Krumholz. Foley Artists: Joan Rowe, Jerry Trent. Re-Recording Mixers: Chris Jenkins, Gary Alexander, Steve Pederson. Scoring Engineers: Wayne Yurgelin, Richard Alderson. Dolby Consultant: Douglas Greenfield. Negative Cutter: Donah Bassett. Accounting Assistant: Donna Santora. Production Assistants: Brian Puudo, Michael De Casper, Douglas S. Ornstein, Edward Ioffreda. DGA Trainee: Gina Leonetti. Camera Trainee: Bobby Mancuso. Security: Tom Cassidy. Security for Mr. Fox: Pat Santino. Assistant to Mr. Fox: Erica Lawson. Assistant to Mr. Bridges: Stephanie Saunders, Penny McCarthy. Secretaries to the Producers: Donna Ostroff, Linda Labov. Original Score Orchestrations: Donald Fagen and Rob Mounsey. Title Design: Wayne Fitzgerald. Titles and Opticals: Pacific Title. Color by Du Art Film Laboratories. Prints by Technicolor.

    Cast: Michael J. Fox (Jamie), Keifer Sutherland (Tad), Phoebe Cates (Amanda), Swoosie Kurtz (Megan), Frances Sternhagen (Clara), Tracy Pollan (Vicky), John Houseman (Mr. Vogel), Charlie Schlatter (Michael), Jason Robards (Alex Hardy), Dianne Wiest (Mother), David Warrilow (Rittenhouse), Alec Mapa (Yasu Wade), William Hickey (Ferret Man), Gina Belafonte (Kathy), Sam Robards (Rich), Zette (Steve), Marika Blossfeldt (Bald Girl), Jessica Lundy (Theresa), Kelly Lynch (Elaine), Peter Boyden (Maître d'), Annabelle Gurwitch (Barbara),

Russell Horton (Walter Tyler), Maria Pitillo (Ponytail Girl), Susan Traylor (Leather Lady), Michael Fischetti (Mannequin Draftsman), Harvey Waldman (Deli Man), David Hyde Pierce (Bartender at Fashion Show), Jim Babchack (Bartender at Disco), Peg Murray (Receptionist), Barbara Rucker (Elegant Lady), Pat Santino (Security Guard), Mike Bacarella (Bakery Man), Josie Bell, Anne Bezamat, Lynn Howland, Sheila Johnson, Melanie Landestoy, Marisol Massey, Jennifer Houser, Alva Chinn, Dianne de Witt, Isabelle, Andrea Sande, Natalie Gabrielli, Maud, Maria von Hartz, Joko Zohrer (Runway Models), Marvin Braverman, Leigh French, Tom Brunelle, Nicholas Guest, Fred Newman, Luisa Leschin, Andrew Masset, Tracy Newman, Wendy Schaal, Arnold Turner, Anna Mathias, Reni Santoni, Jonathan Stark, Claudette Wells (Additional Voices)

Music Credits: "Love Attack"— Performed by Konk; Courtesy of Dog Brothers Records; Produced by Shannon Dawson and G. "Love" Jay; Words and Music by Shannon Dawson and G. "Love" Jay. "Pump Up the Volume"— Performed by M/A/R/R/S; Courtesy of Island Records/4 ADduced by Martyn Young; Words and Music by Martyn Young and Steve Young. "Bill"— Performed by Oscar Peterson; Courtesy of Polygram Special Projects. A Division of Polygram Records, Inc.; Words and Music by Jerome Kern, Oscar Hammerstein II, P.G. Woodhouse; Produced by Norman Granz. "Bright Lights, Big City"— Performed by Jimmy Reed; Courtesy of Vee Jay Records; Written by Jimmy Reed. "BNT Blues"— Performed by Bobby Forester; Produced by Donald Fagen; Music by Bobby Forester and Clarence "Tootsie" Bean. "True Faith"— Performed by New Order; Courtesy of Qwest Records/Factory Records; Produced by Stephen Hague and New Order; Words and Music by New Order and Stephen Hague. "Good Love"— Performed by Prince; Courtesy of Paisley Park Records; Words and Music by Prince; Produced by Prince. "Kiss and Tell"— Performed by Bryan Ferry; Courtesy of Reprise Records; By arrangement with Warner Special Projects. Virgin Records Limited; Produced by Patrick Leonard, Chester Kaman and Bryan Ferry; Words and Music by Bryan Ferry. "Lovely to Look At"— Performed by Oscar Peterson; Courtesy of Polygram Special Projects, A Division of Polygram Records, Inc.; Produced by Norman Granz; Words and Music by Jerome Kern, Dorothy Fields, Jimmy McHugh. "Vivaldi's Concerto in C Major for Guitar and Strings"— Performed by I Solisti Di Zagreb. Alirio Diaz, guitar. Antonio Jangro, conductor; Courtesy of Vanguard Records (A division of the Welk Record Group). "Ice Cream Days"— Performed by Jennifer Hall; Courtesy of Warner Bros. Records, Inc. by arrangement with Warner Special Products; Produced by Alan Tarney; Words and Music by Jennifer Hall and Alan Tarney. "Jaime and Vicky"— Produced by Curt Sobel; Music by Curt Sobel. "Let's Have Another Cup of Coffee"— Performed by Michael Feinstein; Courtesy of Elektra/Asylum Records; By arrangement with Warner Special Products; Words and Music by Irving Berlin. "Obsessed"— Performed by The Noise Club; Produced by Oliver Leiber; Words and Music by Oliver Leiber. "Century's End"— Performed by Donald Fagen; Courtesy of Warner Bros. Records; Produced by Donald Fagen and Gary Katz; Words by Donald Fagen and Timothy Meher; Music by Donald Fagen. "Pleasure, Little Treasure"— Performed by Depeche Mode; Courtesy of Sire Records; By arrangement with Warner Special Products; Produced by Depeche Mode and David Bascombe; Additional production by Daniel Miller; Words and Music by M.L. Gore. "Divine Emotions"—

Performed by Narada; Courtesy of Reprise Records; By arrangement with Warner Special Products; Produced by Narada Michael Walden; Additional production by Shep Pettibone; Words and Music by Narada Michael Walden and Jeffrey Cohen. "Bright Lights, Big City"— Performed by Donald Fagen; Courtesy of Warner Bros. Records; Produced by Donald Fagen; Words and Music by Jimmy Reed. "Nun will die Sonn' so hell aufgeh'n"— From Gustav Mahler's "Kindertotenlieder" Dietrich Fischer-Dieskau, baritone; Berlin Philharmonic Orchestra, conducted by Karl Bohm; Deutsche Grammophon/Polydor International GmbH.; Used courtesy of Polygram Special Projects, A Division of Polygram Records, Inc.

4. *Scrooged* (1988)
   Paramount. Art Linson Production in association with Mirage Productions. Genre: Comedy/fantasy. Running time: 101 minutes. Rating: PG-13. Color. Released: November 23, 1988. Available on videocassette and laserdisc.

   Credits: Producer: Richard Donner and Art Linson. Executive Producer: Steve Roth. Screenplay: Mitch Glazer and Michael O'Donoghue. Suggested by "A Christmas Carol" by Charles Dickens. Director: Richard Donner. Associate Producer: Jennie Lew-Tugend. Music Score: Danny Elfman. Production Designer: J. Michael Riva. Director of Photography: Michael Chapman. Editors: Fredric and William Steinkamp. Co-producer: Ray Hartwick. Casting: David Ruben. Costume Design: Wayne Finkelman. Unit Production Manager: Ray Hartwick. 1st Assistant Director: Chris Soldo. 2nd Assistant Director: James W. Skotchdopole. Post Production Consultant: Stuart Baird. Music Supervisors: David Anderle, Jimmy Iovine. Production Associate: Peter Frankfurt. Set Decorator: Linda DeScenna. Art Director: Virginia L. Randolph. Camera Operator: Michael A. Genne. 1st Assistant Photographers: Larry Hezzelwood, Scott Sakamoto. 2nd Assistant Photographer: Gregory Walters. Steadicam Operator: Stephen St. John. Production Mixer: Willie Burton. Boom Operator: Marvin Lewis. Cable Person: Robert Harris. Additional Boom Operator: Winifred Tennison. Assistant Film Editors: Karl F. Steinkamp, Michael T. Wilson, Debra Goldfield. Assistant to Stuart Baird: William Meshover. Music Editor: Bob Badami. Supervising Sound Editors: Robert George Henderson, Alan Robert Murray. Sound Editors: Teri E. Forman, D. Michael Horton, Joseph A. Ippolito, Virginia Cook-McGowan, Walter Newman, Marshall Winn. Assistant Sound Editors: Brooke Henderson Ward, Karen Minahan. Re-Recording Mixers: Les Fresholtz, Vern Poore, Dick Alexander. Scenic Artist: Ron Strang. Set Desginers: William J. Teegarden, Nancy Patton, Dianne Wager. Illustrators: Edward S. Verreaux, Thomas Southwell. Art Department Coordinator: Leslie C. Warren. Research Coordinator: Mark Snovell. Property Master: Erik Nelson. Assistant Property Masters: David Glazer, Jack E. Ackerman. Lead Person: Ric McElvin. Property Persons: Tom McCown, Tony Piller, Lee Orlikoff, Richard Leon. Chief Lighting Technician: Gary B. Tandrow. Assistant Chief Lighting Technician: Steve McGee. Lamp Operators: Walt Berry, George Dunagan, Brad Emmons, Phelt Saucier. Chief Rigging Electrician: Kevin J. Lang. 1st Company Grip: Alexander La Verde. 2nd Company Grip: Rand R. Vargas. Dolly Grip: Clay Wilson. Grips: Ed Jackson, Ty Suehiro. Supervising Makeup

Artist: Robert Norin. Supervising Hairstylist: Marlene Williams. Hairstylist: Stephen Robinette. Costume Supervisor: Jennifer Parsons. Costumers: Antonio Martinez, Jennifer Butler. Assistant Costumer: Nava Sadan. Special Makeup Effects Created and Designed by: Thomas R. Burman and Bari-Dreiband-Burman. Special Effects Coordinator: Allen L. Hall. Special Effects Foreperson: Albert Delgado. Special Effects: Steven Foster, G. L. Karas, Joe Montenegro. Stunt Coordinator: Mic Rodgers. Script Supervisors: Jan Kemper, Patricia Dalzell. Production Office Coordinator: Shari Leibowitz. Assistant Production Office Coordinator: Michele Imperator. Production Secretary: Carolyn Rothstein. Production Assistants: James Vatis, Richard Harner. Production Auditor: Louis B. Phillips. Assistant Production Auditor: Susan Towner. Accounting Assistant: Tad Driscoll. Unit Publicist: Marsha Robertson. Still Photographer: John Shannon. Location Manager: Lynn M. Kuwahara. 2nd 2nd Assistant Director: Gabriela Vazquez. Additional 2nd Assistant Directors: Adele Simmons, Thomas Burns. Assistant to Richard Donner: Alexander B. Collett. Secretaries to Richard Donner: Ilyse Selwyn, Cynthia Neber. Assistant to Art Linson: Patti Roberts Nelson. Assistants to Bill Murray: Rebecca Baehler, June Popowich. Casting Assistant: Lisa Beach. Celebrity Look-alikes provided by Ron Smith Celebrity Look-alikes. "Solid Gold" choreography by Lester Wilson. Ballet Choreographer: Jullian Hessel. Orchestrator: Steve Bartek. Additional Orchestrations: Steven Scott Smalley. Music conducted by Shirley Walker. Music Scoring Mixer: Robert Fernandez. Music recorded at: The Burbank Studios. Supervising ADR Editor: Jay Engel. ADR Editor: Denise R. Whiting. Assistant ADR Editor: Carmen Hocson. Foley by: Taj Soundworks. Foley Artists: John Roesch, Alicia Stevenson. Foley Recorded by: Greg Orloff. Electronic Sound FX: John Paul Fasal. Construction Coordinator: Bob Scaife. Construction Supervisors: John Villarino, Ken Scaife. Construction Forepersons: Michael Villarino, Terry Scott. Labor Forepersons: Tony Feola, Matt Thompson. Paint Foreperson: Clyde Zimmerman. Set Plasterer: Alex Scutti. Production Painter: Paul J. Campanella. Transportation Coordinator: Dan Anglin. Transportation Captain: Ron Hinsley. Studio Teacher: Gloria Hoffman. Craft Service: Craig Harris. Negative Cutting: Reel People, Inc. Color Timer: Terry Haggar. Dolby Stereo Consultant: Thom Ehle. Network Computer Animation: Jim Dixon, Pacific Data Images, Inc. Title Design: Anthony Goldschmidt. Opticals: Pacific Title. Special Visual Effects: Dream Quest Images. Visual Effects Supervisor: Eric Brevig. Effects Production Supervisor: Craig Newman. Motion Control Photography: Mike Shea. Optical Supervisor: Jeff Matakovich. Rotoscope Supervisor: James Valentine. Model Shop Supervisor: Dave Goldberg. Visual Effects Editor: Marie Davis. Video Supervisor and Layout: Michael Thau. Video Coordinator: Scott Nimerfro. Clip Clearance: Tory Herald, Marla Tate. 24 Frame Video Displays by Video Image: Rhonda C. Gunner, Richard E. Hollander, Gregory L. McMurray, John C. Wash. Video Image Crew: Aaron Katz, Pete Martinez, Dave Katz, Jerry Smith, Monte Swann, Fred Donelson, Mike Keeler, Greg Harms, Bruce Shultz.

New York Crew: Unit Production Manager: Roger Paradiso. 2nd 2nd Assistant Director: Donald J. Lee, Jr. Additional 2nd Assistant Director: Richard D. Patrick. 1st Assistant Director, 2nd Unit: Gaetano Lisi. Art Director: Thomas Warren. Set Decorator: John Alan Hicks. Additional Director of Photography:

Peter Norman. Camera Operator: Thomas Priestley, Jr. 1st Assistant Photographer: Anthony S. Brooke. 2nd Assistant Photographer: Paul Postelnicu. Steadicam Operator: Ted Churchill. Sound Mixer: Al Mian. Property Master: Michael Bird. Chief Lighting Technician: Richard J. Quinlan. 1st Company Grip: Edwin Quinn. Scenic Chargeperson: Ralph Cava. Special Effects: William Traynor. Location Liaison: Vibeke Arntzen. Production Coordinator: Ellen Hillers. Men's Costumer: Guy Tanno. Women's Costumer: Rose Cuervo. Makeup Artist: Edward Jackson. Hairstylist: Robert Grimaldi. Still Photographer: Louis Goldman. Transportation Captain: Harry Leavey. Art Department Production Assistant: John-Paul Riva. Video Assistant: Joe Trammell.

Cast: Bill Murray (Frank Cross), Karen Allen (Claire Phillips), Alfre Woodard (Grace Cooley), David Johansen (Cabby/Ghost of Christmas Past), Carol Kane (Ghost of Christmas Present), Bobcat Goldthwaite (Eliot Loudermilk), Robert Mitchum (Preston Rhinelander), Nicholas Phillips (Calvin Cooley), John Forsythe (Lew Hayward), John Glover (Brice Cummings), Brian Doyle-Murray (Earl Cross), Mabel King (Gramma), John Murray (James Cross), Michael J. Pollard (Herman), Jaime Farr (Jacob Marley), Robert Goulet (Himself), Buddy Hackett (Scrooge), John Houseman (Himself), Lee Majors (Himself), Pat McCormick (Ghost of Christmas Present), Mary Lou Retton (Herself), Al "Red Dog" Weber (Santa Claus), Jean Speegle Howard (Mrs. Claus), June Changler (June Cleaver), Michael Eidam (Wally Cleaver), Mary Ellen Trainor (Ted), Bruce Jarchow (Wayne). Sanford Jensen, Jeffrey Jospeh, Dick Blasucci (Executives). Peter Bromilow (Archbishop). IBC Guards: Bill Marcus, Cal Gibson. Damon Hines (Steven Cooley), Tamika McCollum (Shasta Cooley), Koren McCollum (Randee Cooley), Reina Kind (Lanell Cooley), Paul Tuerpe (Stage Manager), Lester Wilson (Choreographer), Ronald Strang (Art Director), Kate McGregor-Stewart (Lady Censor), Jack McGee, Bill Hart (Carpenters), Kathy Kinney (IBC Nurse), Ralph Gervais (Mouse Wrangler), Alvin Hammer (Foreman), Tony Steedman (Headwaiter), Lisa Mende (Doris Cross), Ryan Todd (Frank as a Child), Rebeca Arthur (Tina), Selma Archerd (Mrs. Claus at Party), Jay Byron (Man #2 at Party), Harvey Fisher (Party Guest), C. Ransom Walrod (Party Animal), James R. Miller (Security Guard at Party), Jennie Lew-Tugend (Foo-Ling), Roy Brocksmith (Mike the Mailman), Shawn Michaels (Stage Manager "Frisbee"), Stella Hall (Lew Hayward's Secretary), Sachi Parker (Belle), Delores Hall (Hazel), Anne and Logan Ramsey (Woman and Man in Shelter), Sydna Scott (Woman #2 in Shelter), Wendie Malick (Wendie Cross), Joel Murray, Mitch Glazer, Susan Isaacs, Lauri Kempson (Guests), Chaz Conner, Jr. (Ghost of Christmas Future [TV]), Miro Polo (Mary Lou's Coach), Ralph Bruneau (Nephew), Maria Riva (Mrs. Rhinelander), Hames E. Kindelon (Butler), Raphael Harris (Older Calvin), Wayne Finkelman (Orderly), Susan Barnes, Lynne Randall (Harpies), Gilles Savard (Waiter), Michael O'Donoghue (Priest), Dick McGarvin (Announcer), Tom Doak (Video Tape Director), Sam Drummy (Cameraman on Crane), Winfred Tennison (Marvin), Stephen Kahan, Norm Wilson, Henry V. Brown, Jeanine Jackson, Amy Hill (Technicians), Miles Davis, Larry Carlton, David Sanborn, Paul Shaffer (Street Musicians), The Caroling Company (Carolers), "Solid Gold" Dancers (Scroogettes).

Music Credits: "Brown Eyed Girl"— By Van Morrison; Performed by Buster

Poindexter; Produced by Hank Medress; Courtesy of RCA Records. "Christmas Must Be Tonight"—Written, performed and produced by Robbie Robertson; Courtesy of Geffen Records. "The Christmas Song (Chestnuts Roasting on an Open Fire)"—By Mel Torme and Robert Wells; Performed by Natalie Cole; Produced by Jimmy Iovine; Courtesy of EMI, a division of Capitol Records, Inc. "Get Up 'N' Dance"—By L. Mallison, M. Dewese and R. Isaacs; Performed by Kool Moe Dee; Produced by LaVaba, M. Dewese and Radcliff; Courtesy of Jive Records. "Hallelujah Chorus"—From *Messiah* by Handel; Courtesy of the Special Music Co. "I Second That Emotion"—By William Robinson and Alfred Cleveland; Performed by Smokey Robinson and the Miracles; Courtesy of Motown Record Company, L.P. "It's Howdy Doody Time"—By Edward G. Kean. "The Love You Take"—Written and produced by Dan Hartman; Performed by Dan Hartman and Denise Lopez; Courtesy of A&M Records. "Put a Little Love in Your Heart"—By Jackie De Shannon, Randy Myers and Jimmy Holiday; Performed by Annie Lennox and Al Green; Produced by David A. Stewart; Courtesy of RCA Records, a Bertelsmann Music Group Company, and A&M Records. "Rudolph the Red-Nosed Reindeer"—By Johnny Marks. "Santa Claus is Coming to Town"—By Haven Gillespie and J. Fred Coots. "Silver Bells"—By Livingston and Ray Evans; Performed by Robert Goulet. "Smile, You're on Candid Camera"—By Alan Scott and Keith Textor. "Sweetest Thing"—By U2; Performed by New Voices of Freedom (Featuring Adriane McDonald and George Pendergrass); Produced by Jimmy Iovine, Dennis Bell and Christopher Bell. "The Toy Parade (*Leave It to Beaver* Theme)"—By David Kahn, Mort Greene and Melvyn Lenard. "We Three Kings of Orient Are"—Performed by Miles Davis, Larry Carlton, David Sanborn and Paul Shaffer; Produced by Marcus Miller; Courtesy of Warner Bros. Records, Inc., MCA Records, Reprise Records, and Capitol Records, Inc. "A Wonderful Life"—Written and produced by Judson Spence and Monroe Jones; Performed by Mark Lennon. "Wooly Bully"—By Domingo Samudio; Re-recorded by Sam the Sham and the Pharaohs; Courtesy of Dominion Entertainment, Inc. "Put a Little Love in Your Heart" (Finale)—By Jackie De Shannon, Randy Myers and Jimmy Holiday; Performed by the Cast.

5. *Major League* (1989)

Paramount Pictures. A Morgan Creek/Mirage Production. Genre: Sports. Running time: 107 minutes. Rating: R. Color. Released: April 7, 1989. Available on videocassette and laserdisc.

Credits: Producers: Chris Chesser, Irby Smith. Co-Producer: Julie Bergman. Executive Producer: Mark Rosenberg. Written and directed by David Ward. Casting: Joanne Zaluski, Wallis Nicita Associates. Music: James Newton Howard. Costume Designer: Erica Edell Phillips. Editor: Dennis M. Hill. Production Designer: Jeffrey Howard. Director of Photography: Reynaldo Villalobos. Unit Production Managers: Irby Smith, Edward Markley. 1st Assistant Directors: Jerry Grandy, Louis D'Esposito. 2nd Assistant Directors: Christine Larson, Richard Patrick. Film Editor: Tony Lombardo. Production Associate: Lisa C. Cook. Location Manager: Frederick Bodner. Production Coordinator: Susan Vanderbeek. Assistant Production Coordinator: Shannon Kesey-Smith. Script Supervisor:

Leslie Park. Camera Operators: Christopher Hayes, George Kohut, James Blanford. 1st Assistant Cameraman: Reynaldo Villalobos, Jr., Mauricio Gutierrez. 2nd Unit Director: Irby Smith. 2nd Unit Director of Photography: James Pergola. Paraglide Operator: Gregory Lunsgaard. Artist Photographer: Bill Hedenberg. Aerial Camera Assistant: Robert P. Sanchez. Gaffer: Hugo Cortina. Best Boy Electric: Blaise R. Dahlquist. Electricians: Steven C. Hodge, John Graf, Jeff Strong. Key Grip: Lloyd Barcroft. Best Boy Grip: Johnny London, Jr. Dolly Grip: Tony Garrido. Grips: Pat Omara, John Altendorf, Rob Ingenthron, Dennis Wojtecki. Art Director: John Krenz Reinhart, Jr. Set Designer: Bill Rea. Set Decorator: Celeste Lee. Assistant Set Decorator: Patrick Thomas Cassidy. On-Set Dresser: Adam Silverman. Scenic Artist: Amanda Flick. Art Dept. Coordinator: Roger B. Meryett. Storyboard Artist: Jack Johnson. Conceptual Artist: Tom Southwell. Construction Foreman: Gary Gagliardo. Lead Carpenter: John M. Holiday. Leadman: Paul Arthur Hartman. Swing: Rick Henning. Carpenters: Jon Reeves, James Risch. Property Master: Peter Bankins. Assistant Prop Masters: David L. McGuire, Loyd Brown. Prop Assistants: Eian Bankins, C. Randall Ott, Deb Navins. Special Effects: Dieter Sturm. Sound Mixer: Susumu Tokunow. Boom Operator: Laura Derrick. Cable Person: Fontaine Stevens. Costume Supervisor: Michael Becker. Wardrobe Supervisor: Laurie L. Hudson. Wardrobe Assistants: Sherrie Brody, Patti Cameron. Seamstresses: Andrea Barrier, Hariett Engler. Hairstylist: Frances Mathias. Makeup Artist: Joann Wabisca. Makeup/Hair Assistants: Peggy Teague-Tamme, Judith Anne Denny. Production Controller: Sheldon M. Katz. Production Accountant: Jette Sorensen. Assistant Accountant: Ira J. Friedlander. Administrator/Morgan Creek: Gail Haigh. Accounting Assistant: Kandace Hewitt. Transportation Coordinator: George Schneider. Transportation Captain: Gregg Goodwin. Technical Advisor: Steve Yeager. Casting Coordinator: Nicole Arbusto. Chicago Casting: Jane Alderman, Shelley Andreas. Extras Casting: Lisa S. Beasley. Extras Casting Associate: Nancy King. Extras Casting Assistants: Linda M. Thomas, Mark Van Ert, Mike Walczak, Hugh R. Ross. Unit Publicist: Rob Harris. Still Photographer: Joyce Rudolph. Post Production Services: Acme Film Editing. Post Production Supervisor: Robin Forman. Post Production Coordinator: Karen Marmer. 1st Assistant Film Editor: Maysie Hoy Marlett. Optical Editor: John Lafferty. Assistant Film Editors: Moonstar Greene, James B.J. Hill. Apprentice Film Editors: Gary Simon, Adrienne Daniels. Negative Cutter: Donah Bassett. Supervising Sound Editor: J. Paul Huntsman. Dialogue Editor: Matthew G. Sawelson. Sound Effects Editor: John Haeny. ADR Supervisor: James Beshears. ADR Editor: Lauren J. Palmer. Foley Editors: Bruce Lacey, Lucy Coldsnow. Music Editor: Ellen Segal. Assistant Music Editor: Eeda Kitto. Contributing Sound Editor: George Anderson. Sound Effects Assistant: Carolann S. Sanchez. Sound Effects Apprentice: Patrick English. Foley Artists: Robin Harlan, Kevin Bartnoff. Score Recording Engineers: Ross Pallone, Robert Schaper. Assistant Engineer: Michael Mason. Re-Recording Mixers: Buzz Knudson, Don Digirolano, Bob Glass, Thiederman. Re-recorded by: Todd AO/Glen Glenn Studios. DGA Trainee: Michael McCloud Thompson. Key Production Assistant: Jay Smith, Frank Serrano, Dawn Leslie Allen. Production Assistants: Patrick Hewitt, Charlene Norman, David Marcus, Scott Crabbe, Bob Hume, Kate Amer. Film Runners: Kimberly A. Boyd, Lawrence Amenda, Jr. Stadium

Entertainers: Bill Leff, Jerry Saslow, John Lehr. Craft Service: Paul Gracyalny, James C. Telford. Caterer: Chow Biz Catering. Set Medic: Rob Mook/Bell Ambulance. Athletic Trainer: Bill Lemke. Assistant to Mr. Ward and Mr. Chesser: Julia Miller. Assistant to Joe Roth: Jami Abell. Assistant to James G. Robinson: Janet West. Secretaries to the Producers: Donna Ostroff, Linda Labov, Lisa Bellomo. Stunt Coordinator: Rick Le Fenour.

Tucson Unit: Camera Operator: Ray J. de la Motte. 2nd Assistant Cameraman: Marco Pennacchini. Grip: Mansur Johnson. Cable Man: John Peate. Wardrobe Assistant: Charlotte Laughon. Transportation Captain: Harold Martin. Set Dresser: Carla Curry. Landscape Design: Steve Chesser. Construction: Robert Detweiler. Crowd Promotion: Christen Carr. Extras Casting: Frank Kennedy. Accounting Production Assistant: Bryan Ambacher. Office Production Assistant: Mike Rom. Production Secretary: Tod Swindell. Security: Leonard Boswell. Craft Service: Wendy Wolverton. Craft Service Assistant: Kip Wolverton. First Aid: Marty Caldwell. Sign Painter: Joanne Brown. Sound Effects by Todd AO/Glen Glenn Studios. Titles and Opticals by Pacific Title. Color by Astro Color Labs.

Cast: Tom Berenger (Jake Taylor), Charlie Sheen (Ricky Vaughn), Corbin Bernsen (Roger Durn), James Gammon (Lou Brown), Wesley Snipes (Willie Mays Hayes), Charles Cyphers (Charlie Donovan), Margaret Whitton (Rachel Phelps), Rene Russo (Lynn Wells), Dennis Haysbert (Pedro Cerrano), Bob Uecher (Harry Doyle), Chelcie Ross (Eddie Harris), Andy Romano (Pepper Leach), Steve Yeager (Duke Temple), Peter Vucovich (Haywood), Stacy Carroll (Suzanne), Richard Pickren (Tom), Kevin Crowley (Vic Bolito), Mary Seibel (Thelma), Bill Leff (Bobby James), Mike Bacarella (Johnny Wynn), Skip Griparis (Colorman), Gary Houston (Russ), Ward Ohrman (Arthur Holloway), Marge Kotlisky (Claire Holloway), Tony Mockus, Jr. (Beast Bowden), Deborah Wakeham (Janice), Neil Flynn (Longshoreman), Keith Uchima (Groundskeeper #1), Kurt Uchima (Groundskeeper #2), William M. Sinacore (Coleman), Richard Baird (Hal Charles), Julian Milaris (Arlene), Roger Unice (Resman), Michael Thoma (Gentry), Patrick Dollymore (French Waiter), Joseph Liss (Gay in Bar), Gregory Alan Williams (Bull Pen Guard), Peter Ruskin (Gateman), Michael Hart (Burton), James Deuter (Phil Butler), Jack McLaughlin-Gray (Jerry Simmons), Tim Bell (Body Building Assistant), Joe Soto (Security), Ted Noose (Lyle Matthews), Lenny Rubin (Clubhouse Man), Thomas Purdoff (Umpire #1), Jeffrey J. Edwards (Umpire #2), Alexandra Villa (Hostess), Michelle Minyon (Working Class Bar Patron), George Aguilar, Alex Flores, Stacey Logan, Michael F. Twarog, Ted White (Stuntmen). *Indians:* Gregory Ashburn, Mark Cibrario, Jeff Dickert, Larry Duncan, Luke Fera, Mark Gaynor, Dave Globig, David Huff, Steve Janacek, Roy Jeske, Todd Johnson, Paul Keltner, Michael Kuster, John Liberger, John Meier, Bill Mosser, Jim Pandl, Pascual Rodriguez, David Roscoe, Brian Sienko, John Silbernagal, Slade Smith, Timothy Sweeny, Peter Whalen. *Yankees:* Jerry Augustine, Scott Brooks, Jim Burian, Chris Chesser, Sean Cooney, Charles Crook, Con Geary, Phillip Higgins, Jeff Hirschinger, Jay Jaster, Steve Knurowski, Randy Little, John Letz, Marty Meyers, Dan Mikorski, Willie Mueller, Ron Nedset, Earl Neibaur, George Prince, Art Rink, Bob Sanders, Dave Scharlat, Todd Schneider, Ken Senft, Paul Sikorski, Chris Stadler, Dan Wnuk, Dale Wnuk, Dave Wnuk, Jim Wolff, Steve Zimmerman.

Spring Training: Tim Brunenkant, Mike Chandler, Sean Christian, Alex Flores, Luis Graterol, Billy Ireland, Andre Jackson, Mike Johnson, Gil Juarez, Dave Ligerman, Randy Linsey, David Markzon, Jim Minor, Rusty Pennoc, Rick Rupkey, Roger Sands, Don Seidenholz, Dale Sumner, Mike Thorell, Mike Twarog, Manny Valencia, Ted White, Gene Whitney, Kevin Williamson. *Umpires:* Phil Brabant, Michael Hughes, Bill Brown, Dewey Schiele, Ron Tourtillott, Bob Hoskins, Bill Hugin, Bill McQuerry, John Schwab, Ray Bellican, Frank Mesa, Carlos Guerra, Alan Haynes, Shawn Carlson, Jerry Colver, Jeff Edwards, Hector Garcia, Ray Kovell, Tim Purdoff. *Standins:* Bill Lund, Ted Schmitz, Leonard Williams, Ramon Guzmon, Tim Cole, Terry Gearhart. *Trainers:* Bill Lemke, Greg Goodwin, Mike Walzak, Marty Caldwell.

Music Credits: "Most of All You"—Lyrics by Alan and Marilyn Bergman; Music by James Newton Howard; Performed by Bill Medley; Produced by James Newton Howard. "Wild Thing"—By Chip Taylor; Performed by X.; Courtesy of Elecktra/Asylum Records by arrangement with Warner Special Products. "How Can the Girl Refuse"—Lyrics by Glen Ballard; Music by James Newton Howard; Performed by Beckett; Produced by Michael Lloyd; Courtesy of Curb Records. "U.S. Male"—By Phillip Kennard and Ron Aniello; Performed by Lonesome Romeos; Produced by Ron Aniello; Courtesy of Curb Records. "Burn On"—Written and performed by Randy Newman; Courtesy of Reprise Records by arrangement with Warner Special Products. "The Nearness of You"—By Hoagy Carmichael and Ned Washington. "Walk away"—By Kenny Greenberg, Gary Nicholson, and Wally Wilson; Performed and produced by the Snakes; Courtesy of Curb Records. "Isn't It Romantic"—By Richard Rodgers and Lorenz Hart. "Oh You Angel"—By Ron Aniello; Performed by Lonesome Romeos; Produced by Lonesome Romeos; George Tutko and Phil Gernhard; Courtesy of Curb Records. "Mozart: Eine kleine Nachtmusik"—Performed by Bamberger Symphoniker; Conducted by Joseph Keilberth; Courtesy of Teldec Record Service GmbH by arrangement with Warner Special Products. "Cryin Shame"—Written and performed by Lyle Lovett; Produced by Tony Brown, Billy Williams and Lyle Lovett; Courtesy of MCA/Curb Records. "Beyond the Blue Horizon"—By Leo Robin, Richard A. Whiting, and W. Franke Harling. "Hideaway"—By Joey Harris; Performed and produced by The Beat Farmers; Courtesy of MCA/Curb Records.

6. *The Fabulous Baker Boys* (1989)
20th Century–Fox. A Mirage Production. Genre: Comedy/drama. Running time: 113 minutes. Rating: R. Color. Released: October 13, 1989. Available on videocassette and laserdisc.

Credits: Producers: Paula Weinstein and Mark Rosenberg. Executive Producer: Sydney Pollack. Co-Producer: William Finnegan. Screenplay: Steve Kloves. Director: Steve Kloves. Casting: Wallis Nicita. Costume Design: Lisa Jensen. Executive Music Producer: Joel Sill. Music: Dave Grusin Editor: William Steinkamp. Production Designer: Jeffrey Townsend. Director of Photography: Michael Ballhous. Unit Production Manager: William Finnegan. 1st Assistant Director: Myers. 2nd Assistant Director: Tracy Rosenthal. Production Executive:

Ken Ryan. Associate Producers: Robin Forman, Julie Bergman. Location Manager: Robin Citrin. Assistant Location Managers: Jody Hummer, John S. Agoglia. Production Coordinator: Margaret E. Fannin. Script Supervisor: Trudy Ramirez. 2nd 2nd Assistant Director: Cherylanne Martin. Camera Operator: David Dunlap. 1st Assistant Camera: Florian Ballhous. 2nd Assistant Camera: Pamela Katz. Additional Camera Assistant: Zeph R. Makgetla. Gaffer: Jim Tynes. Best Boy Electric: John "Fest" Sandau. Electricians: Charles H. McIntyre, III., R. Joe Pure, Jr., Woogie Thomas, Branch M. Brunson, John L. Demps, Jr. Pre-Rig Rigging Gaffers: John J. Doherty, Steve Schwaer. Key Grip: Steve Smith. Best Boy Grip: Bruce Byall. Dolly Grip: Arthur Blum. Grips: Timothy P. Collins, Robert Meckler, Todd Griffith, William D. Harris, Mark Sannes, William A. Shea. Key Rigging Grip: John W. Murphy. Set Decorator: Anne H. Ahrens. Assistant Art Director: Michael Perry. Senior Set Designer: Don Gibbon, Jr. Lead Man: Michael Mulhfriedel. Set Dressers: Amy Feldman, Ross Harpold. On Set Dresser: Bruce Bellamy. Scenic Artist: Chris Winslow. Swing Gang: Charles T. Gray, Eric Hice, Korey Pollard, Peter Sykes. Art Coordinator: Clay A. Griffith. Special Photography: Karen Miller. Construction Coordinator: Curtis Yomtob. Construction Foreman: Joseph H. Cathull. Wardrobe Supervisor: Marsha Perloff. Costumer: Jill Sharaf. Hairdresser: Jeanne Van Phue. Makeup Artist: Ronnie Specter. Assistant Makeup Artist: Tammy Kusian. "Makin' Whoopee" choreographed by: Peggy Holmes. Property Master: Walter Wall. Assistant Props: Paul Rylander. Special Effects: Robert E. Worthington. Sound Mixer: Stephen Von Hase. Boom Man: Ian C. Wright. Cable: Glen Aulepp. Transportation Coordinator: Howard Small. Transportation Captain: Bob White. Production Accountant: Mayda Renizzi-Holt. Accounting Assistant: Kay Jordan. Casting Associate: Joanne Zaluski. Casting Coordinator: Christina Sanchez. Extras Casting: Reatha Grey/Grey Images. Publicist: Spooky Stevens. Still Photographer: Lorey Sebastian. Voice Casting: Barbara Harris. Supervising Sound Editor: J. Paul Huntsman. Music Editorial Consultant: Else Blangsted. Music Editor: Bunny Andrews. Assistant Editor: Michael Wilson. Apprentice Editor: Susan Alexander. Post Production Coordinator: Karen Marmer. Dialogue Editors: Matthew G. Sawelson, Robert Macksten. Sound Effects Editor: John Haeny. ADR Editor: Gregg Baxter. ADR Mixer: Wallace R. Bearden. Foley Editors: Efraim Reuveni, Susan Dudek. Foley Artists: Robin Harlan, Kevin Bartnof. Sound Assistants: Carolann S. Sanchez, Patrick English. Music Recording Engineer: Don Murray. Re-Recording Mixers: Chris Jenkins, Gary Alexander, D.M. Hemphill. Re-recorded by: Todd AO/Glen Glenn Studios. Jeff Bridges Piano Performance by Dave Grusin. Beau Bridges Piano Performance by: John F. Hammond. Sideline Piano Supervisor: John E. Oliver. Piano Coaches: Lou Foresteri, Joyce Collins. Vocal Coach to Ms. Pfeiffer: Sally Stevens. Music Clearance: Jill Meyers. Music Preparation: Jo Ann Kane. Musicians Contractor: Sandy De Crescent. Score Performed by: Ernie Watts, Saxophone; Sal Marquez, Trumpet; Lee Rittenour, Guitar; Brian Bromberg, Bass; Harvey Mason, Drums; Dave Grusin, Keyboards. Stunt Coordinator: Jon Pochron. Propmasters: J. Douglas Burch, David Cannon, Ronald Wayne Cox, Mark Fite, Scott Anthony Lynk, Joshua J. Ott, David Stawecki, Rick Welden, Gary Wortman. Painters: Chris Gibbin, Kenneth Hardy, Suzanne Joffe, Renee Prince, Randy Sanchez, Wayne Shepherd. Construction Laborer: Eugene Freiburger. Drivers: Richard M.

Brasic, Anthony J. Brazas, Lewis Cundiff, Thomas C. Kimmel, Mike Labeaune, Eric W. Mizen, Joseph Kelly Padovich, Mike Padovich, Marvin Palenske, Olin Rushin, Gary Small, Anthony Charles Steere. Production Secretary: Jeffrey K. Ausmus. Production Assistants: Sebastian Ballhaus, Bart Carpenter, Bryan Curry, Ashley R. Friedman, Laura Ann Petticord, Roberto Santana, Suzanne Spangler, Jordan J. Stone. Assistant to Jeff Bridges: Lloyd Catlett. Stand-in/Michelle Pfeiffer: Sandra Fear. Stand-in/Beau Bridges: Creed Bratton. Dog Trainer: Dennis E. Grisco. Craft Service: Denny Hans. Caterer: 4-Star Catering. Studio Teachers: Nancy Pyne-Hapke, Barbara L. Bass. Assistants to the Producers: Linda Labov, Donna Ostroff, Alexandra Stone.

Seattle Crew: Production Coordinator: Valerie Ross. Office Production Assistant: Lynette Goto. Production Assistant: Peter Hirsch. Location Assistant: Tony Grob. Set Dresser: Ed Dupra. Transportation Captain: John McCarthy. Electricians: Don McConald, Jr., Bruce Martin. Grips: Chris Feringer, Mike Steward. Propmasters: Jonathan Hackett, Paul Pembrook. Laborer: Tom Bleckov. Craft Service: Peter Gant. Tutor: Clinton Pozzi, Jr. Drivers: Bob Chestnut, George Evans, Jim Jones, George Kramer, Don Penick, Gary Shepard, Bob Sullivan. Music Supervision: Windswept Pacific. Production Services: Finnegan-Pinchuk. Sound Effects: Todd AO/Glen Glenn Studios. Music Recorded at Sunset Sound. Negative Cutting: Donah Bassett and Associates. Titles and Opticals: Pacific Title. Color by Deluxe. Public Relations Representatives: Rogers and Cowan, Dennis Davidson Associates. Insurance provided by: Albert G. Ruben and Co. Completion Bond: Completion Bond Co. Financial Consultants: Frans J. Afman, Credit Lyonnais Bank, Nederland NV.

Cast: Jeff Bridges (Jack Baker), Beau Bridges (Frank Baker), Michelle Pfeiffer (Susie Diamond), Ellie Raab (Nina), Xander Berkeley (Lloyd), Jennifer Tilly (Monica), Dakin Matthews (Charlie), Ken Lerner (Ray), Albert Hall (Henry), Terri Treas (Girl in Bed), Gregory Itzin (Vince), Bradford English (Earl), David Coburn (Kid at Vet), Todd Jeffries (Theo), Jeffrey J. Nowinski (Hotel Manager), Nancy Fish (Laughing Bar Person), Beege Barkette (Waitress), Del Zamora (Man with Cleaver), Howard Matthew Johnson (Bathroom Attendant), Stuart Nisbet (Veterinarian), Robert Henry (Doorman), Drake (Eddie), Martina Finch, Lisa Raggio, Winifred Freidman, Vickilyn Reynolds, Wendy Goldman, Karen Hartman, D.D. Howard, Carole Ita White, Krisie Spear (Singers), Steve Alterman, John La Fayette, Bach August, Tina Lifford, Greg Finley, Arlin Miller, J.D. Hall, Paige Nan Pollack, David J. Randolph, Doris Hess, Rosanna Huffman, Stephani Ryan (Background Voices)

Music Credits: "People"— Performed by Dave Grusin and John Hammond; Written by Jule Styne and Bob Merrill. "Jingle Bells"— Performed by Ellie Raab. "The Girl from Ipanema"— Performed by Dave Grusin and John Hammond; Written by Antonio Carlos Jobim, Norman Gimbel, Vinicius De Moraes "The Candy Man"— Performed by Jennifer Tilly; Written by Leslie Bricusse and Anthony Newley. "My Way"— Performed by Lisa Raggio; Written by Paul Anka, Gillis Thibault, Claude François, and Jacques Revaux. "Up Up and Away"— Performed by D.D. Howard; Written by Jimmy Webb. "I Go to Rio"— Performed by Wendy Goldman; Written by Peter Allen and Adrienne Anderson. "Tiny Bubbles"— Performed by Carole Ita White; Written by Leon Pober. "I'm So Excited"— Performed by

Krisie Spear, Martina Finch, Vickilyn Reynolds and Karen Hartman; Written by Anita Pointer, June Pointer, Ruth Pointer and Trevor Lawrence. "Feelings"—Performed by Winifred Freidman and Michelle Pfeiffer; Music and Words by Mauricio Kaiserman and Morris Albert. "Bluebird"—Written by A. Hawkshaw. "More Than You Know"—Performed by Michelle Pfeiffer; Written by Edward Eliscu, Billy Rose and Vincent Youmans. "Can't Take My Eyes off You"—Performed by Michelle Pfeiffer; Written by Bob Crewe and Bob Gaudio. "Jingle Bells"—Arranged and adapted by Jon Charles. "Ten Cents a Dance"—Performed by Michelle Pfeiffer, Jeff Bridges and Beau Bridges; Written by Richard Rodgers and Lorenz Hart. "Perdido"—Performed by the Duke Ellington Orchestra; Courtesy of GRP Records, Inc.; Produced by Michael Abene and Mercer Ellington; Written by Juan Tizol. "Lullaby of Birdland"—Performed by Louis Spears, Kenny Dennis and Joel Scott; Music by George Shearing; Words by B.Y. Forster. "The Look of Love"—Performed by Michelle Pfeiffer; Written by Burt Bacharach and Hal David. "Prelude to a Kiss"—Performed by the Duke Ellington Orchestra; Courtesy of GRP Records, Inc.; Produced by Michael Abene and Mercer Ellington; Written by Edward Kennedy "Duke" Ellington, Irving Gordon and Irving Mills. "Moonglow"—Performed by the Benny Goodman Quartet; Courtesy of RCA Records; Written by Will Hudson, Eddie De Lange, Irving Mills. "Do Nothin Till You Hear from Me"—Performed by the Duke Ellington Orchestra; Courtesy of GRP Records Inc.; Produced by Michael Abene and Mercer Ellington; Written by Edward Kennedy "Duke" Ellington, Irving Gordon, and Irving Mills. "Makin Whoopee"—Performed by Michelle Pfeiffer; Written by Walter Donaldson, Gus Kahn. "Solitude"—Performed by Tony Bennett; Courtesy of CBS Records Music Licensing Department; Written by Edward Kennedy "Duke" Ellington, Eddie De Lange and Irving Mills. "Sweet Georgia Brown"—Whistler—Rick Riccio. Written by Ben Bernie, Maceo Pinkard, Kenneth Casey. "The Pea Song"—Performed by Michelle Pfeiffer; Words by Steve Kloves; Music by Michelle Pfeiffer. "You're Sixteen, You're Beautiful and You're Mine"—Performed by Jeff Bridges and Beau Bridges; Written by Robert Sherman and Richard Sherman. "My Funny Valentine"—Performed by Michelle Pfeiffer; Written by Lorenz Hart and Richard Rodgers.

7. *White Palace* (1990)

Universal Pictures. A Mirage/Doubleplay Production. Genre: Drama/romance. Running time: 103 minutes. Rating: R. Released: October 19, 1990. Available on videocassette and laserdisc.

Credits: Producers: Mark Rosenberg, Amy Robinson, Griffin Dunne. Executive Producer: Sydney Pollack. Associate Producer: Robin Foreman. Co-Producer: Bill Finnegan. Screenplay: Ted Tally and Alvin Sargent. Based on the novel by Glenn Savan. Director: Luis Mandoki. Casting: Nancy Nayor. Executive Music Producer: Joel Sill. Music: George Fenton. Costume Design: Lisa Jensen. Editing: Carol Littleton. Production Design: Jeannine Oppewall. Director of Photography: Lajos Koltai. Unit Production Manager: Chuck Murray. 1st Assistant Director: Chris J. Solda. 2nd Assistant Director: Gabriela Vazquez. 2nd 2nd Assistant Director: Donald J. Lee, Jr. Production Coordinator: Lisa Matsukawa. Assistant Production Coordinator: Alexandra Stone. Production Coordinator (LA):

Margaret Fannin. Script Supervisor: Cynthia Upstill. Assistant to Mr. Mandoki: Rosalia Salazar. Camera Operator: Michael Stone. 1st Assistant Camera: Rick Tschudin. 2nd Assistant Camera: Richard Clarkson. Camera Loader: Zeph Makgetla. Gaffer: Stuart Spohn. Electrical Best Boy: Randy Woodside. Electricians: Chris Napolitano, Tim Durr, Bruce Pearn, Kevin Ort. Key Grip: Steve Smith. Best Boy Grip: Rob Meckler. Dolly Grip: Arthur Blum. Grips: Tim Collins, Michael Dougan, Eric Nulsen. Sound Mixer: Stephen Von Hase. Boom Operator: Dennis Fuller. Cableman: Adam Reisz. Assistant Editors: Raul Davalos, Christy Richmond. Apprentice Editor: Suzanne Spangler. Supervising Sound Editor: Bob Grieve. Music Editor: Sally Boldt. ADR Editor: J. Paul Huntsman. Dialogue Editor: Matt G. Sawelson. Sound Effects Editor: John Haeny. Sound Editor: Daniel Yale. Foley Artist: Terry Burke. Sound Assistant: Margi Bentley. Sound Apprentice: Paul Parsons. Assistant Music Editor: Alexander Gibson. Re-Recording Mixers: Andy Nelson, Don Digirolamo, Steve Pederson. Re-Recordists: Samuel F. Kaufman, Ronnie Budwig. ADR Mixer: Paul Zydel. Foley Mixer: Dean Drabin. Re-recorded at: Todd AO/Glen Glenn Studios. Post Production Supervisor: Carol Dantuono. Location Supervisor: Steven Charles. Location Managers: Kathryn M. Griege, Ricki Renna. Location Coordinator: Pamelah Oakey. Location Scout: Linda Diamond. Art Director: John Wright Stevens. Set Decorator: Lisa Fischer. Construction Coordinator: Ed England. Leadman: John Rozman. Graphic Designer: Christine Castigliano. Draftsman: Jay Ferger. Greensman: Richard Poynter. Art Deptartment Coordinator: Andy Milner. Swing Gang: Robert Heizler, Martin McManus. Wardrobe Supervisor: Marsha Perloff. Costumer: Joyce Kogut. Seamstress: Pat Eby. Makeup: Ronnie Specter. Hair: Leslie Anderson. Assistant Makeup/Hair: Karl Wesson. Property Master: Trisha Gallaher. Assistant Property Master: Joann Hicks. Property Assistant: Tim McDonald. Special Effects: Mack Chapman. Special Effects Assistant: Adam Cook. Casting Associate: Kimba Hills. Casting Assistant: Donna Larson. Location Casting: Avy Kaufman. Extras Casting: Carrie Houk. Assistant Extras Casting: Doree Wren. Voice Casting: Barbara Harris. Negative Cutter: Gary Burritt. Color Timer: Steve Sheridan. Carpenters: John Gordon, Sam Bertone, Tim Osman, Troy Osman, Tyler Osman. Construction Assistant: Lori Bertone. Painters: Patrick Gomes, Nancy Gomes. Standby Painter: David Kruger. Caterer: Variety Cinema Catering. Craft Service: Jule Ballard. Production Assistants: Jordan Stone, Steve Cowie, Thomas Gross, Joshua Hancock, Keith Ogier. Production Secretary: Louise Maffitt. Secretaries to the Producers: Jo Berman, Dauri Chase, Linda Labov, Donna Ostroff. Transportation Coordinator: Ed Arter. Transportation Captains: Ronn Hejna, Rick Mercier. Production Accountant: Roberta Rose. Production Controller: Lori Taub. Assistant Production Accountant: Laurie Hindenach. Post Production Accountant: Steven Rosen. Payroll: Jeff Behlendorf. Publicist: Spooky Stevens. Still Photographer: Lorey Sebastian. Music recorded at Evergreen Recording Studios. Scoring Mixer: John Richards. Musicians Contractor: Sandy DeCrescent. Orchestrator: Jeff Atmajian, Soloists: Michael Lang, Daniel Higgins, Timothy May. Music Clearance: Jill Meyers, Bonnie Greenberg. Music Supervision: Windswept Pacific. Production Services provided by Finnegan-Pinchuk. Production Equipment provided by Cinelease. Legal Services provided by Armstrong and Hirsch. Titles and Opticals by Pacific Title. Special Effects by Todd AO/Glen Glenn Studios. Color by Deluxe.

New York Crew: Location Manager: Ann Reddington. 2nd Unit Director of Photography: Michael Stone. Sound Mixer: Dennis Maitland. Boom Operator: Danny Rosenbloom. Gaffer: Bob Dolan. Key Grip: Joe Carroll. Assistant Property Master: Eric Stepper. Helicopter Pilot: Al Cerullo. Transportation Captain: Eddie Iacobelli.

Cast: Susan Sarandon (Nora Baker), James Spader (Max Baron), Jason Alexander (Neil), Kathy Bates (Rosemary), Eileen Brennan (Judy), Steven Hill (Sal Horowitz), Rachel Levin (Rachel), Corey Parker (Larry Klugman), Renee Taylor (Edith Baron), Barbara Howard (Sherri Klugman), Kim Meyers (Heidi Soloman), Jonathan Penner (Marv Miller), Hildie Brooks (Ella Horowitz), Mitzie McCall (Sophie Rosen), K.C. Carr (Stripper), Glenn Savan (White Palace Customer), Fannie Belle Lebby (Marcia), Vernon Dudas (Jimmy the Bartender), Maryann Kopperman (Reba), Maria Pitillo (Janey), Jeremy Piven (Kahn). Bachelor Party Men: Robert Bourgeois, Lantz Harshbarger, Jordan Stone. William Oberbeck (Eddie Lobodiak), John Flack (Advertising Executive), Wilma Myracle (Helen), Jospeh Rosenbloom (Rabbi), Michael E. Arnett (Country Western Singer), Janet Lofton (Supermarket Checker), Sherry Grogan (Mrs. Goodman), Patrick S. Harrigan (Mr. Goodman), Adrienne Brett (Brunch Guest), Toni Lynn (Hostess), Ellen Cantalupo (Waitress), Jonathon Ames (Restaurant Customer), Louis Brill (Elderly Man), Blanche Brill (Elderly Woman). Gary Hymes, Jerry Spicer, Ike Mizen (Stunts) Carlo Allen, Charles Bazaldua, Bart Braverman, Joan Crosby, Judi Durand, Greg Finley, Javier Grajeda, Rosanna Huffman, Barbara Iley, Harvey Jason, Marsha Kramer, David McCharen, Paige Nan Pollack, Jan Rabson, David J. Randolph, Noreen Reardon, Stephani Ryan, Gary Schwartz, Suzanne Stone (Additional Voices)

Music Credits: "Love or Money"— Performed by Slater Sealove Band; Courtesy of Reata; Written by James Slater and Carl Sealove. "What Would It Take" and "Guardian Angel"— Performed by The Centurian Players; Written by David Lee. "Boogie Woogie Baby"— Performed by The Centurian Players; Written by Ken Wesley and J. Remington Wilde. "Tulsa Time"— Performed by The Centurian Players; Written by Daniel Flowers. "Good Hearted Woman"— Performed by The Centurian Players; Written by Willie Nelson and Waylon Jennings. "O Mio Babbino Caro"— Aria from the opera "Gianni Schicchi"; Performed by the Münchner Rundfunkorchester; Conducted by Karl Eichhorn, Soprano by Lucia Popp; Courtesy of Acanta Records/Sounds of Film Ltd; Written by Giacomo Puccini. "Wie nahte mir Der Schlummer"— Aria from the opera "Der Freischütz"; Performed by the Munchner Rundfunkorchester; Conducted by Karl Eichhorn, Soprano by Lucia Popp; Courtesy of Acanta Records/Sounds of Film Ltd.; Written by Carl Maria von Weber. "Younger Men"— Performed by K.T. Oslin; Courtesy of RCA Records; Written by K.T. Oslin. "For All We Know"— Performed by The Bottom Line; Written by Robb Wilson, James Griffin and Fred Karlin. "Your Reputation" and "Highway Warriors"— Performed by Shona Laing; Courtesy of Virgin Records Australia Pty Bkgd., Ltd.; Written by Shona Laing.

8. *King Ralph* (1990)

Universal Pictures. Mirage/Jbro Production. Genre: Comedy. Running time: 97 minutes. Rating: PG. Color. Released: February 1990. Available on videocassette and laserdisc.

Credits: Producer: Jack Brodsky. Executive Producers: Sydney Pollack and Mark Rosenberg. Co-Producers: Julie Bergman and John Comfort. Written and directed by David Ward. Based on the novel *Headlong* by Emlyn Williams. Casting: Mary Selway. Music: James Newton Howard. Costume Designer: Catherine Cook. Editing: John Jympson. Production Designer: Simon Holland. Director of Photography: Kenneth MacMillan. Unit Production Manager: John Comfort. 1st Assistant Director: Derek Cracknell. 2nd Assistant Directors: Melvyn Lind, Julian Wall. Sound Designer: Ivan Sharrock. Boom Operator: Don Banks. Sound Maintenance: David Motta. Sound Trainee: Jo Crilly. Location Managers: William Lang, Peter Elford. Production Coordinator: Janine Lodge. Script Supervisor: Diana Dill. Camera Operator: Mike Proudfoot. Focus Puller: David Morgan. Clapper Loader: Jonathan Earp. Camera Grip: Tony Turner. Camera Trainee: Katrina Thurston. Gaffer: Tommy Brown. Electrical Best Boy: John Clark. Associate Editor: William Webb. Assistant Editors: Jonathan Lucas, Robert Frazen, Alex Renskoff. Editorial Trainee: Joss Agnew. Post Production Supervisor: Carol Dantuono. Supervising Sound Editor: Scott Hecker. Music Editors: James L. Weidman, Dina Eaton. ADR Editor: Bill Voightlander. Dialogue Editors: Bobby Mackston, Matt Sawelson. Special Effects Editor: Joel Valentine. Foley Editors: Chris Flick, Dave Arnold. Foley Artists: Gary Hecker, Katie Rowe. Foley Mixer: Dean Drabin. Sound Effects Recordist: John Paul Fasal. Assistant Sound Editors: Doug Kent, Carol-Anne Sanchez-Shapiro. Music Assistant: David M. Olson. Re-Recording Mixers: Chris Jenkins, Mark Smith, Doug Hemphill. Re-Recordists: Rudy Lara, Tony Jenkins. Re-recorded at: Todd AO/Glen Glenn Studios. Negative Cutter: Gary Burritt. Color Timer: Steve Sheridan. Art Director: Clinton Cavers. Set Decorator: Peter Walpole. Draughtsman: Peter Russell. Draughtswoman: Suzanna Smith and Lucy Richardson. Art Department Assistant: Elli Griff. Construction Manager: Jack Carter. Construction Super: John Hedges. Chargehand Carpenters: Kelvin Carter, Trevor Dyer, Reg Richards. Chargehand Stangehand: Kenneth Langridge. Supervising Painter: Michael Jones. Chargehand Painter: Ken Welland. Chargehand Rigger: John Field. Master Sculptor: Fred Evans. Sculptors: Peter Voysey, Janet Stevens. Wardrobe Supervisor: Annie Crawford. Wardrobe Assistants: Lindsay Pugh, Jennie Hawkins, Joe Hobbs, Dave Whiting. Makeup Supervisor: Peter Robb-King. Makeup: Jane Royle. Hairdresser Supervisor: Elaine Bowerbank. Hairdresser: Betty Glasow. Property Master: Bruce Bigg. Chargehand Prop Man: Ray Rose. Chargehand Standby Prop Man: Danny Hunter. Standby Propman: Colin Burgess. Chargehand Dressing Props: Alfie Smith, Ted Stickley. Dressing Props: Peter Bigg, Barry Gibbs. Property Buyer: Judy Farr. Drapes Master: Graham Caulfield. Special Effects Super: John Morris. Choreo: Pat Garrett. Stunt Coordinator: Greg Powell. Casting Assistant: Caitlin Rhodes. Production Assistant: (UK) Joanna Burn. Assistant to David Ward: Jason Grode. Assistant to the Producers: Lisa Bellomo, Rita Joelson, Linda Labov, Donna Ostroff. Production Runner: Ben Jenkins. Post Production Runner: Elizabeth Dewey. Caterer: 1st Unit Caterers. Unit Drivers: Roy Clarke, Dave Manning, Colin Morris, Michael "Sparrow" Broadway, Tommy Lee, Peter Graovac. Camera Car: Martin Lewis. Standby Construction: Chalky White. Production Accountant: Rex Mitchell. Post Production Accountant: Howard Baral. Assistant Accountants: Della Moore, Andrew Noakes, Lauri Mayberry. Accounting Secretary: Sarah Dean. Publicist: Patricia Johnson. Still Photographer:

Frank Connor. Music recorded at Columbia Recording Studios. Scoring Mixer: Shawn Murphy. Scoring Conductor: Marty Paich. Supervising Scoring Coordinator: Michael Mason. Score Recording Engineers: Robert Schaper, Ross Pallone. Musicians Coordinator: Sandy DeCrescent. Orchestrators: Brad Dechter, Chris Boardman. Music Clearances: Jill Meyers, Bonnie Greenberg. Filmed on location and at Pinewood Studios, London, England. Originated on Eastman Colour Film from Kodak. Lighting Equipment supplied by Lee Lighting Limited. Westcam provided by CRM Group Inc. Post production facilities provided by Big Time Picture Co. Sound Effects by Todd AO/Glen Glenn Studios. Titles and Opticals by Pacific Title. Panavision. Color by Rank Film Laboratories.

Cast: John Goodman (King Ralph), Peter O'Toole (Willingham) John Hurt (Graves), Camille Coduri (Miranda), Richard Griffiths (Phipps), Leslie Phillips (Gordon), James Villiers (Hale), Joely Richardson (Princess Anna), Niall O'Brien (McGuire), Julian Glover (King Gustav), Judy Parfitt (Queen Katherine), Ed Stobart (Dysentery), Gedren Heller (Punk Girl), Rudolph Walker (King Mulamboo), Michael Johnson (Hamilton), Ann Beach (Miranda's Mother), Jack Smethurst (Miranda's Father), Roger Aston Griffiths (Royal Photographer), Brian Greene (Ed Mayes), Dallas Adams (MC Strip Club), Adele Lakeland (Fanny Oakley), Joanne Haydon-Pearce, Vanessa Lee Hicks, Jazzi Northover, Charlotte Pyecroft, Dawn Spence (Chorus girls), Guy Fithen (Bouncer), Ian Gelder (Writing Instructor), Cameron Blakely (Graves Photographer), Carolyn Paterson (Counter Girl), Sally Nesbitt (Onlooker), Richard Whitmore (Male Newscaster), Jennie Stoller (Female Newscaster), Kirk St. James (Sax Player), Tim Seely (King of England), Alison McGuire (Queen of England), Gareth Forwood (Duke), Alan McMahon (Assistant Photographer), Richard Bebb (Gamekeeper), David Stoll (Butler), Chantel-Claire, Topaze Hasfal-School, Charlotte Pyecroft (Dukettes Backup Singers), Paul Beech (Tailor), Angus McKay (Assistant Tailor), Jason Richards (Baby Ralph II)

Music Credits: "Tiny Bubbles"—Written by Leon Pober; Performed by John Goodman. "Be Bop a LuLa"—Written by Gene Vincent and Sheriff Tex Davis; Song from Moulin Rouge. "Where Is Your Heart"—Written by William Engvick and George Auric. "In the Mood for Love"—Written by Dorothy Fields and Jimmy McHugh. "Good Golly Miss Molly"—Written by Robert Blackwell and John Marascalco; Performed by John Goodman. "Duke of Earl"—Written by Earl Edwards, Eugene Dizon and Bernice Williams; Performed by John Goodman. "Good Golly Miss Molly"—End Title Performance by Little Richard; Produced by Jeff Lyne.

9. *Presumed Innocent* (1990)

Warner Bros. A Mirage Production. Genre: Crime/mystery. Running Time: 127 minutes. Rating: R. Color. Released: July 27, 1990. Available on videocassette and laserdisc.

Credits: Producers: Sydney Pollack and Mark Rosenberg. Screenplay: Frank Pierson and Alan J. Pakula. Based on the novel by Scott Turow. Director: Alan Pakula. Director of Photography: Gordon Willis. Editing: Evan Lottman. Music: John Williams. Lyrics: Shamus O'Connor, John J. Stamford, Red Latham, Wamp Carlson, Guy Bonham, Richard Wolf, Bret Mazur, Y.C. Smith. Production

Design: George Jenkins. Art Director: Bob Guerra. Set Design: Carol Joffe. Costume Design: John Boxer. Technical Effects: William N. Fordes. Unit Production Manager: David Starke. 1st Assistant Director: Alex Hapsas. 2nd Assistant Director Tony Adler. Production Comptroller: Deborah Johnson. Assistant Unit Production Manager: Celia Costas. Assistant Art Directors: Mary Beth Kuhn, Teresa Carriker. Assistant Set Decorator: Steven Gamiello. Master Scenic Artist: Patricia A. Walker. Chief Set Dresser: Dick Tice. Art Department Coordinator: Catherine Solt. Property Master: Janet Shaw. Assistant Property Masters: Loren Levy, Bob Wilson, Jr. Assistant Property Master (Detroit): Michele Poulik. Camera Operator: Craig DiBona. 1st Assistant Camera: Douglas C. Hart. 2nd Assistant Camera: Richard Crudo. 2nd Assistant Camera (Detroit): Val Sklar. Still Photographer: John Seakwood. Script Supervisor: Karen Hale Wookey. Makeup Artist: Fern Buchner. Assistant Makeup: Vincent Callaghan. Hairstylist: Colleen Callaghan. Assistant Hairstylist: Judi Goodman. Assistant Costume Designer: Suzanne Schwarzer. Wardrobe Supervisor: Ross Trimarco-Cuervo. Wardrobe: Guy Tanno, Robert Musco, Mark Klein. Production Sound Mixer: James Sabat. Recordist: Frank Graziadei. Recordist (Detroit): Gail Carroll-Coe. Video Technicians: Bob Gaulin, Richard Mader, Jr. Joseph Trammell. Chief Lighting Technician: James Fitzpatrick. Assistant Chief Lighting Technician: Kevin Fitzpatrick. Assistant Chief Light Technician (Detroit): Robert Hayward. Key Grip: George Patsos. 2nd Grip: William Patsos. 2nd Grip (Detroit): Timothy O'Dea. Dolly Grip: James Pollard. Construction Coordinators: Anthony Zappia, Gilbert Gertsen. Construction Foreman: Don Zappia. 1st Assistant Film Editor: Lee Fonvielle. Assistant Film Editor: Gregory Dagostino. Supervising Sound Editor: Ron Bochar. Dialogue Editors: Jeffrey Stern, Laura Civello. ADR Editor: Darrell Hanzalik. ADR Mixer: Paul Zydel. Music Editor: Ken Waninberg. New York Music Editor: Todd Kasow. Orchestrators: Herbert Spencer, John Neufeld. Music Recording Engineer: Armand Steiner. Foley Editors: Bruce Pross, Steven Visscher. Assistant Sound Editors: Kan Chan, Chris Fielder, Yvette Nabel, Joan Franklin. Re-Recording Mixer: Richard Portman. SFX and Foley Design: C5, Inc. Legal Technical Consultant: William N. Fordes, Esq. Legal Research Associate: Beth Minsky. Coordinator for Mr. Pakula: Catherine Hall. Production Associate: Jody Cregan Henry. Assistant to Mr. Pakula: Stephanie Koules. Assistant to Mr. Solt: Robert I. Smith, Jr. Production Office Coordinator: Jane Raab. Assistant Production Office Coordinators: Diana Schmidt, Roe Dressen-Soto. Assistant P.O.C. (Detroit): Lois Nalepka. Production Accountants: John Richardson, Robert Palo. Production Aides: Martha Appel, John Michael Maas, Abby Margolis, Ted Shuttleworth, Matthew Weiner. Production Office Assistants: Jonathan Oliver, Robert McClung. Art Department Assistant: Patty Shelley. Location Manager: Peter Pastorelli. Location Coordinator: Richard W. Dooley. Location Coordinator (Detroit): Catherine Thomas. Location Assistants: Matt Widman, Linda Marshall-Smith. 2nd 2nd Assistant Director: Randy Barbee. DGA Trainee: Lisa Stein. Casting Assistant: Lisa M. Marfleet. Extras Casting: Joy Todd. Unit Publicist: Eric Myers. Teamster Captain: James P. Whalen. Co-Captain: Francis Connolly, Jr. Craft Service: Jude Aubrey Hindle, Frank McKenna. Craft Service (Detroit): Barbara Gurski. Negative Cutting: Donna Bassett. Color Timer: Bob Kaiser. Multidimensional Sound: B.A.S.E. Titles and Opticals: The Effects House, NY. Post Production Facilities: Todd/AO Studios

East. Camera Package: General Camera Corp., NY. Color: Du Art Film Labs, NY. Prints by Technicolor. Lenses and Paniflex Camera by Panavision.

Cast: Harrison Ford (Rusty Sabich), Greta Scacchi (Carolyn Polhemus), Brian Dennehy (Raymond Horgan), Raul Julia (Sandy Stern), Bonnie Bedelia (Barbara Sabich), Paul Winfield (Judge Larren Lyttle), John Spencer (Detective Lipranzer), Joe Grifasi (Tommy Molto), Tom Mardirosian (Nico Della Guardia), Anna Maria Horsford (Eugenia), Sab Shimono ("Painless" Kumagai), Bradley Whitford (Jamie Kemp), Christine Estabrook (Lydia "Mac" MacDougall), Michael Tolan (Mr. Polhemus), Madison Arnold (Sgt. Lionel Kenneally), Ron Frazier (Stew Dubinsky), Jesse Bradford (Nat Sabich), Joseph Mazzello (Wendell McGaffney), Tucker Smallwood (Detective Harold Greer), Leland Gantt (Leon Wells), Teodorina Bello (Ernestine), David Wohl (Morrie Dickerman), John Michael Bennett (Guerasch), Bo Rucker (Mike Duke), Peter Appel (Glendenning), John Ottavino (Chet), Robert Katims (Cody), Joseph Carberry (Mr. McGaffney), John Setz (Balestrieri), Bill Winkler (Tom), John Vennema (Judge Mumphrey), Michael Genet (Court Clerk), Richard L. Newcomb (Undercover Cop), Ed Wheeler (Jim, Arresting Detective), Miles Watson (Arresting Detective), DeAnn Mears (Loretta), Julia Meade (Moderator), Thom Cagle (Camp Counselor), Ricky Rosa (Camper), Allison Field, Janis Corsair, Bill Corsair, Carla Goff (Reporters), Rick DeFuria, Victor Truro, Elizabeth Williams, Jeffrey Wright, Ted Neustadt, Kimberleigh Aarn (Prosecuting Attorneys)

Music Credits: "Macnamara's Band"—Written by Shamus O'Connor, John J. Stamford, Red Latham, Wamp Carlson, Guy Bonham. "Let the Drummer Loose"—Written by Richard Wolf, Bret Mazur; Performed by Y.C. Smith.

10. *Dead Again* (1991)
Paramount Pictures. A Mirage Production. Genre: Mystery/Romance. Running time: 107 minutes. Rating: R. Color. Released: August 1991. Available on videocassette and laserdisc.

Credits: Producers: Lindsay Doran and Charles H. Maguire. Executive Producer: Sydney Pollack. Screenplay: Scott Frank. Director: Kenneth Branagh. Director of Photography: Matthew F. Leonetti. Editing: Peter E. Berger. Production Designer: Tim Harvey. Art Director: Sydney Z. Litwack. Set Decorator: Jerry Adams. Costume Design: Phillis Dalton. Casting: Gail Levin. Music: Patrick Doyle. Co-Producer: Dennis Feldman. Unit Production Manager: William C. Gerrity. 1st Assistant Director: Steve Danton. 2nd Assistant Director: Tracy Rosenthal. Set Designers: Henry Alberti, Joseph Hubbard, Eric Orbam. Script Supervisor: Marshall Schlom. 1st Assistant Photographer: Mike Weldon, Steve Ullman. Camera Operator: Robert McBride. 2nd Assistant Photographer: Tim Dunford, Mark Figueroa. Still Photographer: Peter Sorel. Video Assist Operator: Thomas A. Pendell. Sound Mixer: Gerald G. Jost. Boom Operator: Pat Suraci. Cable Person: James Thompson. Assistant Editor: George C. Villasenor. Apprentice Editor: John Robert Coniglio. Supervising Sound Editor: George Watters, II. Sound Editors: Larry Carow, Midge Costin, Joseph A. Ippolito, Frank Howard, Gary Wright. Music Editor: Roy Prendergast. ADR Editors: Fred Stafford, Bobbi Banks. Foley Editors: Victoria Martin, Fred Burke. ADR Sound Effects: Donald

Ortiz, Maggie Ostroff. Apprentice Sound Editor: Christopher C. Schiavo. Foley Artists: Ken Dufva, David Lee Fein, Joan Rowe. Foley Mixers: Marty Church, Greg Curda. ADR Mixer: Bob Baron. Recorder: Denis Blackeady. Re-Recording Mixers: Terry Porter, David J. Hudson, Mel Metcalfe. Music Scoring Mixer: John Richards. Orchestrator: Lawrence Ashmore. Orchestra conducted by William Kraft. Music recorded at Evergreen Recording Studios. Voice Casting: Barbara Harris. Makeup Artist: Dan Striepeke. 2nd Makeup Artist: Leonard Engelman. Effects Makeup: Tom and Bari Burman. Hairstyles: Kathryn Blondell. 2nd Hairstylist: Virginia Hadfield. Costume Supervisor: Sandra Culotta. Costumers: Ann Culotta, Daniel Weinberg, Deborah Hopper. Chief Lighting Technicians: Patrick Dlymyer. Assistant Chief Lighting Technicians: Robert Fillis, Keith Baber. 1st Company Grip: Daniel Reilly. 2nd Company Grips: Russell Reilly, Burt Lindemoen. Dolly Grip: Antonio Garrido. Grip: Don Linsley. Electricians: Patrick Marshall, Kurt Marshall, Terry Neville, Lloyd Gowdy. Property Master: John Zemansky. Assistant Property Masters: Dean Wilson, Glen Feldman. Lead Person: James Husbands. Property Persons: Frank Flores, Gary Daspit. Location Manager: Ned Shapiro. Assistant Location Manager: Serena Baker. Production Office Coordinator: Barbara Spitz. Production Accountant: Michael D. Roberts. Assistant Accountant: Mindy Sheldon. Accounting Auditor: Jana Karas. Production Secretary: Kathleen Melton. Production Office Assistant: Dana Delfs. Assistant to Ms. Doran: Carol King. Assistant to Mr. Maguire: Scott W. Anderson, John McDonald. Assistant to Mr. Branagh: S. W. Schuster. Production Consultant: Hugh Crutwell. Post Production Associate: Karen Marmer Allen. Dialect Coaches: Carla Myer, Susan Hegarty. DGA Trainee: Kate Yurka. Casting Assistant: Liz Jereski. Extras Casting: Central Casting. Special Effects: Frank Toro, Gregg Hendrickson, Steve Foster. Construction Coordinator: Robert Krume. General Supervisor: Bob Sturtevant. Construction Supervisor: Ed Vance. Paint Supervisor: George Stuart. Production Painter: Dennis Ivanjack. Transportation Coordinator: Jim Thornsberry. Transportation Captain: A. C. Steere. Craft Service: Vartan Chakirian. Catering: Michaelson's. First Aid: Barbra Lortie. Unit Publicist: Eileen Peterson. Color Timer: Bob Kaiser. Negative Cutting: Theresa Rapola Mohammed. Title Design: Phill Norman. Titles and Opticals by F Stop Inc., Cinema Research Corp. Dolby Stereo Composer: Thom Ehle. Color by Technicolor. Ultracam 35 Camera Lenses and Equipment provided by the Leonetti Company.

Cast: Kenneth Branagh (Mike Church/Roman Strauss), Emma Thompson (Grace/Margaret Strauss), Andy Garcia (Gray Baker), Lois Hall (Sister Constance), Richard Easton (Father Timothy), Jo Anderson (Sister Madeleine/Starlet), Patrick Montes (Pickup Driver), Raymond Cruz (Clerk), Robin Williams (Doctor Cozy Carlisle), Wayne Knight ("Piccolo" Pete), Patrick Doyle (1st Cop/2nd Party Guest), Erik Kilpatrick (2nd Cop), Gordana Rashovich (Handcuffed Woman), Derek Jacobi (Franklyn Madson), Obba Babatunda (Syd), Christine Ebersole (Lydia Larson), Vasek C. Simek (Otto), Hanna Schygulla (Inga), Gregor Hesse (Frankie), John Gould Rubin (Cafe Owner), Campbell Scott (Doug), Steven Culp (1st Party Guest), Yvette Freeman (Nurse), Steve Boyum, Greg Barnett (Stunt Coordinators), Clarke Coleman, Doug Coleman, Ken Endoso, Jean Epper, Kelly Malone, John Meier, Chad Randall, Jayleen Sun, Mickey White (Stunt Players)

Music Credits: "Lush Life"— By Billy Strayhorn. "Rhapsody on a Theme of

Paganini"—By Sergei Rachmaninoff. "Tangerine"—By Johnny Mercer and Victor Schertzinger. "Isn't It Romantic"—By Richard Rodgers and Lorenz Hart. "Board Review"—By Otis O'Connor.

11. *Leaving Normal* (1992)

Universal Pictures. A Mirage Production. Genre: Drama. Running time: 110 minutes. Rating: R. Color. Released: April 1992. Available on videocassette and laserdisc.

Credits: Producer: Lindsay Doran. Screenplay: Ed Solomon. Director: Edward Zwick. Executive Producer: Sydney Pollack. Director of Photography: Ralf D. Bode. Editing: Victor DuBois. Music: W.G. "Snuffy" Walden. Production Design: Patricia Norris. Art Director: Sandy Cochrane. Set Design: Elizabeth Wilcox. Costume Design: Patricia Norris. Casting: Mary Colquhoun. Associate Producer: Edward Solomon. Line Producer: Fitch Cady. Co-Producer: Sara Caplan. Unit Production Manager: Casey Grant. 1st Assistant Director: Skip Cosper. 2nd Assistant Director: Richard Cowan. Canadian Casting: Stuart Aikins. Unit Manager: Stewart Bethune. Location Manager: Rino Pace. Assistant Location Manager: Scott Harper. Location Production Assistants: Bill Kuchera, Dave Coglin. Alaska Locations: Bob Crockett. Camera Operator: Peter Woeste. 1st Assistant Camera: Andy Wilson. 2nd Assistant Camera: Simon Davis Barry. Camera Trainees: Marty Naucler, Jeremy Testar. Still Photographer: Joe Lederer. Script Supervisor: Christine Wilson. Sound Mixer: Rob Young. Boom Operator: Don Brown. 2nd Assistants: Ruth Huddleston, Tony Giacinti. 2nd 2nd Assistant Director: Judy Slattery. 3rd Assistant Director: Kevin Speckmaier. Trainee: Seanna McPherson. Gaffer: Les Erskine. Lamp Operators: Barry Donlevy, Dave Anderson, Tim Atkins, Rick Buckmaster. Key Grip: Tim Hogan. Dolly Grip: John L. Brown. 2nd Grip: Ken Woznow. Grips: Rick Allen, Ken Hemphill. Assistant Art Director: Ken Rabehl. Assistant Set Decorator: Doug Carnegie. Set Decorator Buyer: Jane Groves. Set Dressers: Matthew Reddy, Gordie Brunner. On Set Dresser: Patrick Kearns. Property Master: Jimmy Chow. Assistant Proprs: Paul Mulder, Cindy Gordon. Assistant Costume Designer: Monique Strana. Costume Supervisor: Debbie Douglas. Assistant to Patricia Norris: Deborah Winship. Makeup Artist: Jayne Dancose. Assistant Makeup Artist: Victoria Down. Hairstylist: Ian Ballard. Construction Coordinator: Thom Wells. Foreman: Duff Chambers, Dick Stewart. Scenic Carpenters: Jim Armstrong, Philip Jean, Don Engel, Ron Clifford, Brian Price, Gary York, Bob Nicholson, Chris Prior. Model Makeup: Sal D'Aquila. Head Scenic Artist: Barry Kootchin. Lead Painter: Susan High. Scenic Artists: Jurgen Gottschlag, Tara Ireland. Scenic Painters: John Hamilton, Robert Foley, Gordon Hughes, Jean-Paul Costaz, Phil Morgan. Standby Painter: Herminio Kam. Head Greensman: Mike Siver. Greens Best Boy: Erich Hepnar. Greensmen: Avo Liva, Gary Brooks, Travis Brooks, Jim Green, Art Green, Phil Lunt. Stunt Coordinator: Betty Thomas. SPFX Coordinator: Bill Orr. SPFX Best Boy: Joel Whist. Production Coordinator: Penny Gibbs. Assistant Production Coordinator: Yvonne Melville. Office Production Assistant: Jim Brebner. Production Accountant: Kathryn M. Drew. Assistant Accountant: Doreen Beaulac. Acct. Clerk: Dana Perlman. 2nd Acct. Clerk: Ann McDonough. Post Production

Assistants: Samantha Mudd, Arthur Borman. Unit Publicist: Brigitte Prochaska. Assistant to Edward Zwick: Deborah Yates. Assistant to Lindsay Doran: Carol King. Assistant to Sarah Coplan: Molly Whelan. Assistant to Producers (Vancouver): Cindy Mjolsness. Assistant to Sydney Pollack: Donna Ostroff. Assistant to Mary Colquohoun: John Brace. Extras Casting: James Forsyth. Canadian Casting Assistant: William Haines. Transportation Coordinator: Dave Bowe. Transportation Captain: John Oliver. Co-Captain: Ed Dykstra. Picture Grip: Nigel Hargood. Drivers: Greg Lawrence, Barry Chapman, Terry Newton. Shotmaker Driver: Chris Summerall. Mechanic: Fred Davie. Catering by Focus on Food. Chefs: Shelley Adams, Maureen Sugrue. Craft Service: Gabrielle Berkovics. Animal Handler: Debra J. Coe. Translator: Oscar Kawagley. Dance Instruction by Dance City Studios, Sallie Wong. 2nd Unit Directors: David Wagreich, Sarah Caplan.

Alberta Unit: Location Manager: Neil Joudrie. Assistant Set Decorator: Jan Goodine. Set Dresser: Bruce Hosick Assistant Props: Dean Goodine. Construction Foreman: Jan Kobylka. Standby Carpenter: Vince Bevans. Standby Painter: Gary Ripley. Assistant Makeup Artist: Al Magallan. Assistant Hair Stylist: Iloe Flewelling. Cable Puller: Kelly Zombor. Grips: Carey Toner, Tom Hansen, Mike Brown. Electric: Jim Gregor, Larry Johnson. Granny Operator: Vete Dorchuk. 2nd Electric: Dean Merrell, Ken Merrell. Lamp Operators: Lee Routley, Gord Schmidt. Special Effects Assistant: Morris Routley. Transportation Coordinator: John Scott. Driver: John Dodds. Visual Effects Consultant: Alan Munro. Matte Painting Effects Produced by Matte World, Marin County, CA. Director of Matte Photography: Craig Barron. Matte Artist Supervisor: Michael Pangrazio. Executive in Charge of Producer: Krystyna Demkowicz. Matte Artists: Brian Flora, Bill Mather. Motion Control Cameraman: Joel Hladecek. Key Grip: Paul Oehlke. Plate Camera Operator: Wade Childress. 2nd Editor: Marty Nicholson. Additional Film Editing: Anthony Sherin, Jane Morrison. Additional Editors (LA): Karen Kory, Nicole Smith. Additional Editors (Vancouver): Michael Smith, Steve Roberts, Charles Robichaud. Post Production Coordinator: Deborah Yates. Edited on Ediflex. Music Editor: Allan K. Rosen. Music Editor Assistant: Patty von Ark. Assistant to W.G. Snuffy Walden: Jo L. Parker. Music Preparation: Julian Bratolyubov. Score Recording Engineer: Ray Pyle. Score Mixing Engineer: Stephen Krause. Supervising Sound Editor: Lon E. Bender. Sound Effects by Soundelux. Sound Editors: Frank T. Smathers, Dan Hegeman, Stuart Copley, Per Hallberg, Pamela J. Yuen, Raoul. Assistant Sound Editors: Karen M. Baker, Lisa Miller. ADR Supervisor: Joe Mayer. ADR Group Coordinator: Leigh French. Digitial Sound Editors: Chris Hogan, Kim Waugh. Foley Artists: Audrey Trent, Jerry Trent. Re-Recording Mixers: Steve Maslow, Robert Beemer. Recordists: Brian Paccassi. Re-recorded at Skywalker Sound, a division of LucasArts Entertainment Company. Special Optical Effects produced by Visual Concept Engineering. Supervisor: Peter Kuran. Camera: Paul Gentry, Bill Conner, Gary George. Opticals: Dave Emerson, Todd Hall, David Tucker, Gary Martin. Animation: Pam Vick. Coordinator: Brian Jochum. Negative Cut by: Sandy Brundage. Opticals: Cinema Research Corp. Titles by Kathie Broyles, Jeffrey Okun. Color Timer: Phil Hetos. Panavision. Color by Deluxe.

Cast: Christine Lahti (Darly Peters), Meg Tilly (Marianne Johnson), Lenny von Dohlen (Harry Rainey), Maury Chaykin (Leon "Crazy-As" Pendleton), Patrika Darbo (66), Eve Gordon (Emily Singer), James Eckhouse (Rich Singer), Brett Cullen (Kurt), James Gammon (Walt), Lachlan Murdoch (Marshall), Robyn Simons (Sarah), Ken Angel (Nuqaq), Darrell Dennis (Clyde), Barbara Russell (Izuzu Mother), Ahnee Boyce (Izuzu Judy), Marc Levy (Dave), Peter Anderson (Spicy), Gordon Tootoosis (Hank Amaruk), Rutanya Alda (Palmer Hospital Nurse), Ray Godshall (Mort), Tom Heaton (Alec), Dierdre O'Connell (Ellen), Gordon Tipple (Danny), John Bear Curtis (Michael), Paul Jarrett (Charlie), Ed Solomon (Jerk in Bar), Andrew Johnston (Nearest Guy), Ben Ratner (Next Nearest Guy), Timothy Webber (Spicy's Friend), Sam Bob (Delivery Guy), Marlane O'Brien (Clara), Brenda McDonald (Motel Clerk), Paul Stanley (Man Customer), Rob Morton (Bartender), Darryl Layne (Topless Dancer), Julie Taggart (Twelve-Year-Old Girl), Ruby Cox (Woman), Desmond Smiley (Minister), Dana Stevens (Marianne's Mother), Ashlee Buhler (Young Marianne), Jenny Drugan (Young Emily). Colin James Munn (Colin James Band). Members: Dennis Marcenki, Richard Hopkins, John Ferreira, Danell Mayes. Trisha Gagnon (Tumbleweed Band), Cathy-Anne Whitworth, Dave Schryver, Chris Stevens (Members), Fione Roeske, Melissa Stubbs (Stunt Players)

Music Credits: "Honky Tonk Special"—Written and performed by Marty Brown; Courtesy of MCA Records. "T for Trouble"—Written by Bill Carter, Ruth Ellsworth and Colin James; Performed by Colin James; Courtesy of Virgin Records America, Inc. "Changing Partners"—Written by Joe Darion, Larry Coleman; Performed by the Tumbleweed Band. "Heaven"—Written and performed by Chris Rea; Courtesy of ATCO Records, Warner Music UK Ltd.; By arrangement with Warner Special Products. "Wicked Game"—Written and performed by Chris Isaak; Courtesy of Warner Bros. Records; By arrangement with Warner Special Products. "Crazy Love"—Written and performed by Van Morrison; Courtesy of Warner Bros. Records; By arrangement with Warner Special Products.

12. *Searching for Bobby Fischer* (1993)

Paramount Pictures. A Scott Rudin/Mirage Production. Genre: Drama. Running time: 110 minutes. Rating: PG. Color. Released: August 1993. Available on videocassette and laserdisc.

Credits: Producers: Scott Rudin, William Horberg. Executive Producer: Sydney Pollack. Written and directed by Steve Zaillian. Based upon the book by Fred Waitzkin. Director of Photography: Conrad L. Hall. Editing: Wayne Wahrman. Music: James Horner. Co-Producer: David Wisnietvitz. Production Designer: David Gropman. Director of Photography: Conrad Hall. Casting: Avy Kaufman. Costume Designer: Julie Weiss. Unit Production Managers: David Coatsworth, Jonathan Filley. 1st Assistant Directors: Tony Gittleson, Burit Harris. 2nd Assistant Director: Walter Gasparivic. Co-Editor: Ronald Roose. Art Director: Gregory P. Keen. Set Designer: Steve Shewchuk. Assistant Art Director: Dennis Davenport. Camera Operator and Additional Photography: Robert Hahn. 1st Assistant Photographer: Tony Guerin. 2nd Assistant Photographer: Ciarin Copelin. Camera Operator: Harold Ortenburger. Camera 1st Assistant Photographer: Perry Hoffmann. Camera 2nd Assistant Photographer: Richard Brown. Steadicam Operators: David Crone, Rick Raphael. Video Playback Operators: Stephen Sebert, David J. Woods. Sound Mixer: David Lee. Boom Operator: Stephen Switzar. Cableperson: Sanjay Mehta. Script Supervisor: Mimi Wolch. 2nd 2nd Assistant Director: Rose Tedesco. 3rd Assistant Director: Grant Lucibello. Assistants to Mr. Rudin: Mike Thompson, Brandon Camp. Assistant to Mr. Horberg: Lisa Medwid. Assistant to Mr. Zaillian: Katrina Cerio. Assistant to Mr. Wisnietvitz: Henry Colas. Assistant to Mr. Pollack: Donna Ostroff. Still Photography: Kerry Hayes. Chief Lighting Technician: James MacCammon, Brian Montague. Assistant Chief Lighting Technician: Ken Wyke. Lighting Technicians: Brian Woodruff, Michael Anderson, Delroy Jarrett. Generator Operator: Herb Reishl. 1st Company Grip: Randy Tambling. 2nd Company Grip: Robert Rice. Dolly Grip: Ron Renzetti. Grips: Hugh Montgomerie, James Cameron, Cesare DiGiulio. Rigging Grip: Roy Elliston. Set Dressers: Denis Kirkham, Bill Woods. Set Decorating Buyer: Roger Baron. Draftsperson: Douglas McLean. Art Production Assistant: Ian Hall. Makeup Artist: Linda Gill. Hairstylist: Paul Elliot. Assistant Costume Designer: Arthur Rowsell. Wardrobe Master: Kim Chow. Wardrobe Assistant: Patti Unger. Wardrobe Production Assistant: Tanya Shuster. 1st Assistant Editor: Debra Kahn. Assistant Film Editors: Mark Sadusky, Lynel L. Moore, Peter Watson, Patricia Lambkin. Apprentice Film Editor: Ellie Brooks. Music Editor: Jim Henrikson. Supervising Sound Editor: Beth Sterner. Sound Effects Editors: Thierry Couturier, Richard Burton, Kim Secrist, Noah Blough. Dialogue Editors: Bobby Mackston, Michael Magill. Supervising ADR Editor: Nick Korda, ADR Editor: Norto Sepulveda. Supervising Foley Editor: Scott Jackson. Foley Editors: Leslie Gaulin, Pat Bietz. Assistant Sound Editors: Chris Ingram, Paul O'Bryan. Re-Recording Editors: Gary Bourgeois, Scott Millan, Elmo Ponsdomenech. ADR Mixer: Bob Baron. Foley Mixer: Eric Gotthelf. Foley Artists: Catherine Rowe, James Moriana, Joan Rowe. Voice Casting: Barbara Harris. Orchestra conducted by: James Horner. Orchestrator: Thomas Pasatieri. Orchestra Contractor: Nathan Kaproff. Music Preparation: Bob Bornstein. Music Scoring Mixer: Shawn Murphy. Construction Coordinator: Jim Halpenny. Assistant Construction Coordinator: Pat McCaffery. Head Carpenter: R. Doug Ingle. Head Scenic Artist: Guenter Bartlik. Production Painter: Karl Schneider. Property Master: Vic Rigler. Assistant Props: Ron Hewitt. Special Effects: Bob Hall. Production Coordinator: Mara McSweeny. Assistant Production Coordinator: Tammy Quin Clarke. Casting Associate: Michele Heilbrun. Toronto Casting: Tina Gerussi. Accountant: Don Petrie. Accounting Assistants: Veronica Miller, Jim Sternberg. Location Manager: Fred Kamping. Assistant Location Manager: Jan Gordon. Publicist: Eric Myers. Transportation Coordinator: Fred Jonson. Transportation Captain: Robert Tenaglia. Production Assistants: Deborah Gibson, Andrew Wells, Stuart Williams, Ryan Lord, Edie Steiner, Lorelie Bearss, Cathy Lew, Kirsten McLean, Kris Lefcoe. Technical Advisor: Bruce Pandolfini. Clearances: Dale Ashcraft. Craft Service: Starcraft. Extras Casting: Scott Mansfield. Camera Trainees: Andrew Peart, Yvonne Collins.

New York Crew: 2nd Assistant Director: Julie A. Bloom. Art Director: Daniel Davis. Set Decorator: Christopher Maya. 2nd 2nd Assistant Director: Juan Ros. A Camera 1st Assistant Photographer: Gary Muller. A Camera 2nd Assistant Photographer: Edwin Effrein. B Camera Operator: Tom Priestley. B Camera 1st

Assistant Photographer: Ralph Brandofino. B Camera 2nd Assistant Photographer: Gerard Sava. Assistant Steadicam Operator: Marc Hirschfeld. Video Playback Operator: Nils Johnson. Sound Mixer: Dennis Maitland. Boom Operator: John Fundus. Cableperson: Kim Maitland. Scenic Change: Bob Topol. Extras Casting: Todd Thaler. Makeup Artist: Paul Gebbia. Hairstylist: Bill Farley. Assistant Costume Designer: Suzanne Schwarzer. Wardrobe Supervisors: Walter Rivera, Rose Cuervo. Wardrobe Production Assistant: Elizabeth Holder. Chief Lighting Technician: Russ Engels. Assistant Chief Lighting Technician: Kenneth Conners. Lighting Technicians: Michael Burke, James Walsh, Jr. Key Grip: Dennis Gamiello. 1st Company Grip: John Lowry. 2nd Company Grip: Brian Fitzsimmons, Bruce Atwater. Property Master: Ann Miller. Assistant Props: Conrad V. Brink, Kevin H. Brink. Set Dresser: Dan Grosso. Art Production Assistant: Joanne Belonsky. Production Coordinator: Alexis Alexanian. Location Manager: Daniel Strol. Assistant Location Manager: Maria Bierniak. Tranportation Captain: Ed Iacobelli. Transportation Co-Captain: James P. Whalen, Sr. Production Assistants: Jim Adler, Robert Albertell, James Traynor, Carol Chambors, John Kuegel, Shelly Keiser, Susanna Graves, Jane Sonders, Joanna Belonsky, Elizabeth Holder. DGA Trainee: Stuart Feldman. Caterer: Something's Cooking. Children's Tutoring provided by On Location Education. Color Timer: Mike Stanwick. Negative Cutter: Theresa Repola Mohammed. Title Design: Robert Dawson. Titles and Opticals by Cinema Research Corporation. Soundtrack Album on Big Screen Records. Dailies by Film House. Prints by Deluxe.

Cast: Joe Mantegna (Fred Waitzkin), Max Pomeranc (Josh Waitzkin), Joan Allen (Bonnie Waitzkin), Ben Kingsley (Bruce Pandolfini), Laurence Fishburne (Vinnie), Michael Nirenberg (Jonathan Poe), Robert Stephens (Poe's Teacher), David Paymer (Kalev), William H. Macy (Tunafish Father), Dan Hedaya (Tournament Director), Laura Linney (School Teacher), Anthony Heald (Fighting Patient), Josh Mostel (Chess Club Regular), Josh Kornbluth (Chess Club Regular), Tony Shalhoub (Chess Club Member), Austin Pendleton (Asa Hoffman), Hal Scardino (Morgan), Vasek Simek (Russian Park Player), Steven Randazzo (Man of Many Signals), Chelsea Moore (Katya Waitzkin), Tom McGowan (Reporter), Ona Fletcher (Reporter). Park Players: Kamran Shirazi, Joel Benjamin, Roman Dzindzichashvili, Jerry Poe McClinton. Matt De Matt Reines (Night Park Player), Vincent Smith (Washington Square Patzers), Jerry Rakow (Washington Square Patzers), William Colgate (Statistician), Tony De Santis (Journalist), R.D. Reid (Final Tournament Director), Anthony McGowan (Park Dealer), Katya Waitzkin (82nd Girl), Ryder Fleming-Jones (Petey), Harris Krofchick (Running Chess Kid), John Bourgeois, Maria Ricossa (Gym Parents), Caroline Yeager (Screaming Mom), Andrew Sardella (Josh's Syracuse Opponent), Nathan Carter (Josh's Teammate), Nicholas Taylor, Jonathan Fazio, Nicky Mellina, Philip Neiman, Elizabeth Gropman (Birthday Friends)

Music Credits: "Rough Enough"—Written and performed by Freddie Foxxx; Courtesy of Flavor Unit/Epic Records; By arrangement with Sony Music Licensing. "Green Grass That Grows All Around"—Performed by Pete Seeger; Courtesy of TRF Music, Inc."All Things Considered Theme Music"—By Donald Voegeli; Courtesy of National Public Radio. "Enough Is Enough"—By Anthony Criss, Kier Gist, Vincent Brown, A. Bahr, J. Ray; Performed by Rottin Razcals; Courtesy of Flavor Unit/Epic Records; By arrangement with Sony Music Licensing. "Salsa #3"—By

John E. Oliver and Louis Forestieri. "Saxophone Concerto"—By John Debney. "Heart and Soul"—By Hoagy Carmichael and Frank Loesser.

13. *Flesh and Bone* (1993)
   Paramount Pictures. A Mirage/Spring Creek Production. Genre: Thriller. Running time: 127 minutes. Rating: R. Released: November 1993. Available on videocassette and laserdisc.

   Credits: Executive Producer: Sydney Pollack. Producer: Mark Rosenberg, Paula Weinstein. Written and directed by Steve Kloves. Co-Producer: G. Mac Brown. Music: Thomas Newman. Costume Design: Elizabeth McBride. Film Editor: Mia Goldman. Production Designer: Jon Hutman. Director of Photography: Philippe Rousselot. Casting: Rita Bramon-Garcia and Joel Bestrop. Unit Production Manager: C. Mark Brown. 1st Assistant Director: Cara Ciallanza. 2nd Assistant Director: Marge Piane. Art Director: Charles Breen. Location Manager: Andrew D. Cooke. Camera Operator: Anastas N. Michos. Sound Mixer: Danny Michael. 1st Company Grip: C. Alan Rawlins. Chief Lighting Technician: Jack English. Property Master: Trisha B. Gallaher. Set Decorator: Samara Schaffer. Supervising Sound Editor: Scott Hecker. Re-Recording Mixers: Andy Nelson, Steve Pederson. Music Editor: Bill Bernstein. Makeup Artists: Leonard Engelman, Dorothy J. Pearl. Hair Stylists: Colleen Callaghan. Production Coordinator: Mary Jo Winkler. Production Accountant: Sue Bokobza. Production Associate: Edward A. Ioffreda. 1st Assistant Camera: Ted Morris. 2nd Assistant Camera: J. Steven Lathan. Still Photograph: Lorey Sebastian. Script Supervisor: Valerie E. Norman. 2nd Editor: Anthony Sherin. Assistant Editors: Heather Persons, Jim Makiej. Assistant Costume Designer: Taneia Lednicky. Set Costumer: Eva Prappas. Lead Set Dresser: John D. Kretschmer. Assistant Art Director: Gary C. Diamond. Assistant Set Decorator: Patty Malone. Art Dept. Coordinator: Beth Bernstein. Scenic Chargeperson: Brian P. Stulz. Construction Coordinator: Tom Dreesen. Special Effects Supervisor: Randy E. Moore. Special Effects Coordinator: Margaret Johnson. Stunt Coordinator: Andy Armstrong. Boom Operator: Andrew Schmetterling. Cableperson: Maurice Jacks, Jr. 2nd Company Grip: Wayne Parker. Dolly Grip: Charles Ashley Sudge. Grips: Michael Alexonis, Steve Belsky, Alan J. Bullard, Rob Hicks. Assistant Chief Lighting Technician: James Babineaux. Lighting Technicians: George M. Chappell, Scott Graves. Rigging Gaffer: Daniel Murphy. Assistant Property Master: Christopher Carlson. Property Assistant: Greg Benge. Post Production Supervisor: Sara Romilly. Supervising ADR Editor: Joe Dorn. Supervising Foley Editor: David Arnold. Sound Effects Editors: Joe Earle, Bruce Tanis, Chris Flick, Simon Coke. Dialogue Editors: Ralph Osborne, Alan Sawelson, Gary Lewis, Pat McCormick. 1st Assistant Sound Editor: Doug Kent. Assistant ADR Editor: Melissa Lytle. ADR Mixer: Bryan Ruberg. Foley Mixer: Dean Drabin. Recordists: Andrea Lakin, Sam Kaufman, Annie Hadsell, Joan Chamberlain. Foley Artists: Sarah Jacobs, Robin Harlan. Voice Casting: Barbara Harris. Orchestrator: Thomas Pasatieri. Music Scoring Mixer: John Vigran. Assistant Engineer: Tom Winslow. Orchestra Manager: Leslie Morris. Music Preparation: Julian Bratolyubov. Wardrobe Assistants: Anne Abbey, Rosemary Bengele, Mary Ellen Fields, Renee Shearer. Sewer: Kristine Kearney. Wardrobe

Buyers: Susan Kistler, Kimmie Rhodes. Set Dressers: Marcus Lee Brown, Jerry King, Shane Patrick, J.P. Schwan, Joe Self, Lisa K. Sessions. Property Buyer: Karen E. Luzius. Greenspersons: Larry Misselhorn, Hap Weaver. Scenic Foreperson: James Onate. Scenic Painters: Peter J. Durand, Mike Alexis Koellner, Richard Riggs, Kelly Brett Stultz. Production Painter: John R. Helton. Storyboard Artist: Mark Lambert Bristol. Casting Associate: Mary Vernieu. Texas Casting by Elizabeth H. Keigley. Extras Casting: Sari E. Keigley. Unit Publicist: Patti Hawn. Assistant Production Coordinator: Elizabeth Alexis Arnold. 1st Assistant Accountant: Sam Bokobza. Accounting Assistant: Jamie Megan Mascena. Assistant Production Accountant: Kevin Buxbaum. Post Production Accountant: Leah A. Palco. Assistant to Mr. Quaid: Gregory Beau Holden. Assistant to Mr. Caan: Suzanne Sherrill. Assistant to Mr. Kloves: Emily Milder. Assistants to Mr. Rosenberg: Linda Labov, Loring A. Sumner. Assistant Location Managers: Eric A. Williams, Michelle K. Romaine. Additional 2nd Assistant Director: Jordon J. Stone. Additional 2nd Assistant Camera: Bill Finder. Additional 1st Assistant Camera: Victoria Lowe. Camera Loader: Brian W. Nordheim. DGA Trainee: Christine Tope. Construction Forepersons: Tom Lemman, David Henry Menefee, Jack E. Thorpe III. Carpenters: Steve Allen, Charles Bates, Neil Dexter Gahm, Don Cross, R. Kim Hawkins, W.S. Hickey, Chris Telschow, Robert Weinberger. Special Effects Assistants: Charles Grimes, Stephen Johnston. Special Effects Assistant/Makeup: David M. Whitley. Video Playback Engineer: Peter J. Verrando. Craft Service Persons: Robert W. Terrill, Craig B. Glaser, Willian Laczko. Medic: Anne Catherine Carr. Transportation Coordinator: Jerry McKnight. Transportation Captain: Cecil D. Evans. Drivers: Julian Arredondo, Kate McCarley, Jack Berggren, Doyle Nelson, Daniel Castanada, Ron Paschall, Henry Castillo, Jack Prince, Isidro Saldivar, Phil Schriber, Bobby Sconci, Timmy Thompson, Wilburn White, Bud Holtzendorf, Joseph Hawkins, Mike Hammett, Charles Griffith, Billy Furrh, Mary Delaney, Ronald Chambers. Animal Wrangler: Karen Holst Prince. Teacher: Cindy Lindaur. Location Assistants: Caroline J. Brock, James Crowley, Mark E. Shelby, John Stobaugh. Key Production Assistant: Derek "Bongo" Johansen. Set Assistants: Ellie Hecter, Patrick Gillis, Diane Gunderson, Stuart Yates. Production Office Assistants: Heather E. McClellan, Brady Dial, Christina Peters, Wade Bartlett, Michael A. Benson. Post Production Office Assistant: Aaron Goldstein. Catering Services provided by Tomkats Catering, Michael Maxwell, Elizabeth Smith Maxwell. Travel Services provided by Kima Travel, NY. Camera Car provided by Camera Cars of Atlanta. Camera Car Operator/Grip: John Schisler. Camera Crane provided by Texas Crane Company. Camera Crane Operator: Greg Reim. Crane and Dollies by Chapman. Camera Package by Victor Duncan-Dallas, John Shrimpf. Lighting and Grip Package by Lighthouse Studio Rentals, Inc. Post Production Sound and Sound Editing provided by Todd-AO/Glen Glenn Studios. Music recorded and mixed at Village Recorder and Todd-AO/ Scoring. Music Clearance: Jill Meyers. Color Timer: Mike Milliken. Negative Cutter: Gary Burritt. Dolby Stereo Consultant: Steve Smith. Titles and Opticals by Pacific Title. Title Design by Nina Saxon Film Designs. Music Consultant: Joel Sill. Footage from Family Feud, courtesy of Mark Goodson Productions Inc. Color by Allied-WBS /film and Video Services, Dallas. Prints by Deluxe Laboratories. Photographed with Eastman EXR Motion Picutre Film. Footage from Home Shopping Network provided by Home Shopping Network, Inc.

Cast: Dennis Quaid (Arlis Sweeney), Meg Ryan (Kay Davies), James Caan (Roy Sweeney), Gwyneth Paltrow (Ginnie), Scott Wilson (Elliot), Christopher Rydell (Reese Davies), Julia Mueller (Sarah Willets), Ron Kuhlman (Glen Willets), Jerry Swindall (Young Arlis), Ryan Bohls (Scotty Willets), Ez Perez (Boy in Suit), Craig Erickson (Tiny Ted), Barbara Alyn Woods (Cindy), Joe Berryman (Plump Man), James Harrell (Woody), Gerardo Johnson (Juan), Hector Garcia (Nestor), Bestsy Brantley (Peg), John Hawkes (Groom), Vic Polizos (Pudge Riley), Nik Hagler (Earl), Travis Baker (Sullen Kid), Angie Bolling (Woman with Crying Baby), Joe Stevens (Kyle), Libbie Villari (Waitress), Gail Cronauer (Emma), Bradley J. Bovee (Stunt Double "Roy"), Charles Bartlett, Noreen Reardon, Patrika Darbo, Bob Neill, Barbara Iley, Doug Burch, Charles Bazaldua, Marina Pincus, Javier Grajeda, Judi Durand, Greg Webb (ADR Voice Artists)

Music Credits: "The Untouchables"—Original TV Series; Written by Nelson Riddle, William Loose, Jack Cookerly, Emil Cadkin. "Sometimes You Just Can't Win"—Written by Smokey Stover; Performed by George Jones; Courtesy of Liberty Records; Under License from CEMA Special Markets. "Blue Moon"—Written by Richard Rodgers and Lorenz Hart. "Blue Moon Revisited"—Written by Marco Timmins and Michael Timmins; Performed by The Cowboy Junkies; Courtesy of EMC Music Canada, Inc. "Stardust"—Written by Hoagy Carmichael and Mitchell Parish; Performed by Willie Nelson; Courtesy of Columbia Records by arrangement with Sony Music Licensing. "Papa Come Quick" (Jody and Chico)—Written by Billy Vera, Rick Hirsch and Ship Taylor; Performed by Gwyneth Paltrow. "Bad to the Bone"—Written by George Thorogood; Performed by George Thorogood and The Destroyers; Courtesy of EMI Records Group. EMI Records; Under license from CEMA Special Markets. "Lilita"—Written by Bill Bernstein; Performed by Desert Star Boys.

14. *Sense and Sensibility* (1995)

Columbia Pictures. A Mirage Enterprises Production. Genre: Romance/comedy/period/adaptation. Premiered: December 13, 1995 in US. Running time: 135 minutes. Rating: PG. Released on video in U.S., June 25, 1996.

Credits: Producer: Lindsay Doran. Co-Producer: James Schamus, Laurie Borg. Executive Producer: Sydney Pollack. Associate Producer: Geoff Stier. Director: Ang Lee. Screenplay: Emma Thompson. Adapted from the novel by Jane Austen. Director of Photography: Michael Coulter. Production Designer: Luciana Arrighi. Editor: Tim Squyres. Costume Designers: Jenny Bevan, John Bright. Music: Patrick Doyle. 1st Assistant Director: Chris Newman. 2nd Assistant Director: Bernard Bellew. Supervising Art Director: Andrew Sanders. Art Director: Philip Elton. Assistant Art Directors: Sophia Mueller, Pippa Marks. Art Department Assistant: Philippa Hart. Set Decorator: Ian Whittaker. Production Buyer: Gill Ducker. Script Supervisor: Libbie Barr. Camera Operator: Philip Sindall. Focus Puller: John Jordan. Clapper Loader: Unikar Bobby Dhillon. Camera Grip: Richard Broome. 2nd Unit Photographer: Chris Plevin. Stills Photographer: Clive Coote. Camera Trainee: Chris Bain. Wardrobe Supervisor: Janet Tebrooke. Wardrobe Mistress: Yvonne Hobbs. Wardrobe Master: Joe Hobbs. Wardrobe

Assistant: Sue Honeyborne, Anna Krystyna Kot. Chief Makeup Artist: Morag Ross. Makeup Artist: Sallie Jaye. Chief Hairdresser: Jan Archibald. Hairdresser: Barbara Taylor, Astrid Schikorra. Choreographer: Stuart Hopps. Gaffer: Terry Edland. Best Boy: Tony Hayes. Electrician: Darren Gattrell. Electricians: Paul Kemp, Ken Monger, Robert Monger, Al Waarson, Andrew Watson, Danny Young. 2nd 2nd Assistant Director: Keith Young. 3rd Assistant Director: Ben Howarth. Production Assistant: Rebecca Tucker. Movement Consultant: Jane Gibson. Special Effects Supervisor: Richard Farns. Special Effects Technician: Jeff Clifford. Production Accountant: Bobbie Johnson. Assistant Accountant: Betty Williams. Post Production Accountant: Joyce Hsieh. Production Coordinator: Carol Regan. Assistant Coordinator: Lesley Keane. Assistant to Ang Lee (David Lee). Assistant to Sydney Pollack: Donna Ostroff. Assistant to Lindsay Doran: Ross Katz. Assistant to James Shamus: Jean Christophe Castelli. Assistant to Producers (United Kingdom): Mona Benjamin. Location Manager: Tony Clarkson. Assistant Location Managers: Andrew Hill, Chris Webb. Location Runners: George Albert Pointer, Nick Waldron. Property Master: Arthur Wicks. Chargehand Standby Propman: Mark Gruin. Standby Propman: Darren Reynolds. Dressing Storeman: Graham Stickley. Chargehand Dressing Propman: Stan Cook. Dressing Propman: Gary Fox, Mark McNeil. Food Stylist: Debbie Brodie. Construction Manager: Jack Carter. Supervising Chargehand: John Hedges. Supervising Painter: Bob Harper. Carpenters: Darryl Carter, Les Hall, Roger Willis. Painters: Anthony Thone, Lee Shelley, Ken Welland. Plasterer: Harold Brust. Stagehands: Kenneth Langridge, Alan Titmuss. Riggers: Keith Batterbee, Mel Sansom. Construction Electrician: Ronnie Rampton. Standby Carpenter: John Behan. Standby Painter: Norman North. Standby Rigger: Sidney Hinson. Standby Stagehand: Roy Biggs. Transportation Captain: Gerry Gore. Unit Drivers: Jed Bray, Peter Brook, Derard Bryson. Rushes Driver: Eddie Kaye. Camera Car Driver: Brian Bassnett. Grips Truck Driver: Sonny Donato. Facilities Driver: Roy Bond. Production Runner: Phil Stoole. Post Production Supervisor: Anthony Bregman. 1st Assistant Editor: Susan Littenberg. Film Conform Assistant: Jan Unger, Andres Hafitz. Assistant Editor (United Kingdom): Larry Richardson. Post Production Assistants: Edward Berger, Jeanette King. Supervising Sound Editor: Steve Hamilton. Music Editor: Roy Prendergast. Production Mixer: Tony Dawe. Boom Operator: Chris Gurney. Sound Assistant: Jaya Bishop. ADR: Paul Carr, Robert Farr. Foley: Cynthia Leigh Heim, Linda Russon. Re-Recording Mixer: Reilly Steele. FX Editor: Thomas O'Shea. Dialogue Editors: Juan Carlos Martinez, Mary Ellen Porto. Foley Editor: Jennifer Ralston. ADR Editor: Steven Kilkensen. Assistant Sound Editor: Pietro Cecchini, Joe Cimino, Andrew Kris. Apprentice Sound Editor: Seth Anderson. Titles Designer: Balsmeyer and Everett Inc. Music Supervisor: Maggie Rodford. Music Recording Facilities: Air Studios Lyndhurst Hall. Music Orchestrator: Lawrence Ashmore. Music Conductor: Robert Ziegler. Music Recording Engineer: Paul Hulme. Orchestra Conductor: Tonia Davall. Music Preparation: Tony Stanton. Horse and Carriage Coordinator: Debbie Kaye. Horsemaster Coordinator, Stunt Coordinator: Nick Wilkinson. Trainer: Mick Hart. Animal Coordinator: Kay Cutts. Coachbuilder: Terry Robertson. Casting Assistant: Suzy Catliff. Stand-Ins: Annie Livings, Steve Rickard, Pippa Grant. Tutor to Emile François: Cecile Cabal. Chaperone to Emile François: Joy Geoghegan. Storyboard Artist: Christina Moore. Unit Publicist: Ginger Corbett. Caterer: Set Meals

Limited, Paul Caldicott, Colin Anderson, Tamara Morris. Unit Paramedic: Paul Newton. Post Production Facilities: Spin Cycle Post. Re-Recording Studio Facilities: Sound-One. ADR Studio: Goldcrest Post Production. Studios: Shepperton Studios. Camera Equipment: Samuelson Film Service London Limited. Lighting and Electrical Gear: Lee Lighting Limited. Grip Equipment: Panavision Grips. Facility Vehicles: Location Facilities Limited, D & D International Limited. Negative Cutter: Stan Sztaba, Patricia Sztaba. Color Timing: Mark Ginsberg. Visual Effects Producer: Balsmeyer & Everett Inc. Visual Effects Supervisor: Randall Balsmeyer. Digital Compositing Supervisor: Daniel Leung. Visual Effects Producer: Kathy Kelehan.

Cast: Emma Thompson (Elinor Dashwood), Alan Rickman (Colonel Brandon), Kate Winslet (Marianne Dashwood), Hugh Grant (Edward Frears), James Fleet (John Dashwood), Tom Wilkinson (Mr. Dashwood), Harriet Walker (Fanny Dashwood), Gemma Jones (Mrs. Dashwood), Emile Françoise (Margaret Dashwood), Elizabeth Spriggs (Mrs. Jennings), Robert Hardy (Sir John Middleton), Ian Brimble (Thomas), Isabelle Amyes (Betsy), Greg Wise (Willoughby), Alexander John (Curate), Imelda Staunton (Charlotte Palmer), Imogen Stubbs (Lucy Steele), Hugh Laurie (Mr. Palmer), Allan Mitchell (Pidgeon), Josephine Gradwell (Maid to Mrs. Jennings), Richard Lumsden (Robert Ferrars), Lone Vidahl (Miss Grey), Oliver Ford Davies (Dr. Harris), Eleanor McCready (Mrs. Bunting).

Music Credits: "Weep You No More Sad Fountains"— Music by Patrick Doyle; Text Anonymous. "The Dreame"— Music by Patrick Doyle; Text by Ben Johnson; End title performed by Jane Eaglen; Courtesy of Sony Classical.

15. *Sliding Doors*
    Miramax and Paramount. Producers: Sydney Pollack, William Horberg, Philippa Braithwaite. Written and directed by: Peter Howitt. Released April 24, 1998.

    Cast: Gwyneth Paltrow, John Hannah, Jeanne Tripplehorn, John Lynch.

16. *The Talented Mr. Ripley* (Scheduled to start 5/98)
    Miramax and Paramount. Producers: Sydney Pollack, William Horberg, Tom Sternberg. Written and directed by: Anthony Minghella.

    Cast: Matt Damon, Gwyneth Paltrow, Jude Law.

17. *Up at the Villa* (No start date)
    Mirage and Intermedia. Executive Producers: Sydney Pollack, Aaron Milchan. Based on the novella by W. Somerset Maugham. Directed by: Phillip Haas. Written by: Belinda Haas and Phillip Haas.

    Cast: Kristin Scott Thomas, Sean Penn.

18. *For Love of the Game* (No start date)
    Universal Pictures

Other Credits

1. *The Young Savages* (1961) (Dialogue director)
United Artists. A Harold Hecht Production. A Contemporary Productions, Inc. Picture. Genre: Drama. Running time: 110 minutes. Black-and-White. Released: May 24, 1961.

Credits: Producer: Pat Duggan. Executive Producer: Harold Hecht. Director: John Frankenheimer. Screenplay: Edward Anhalt and J.P. Miller. Based on the novel *A Matter of Conviction* by Evan Hunter. Director of Photography: Lionel Lindon. Music composed and conducted by David Amram. Executive Production Manager: Gilbert Kurland. Film Editor: Eda Warren. Art Director: Burr Smidt. Set Decorator: James Crowe. Assistant Director: Carter DeHaven, Jr. Sound: Harry Mills. Makeup: Robert Schiffer. Hair Stylist: Joan St. Oegger. Script Supervisor: John Franco. Head Grip: John Lively. Recorder: Eldon Coutts. Property Master: Harry Hopkins. Men's Costumer: Jack Angel. Ladies' Costumer: Roselle Novello. Dialogue Coaches: Thom Conroy and Sydney Pollack.

Cast: Burt Lancaster (Hank Bell), Dina Merrill (Karin Bell), Shelley Winters (Mary di Pace), Telly Savalas (Lt. Richard Gunnison), John Davis Chandler (Arthur Reardon), Edward Andrews (Dan Cole), Milton Selzer (Walsh), Chris Robinson (Pretty Boy), Pilar Seurat (Louisa Escalante), Vivian Nathan (Mrs. Escalante), Larry Gates (Randolph), Jody Fair (Angela Rugiello), Roberta Shore (Jenny Bell), Robert Burton (Judge), David Stewart (Barton), Stanley Kristien (Danny di Pace), Neil Nephew (Anthony Aposto), Luis Arroyo (Zorro), Jose Perez (Roberto Escalante), Richard Velez (Gargantua), William Sargent (Soames), Stanley Adams (Lt. Hardy), William Quinn (Cpt. Larsen), Linda Danzil (Maria Amora), Raphael Lopez (Jose), Henry Norell (Pierce), Jon Carlo (McNally), Bob Biheller (Turtleneck), Mario Roccuzzo (Diavalo), Harry Holcombe (Doctor), Helen Kleeb (Mrs. Patton), Thom Conroy (Mr. Abbeny), John Walsh (Lonnie), Irving Steinberg (Officer Wohlman), Clegg Hoyt (Whitey), Joel Fluellen (Clerk of the Court), Robert Cleaves (Sullivan)

2. *The Leopard* (*Il gattopardo*) Italy-France (1963)
(Post Synching/English Dubbing Supervisor)
Genre: Historical/drama. Running time: 205 minutes. Released in the U.S.: August 13, 1963.

Credits: Producer: Goffredo Lombardo. Director: Luchino Visconti. Screenplay: Luchino Visconti, Suso Cecchi D'Amico, Pasquale Festa Campanile, Enrico Medioli, Massimo Franciosa. Based on the novel *Il Gattopardo* by Guiseppe Tomasi Di Lampedusa. Director of Photography: Guiseppe Rotunno. Editing: Mario Serandrei. Musical Composer: Nino Rota, Giuseppe Verdi. Music Director: Franco Ferrara. Art Director: Mario Garbuglia. Set Designers: Giogio Pes, Laudomia Hercolani. Costumes: Piero Tosi, Reanda, Sartoria Safas. Makeup: Alberto De Rossi.

Cast: Burt Lancaster (Prince Don Fabrizio Salina), Alain Delon (Tancredi), Claudia Cardinale (Angelica Sadara/Bertiana), Rina Morelli (Maria Stella), Paolo

Stoppa (Don Calogero Sedara), Romolo Valli (Father Pirrone), Lucilla Morlacchi (Concetta), Serge Reggiani (Don Ciccio Tumeo), Ida Galli (Carolina), Ottavia Piccolo (Caterina), Pierre Clementi (Francesco Paolo), Carlo Valenzano (Paolo), Anna-Maria Bottini (Governness Mademoiselle Dombreuil), Mario Girotti (Count Cayriaghi), Leslie French (Cavalier Chevally) Olimpia Cavalli (Mariannina), Marino Mase (Tutor), Sandra Chistolini (Youngest Daughter), Brook Fuller (Little Prince), Giuliano Gemma (Garibaldino General), Giovanni Melisendi (Don Onofrio Rotolo), Howard Nelson-Rubien (Don Diego), Lola Braccini (Donna Maugherta), Ivo Ganani (Col. Pallavicino)

3. *The Swimmer* (1968) (Director [uncredited])
   Columbia. A Horizon Picture. Genre: Drama. Running time: 94 minutes. Rating: PG. Released: May 15, 1968.

   Credits: Producers: Frank Perry and Roger Lewis. Directors: Frank Perry and Sydney Pollack (uncredited). Screenplay: Eleanor Perry (based on the short story by John Cheever). Directors of Photography: David Quaid, Michael Nebbia (Technicolor). Editors: Sidney Katz, Carl Lerner, Pat Somerset. Music: Marvin Hamlisch. Art Director: Peter Dohanos. Costume Design: Anna Hill Johnstone, Elizabeth Stewart. Makeup: John Kiras. Production Manager: Joseph Manduke. Assistant Director: Michael Hertzberg. Casting: Alan Shayne Associates, Ltd. Dialogue Coach: Thom Conroy. Production Assistant: Florence Nerlinger. Hairstylist: Ed Callaghan. Sound Mixer: Willard Goodman. Key Grip: Al Stetson. Gaffer: Richard Falk. Property Master: Thomas Wright. Script Supervisor: Barbara Robinson. Scenic Artist: Stan Cappiello. Unit Auditor: Sam Goldrich. Swimwear: Elizabeth Stewart. Automobiles: Pontiac. Orchestrations by: Leo Shuken and Jack Hayes.

   Cast: Burt Lancaster (Ned Merrill), Janet Landgard (Julie Hooper), Janice Rule (Shirley Abbott), Tony Bickley (Donald Westerhazy), Marge Champion (Peggy Forsburgh), Nancy Cushman (Mrs. Halloran), Bill Fiore (Howie Hunsacker), John Garfield, Jr. (Ticket Seller), Kim Hunter (Betty Graham), Rose Gregorio (Sylvia Finney), Charles Drake (Howard Graham), Bernie Hamilton (Chauffeur), House Jameson (Mr. Halloran), Jimmy Joyce (Jack Finney), Michael Kearney (Kevin Gilmartin), Richard McMurray (Stu Forsburgh), Jan Miner (Lillian Hunsacker), Diana Muldaur (Cynthia), Keri Oleson (Vernon), Joan Rivers (Joan), Cornelia Otis Skinner (Mrs. Hammar), Dolph Sweet (Henry Biswanger), Louise Troy (Grace Biswanger), Diana Van Der Vlis (Helen Westerhazy), Alva Celauro (Muffie), Lisa Daniels (Matron), John Gerstad (Guest), Marilyn Langner (Enid Bunker), Ray Mason (Bunkers' Party Guest)

4. *The Making of Tootsie* (1983) (Videorecording)
   Columbia. Documentary. Producer: Rocky Lang. Distributor: Direct Cinema Ltd. 50 min. VHS, Beta 3/4U.

5. *The Forest Through the Trees* (1990) (Narrator)
   Documentary. Isan Film Group. Producer: Frank Green. Written by: Sharon Wood. Narrated by: Sydney Pollack. Distributor: The Video Project, Ben Lomond, California. 58 minutes. VHS, Beta, 3/4U.

Television Credits

Guest Appearances

Unsold Television Pilot — No Air Date

"Now Is Tomorrow." Roncom. Proposed one-half hour anthology. Hosted by Charles Bickford. **Cast**: Robert Culp, Simon Scott, Jack Hogan, Dan Wright, John La Salle, Warren Vanders, David Garcia, Sydney Pollack (Cpt. Stein).

7/3/56   *The Kaiser Aluminum Hour*

"The Army Game." Dramatic anthology. Network: NBC. Directed by: Franklin Schaffner. Written by: Mayo Simons and Loring Mandel. **Cast**: Paul Newman (Danny), George Grizzard (Bert), Edward Andrews (Berman), Patrick McVey (Lassiter), Phillip Abbott (Manken), James Pritchett (Ward), Burt Brinkerhoff (Sugars), Sydney Pollack. 60 minutes. B/W.

11/28/56   *Kraft Television Theater*

"Time Lock." Dramatic anthology. Network: NBC. Written by: Arthur Hailey. **Cast**: Chester Morris, Peter Lazer, Sydney Pollack. Filmed by Distributors Corporation of America. 60 minutes. B/W.

3/12/59 & 3/19/59   *Playhouse 90*

"For Whom the Bell Tolls." Dramatic anthology. Network: CBS. Producers: Martin Manulis, John Houseman, Russell Stoneham, Fred Coe, Arthur Penn. Director: John Frankenheimer. Teleplay by A.E. Hotchner from Ernest Hemingway's novel. Music: George Smith, Robert Allen. **Cast**: Maria Schell, Jason Robards, Jr., Maureen Stapleton, Eli Wallach, Nehemiah Persoff, Steven Hill, Vladimir Sokoloff, Milton Selzer, Marc Lawrence, Herbert Berghof, Joseph Bernard, Nick Colossanto, Sydney Pollack (Andre). 90 minutes. B/W.

6/20/59   *Brenner*

"Family Man." Police drama. Network: CBS. **Regulars:** Edward Binns (Roy Brennan), James Broderick (Ernie Brennan), Joseph Sullivan (Cpt. Laney).

Guests: Martin Balsam (Arnold Joplin), Augusta Dabney (Mrs. Joplin), Collin Wilcox (Elizabeth Joplin), Sydney Pollack (Detective Dunn), Frank Campanella (Detective Stern), Van Dyke Parks (Jay Joplin), Don V. Murphy (Headmaster), Lynne Forrester (Policewoman), Marguerite Lenert (Maid), Michael Dolan (Garage Attendant). 60 minutes. B/W.

9/9/59   *U. S. Steel Hour*

"The Case of Julia Walton." Dramatic anthology. Network: CBS. Adapted by Harold Gast from a screenplay by Jay Ingram. **Cast:** Robert Lansing, Nina Foch, Jeffrey Lynn, Peter Lazer, Alan Baxter, Sydney Pollack. 60 minutes. B/W.

10/28/59   *Armstrong Circle Theater*

"35 Rue du Marche." Anthology. Network: CBS. Producers: Robert Costello, Jacqueline Babbin, George Simpson, Selig Alkon. Written by: Harold Gast. Narrated by: Douglas Edwards. **Starring:** Telly Savalas. **Special Guest:** Lester B. Pearson. **Guests:** Sydney Pollack, among others. 60 minutes. B/W.

1/29/60   *Buick Electra Playhouse*

"The Fifth Column." Dramatic anthology. Network: CBS. Producer: Gordon Duff. Director: John Frankenheimer. Written by: A.E. Hotchner. **Cast:** Richard Burton, Maxmillian Schell, Betay Von Furstenberg, Sally Ann Howes, George Rose, Elisa Loti, Sydney Pollack. 90 minutes. B/W.

10/18/60   *Alfred Hitchcock Presents*

"The Contest for Aaron Gold." Mystery/suspense anthology. Network: NBC. A Shamley Production. Executive Producer: Alfred Hitchcock. Produced by: Joan Harrison. Associate Producer: Norman Lloyd. Director: Norman Lloyd. Teleplay: William Fay. Story by Philip Roth. Photography: John L. Russell. Art Director: Martin Obzina. Editorial Supervisor: David J. O'Connell. Film Editor: Edward W. Williams. Music Supervisor: Frederick Herbert. Sound: James Brock. Assistant Director: James H. Brown. Set Decorators: John McCarthy and Rudy Butler. Costume Supervisor: Vincent Dee. Makeup: Jack Barron. Hair Stylist: Florence Bush. **Cast:** Barry Gordon (Aaron Gold), Sydney Pollack (Bernie Samuelson), Frank Maxwell (Lionel Stern), William Thourlby (Lefty James), John Craven (Herbert Gold), Buddy Lewis (Angelo), Michael Adam Lloyd (Henry), Robin Warga, Phil Phillips. 30 minutes. B/W.

12/9/60   *The Twilight Zone*

"The Trouble with Templeton." Science fiction anthology. Network: CBS. Created by: Rod Serling. Produced by: Buck Houghton. Executive Producer: Rod Serling. Cayuga Productions. Directed by: Buzz Kulik. Written by: E. Jack Neuman. Director of Photography: George T. Clemens. Theme

Music: Marius Constant. **Cast:** Brian Aherne (Booth Templeton), Pippa Scott (Laura Templeton), Charles S. Carlson (Barney Flueger), Sydney Pollack (Willis), Larry Blake (Freddie), Dave Willock (Marcel), John Kroger (Ed Page), David Thursby (Eddie), Sid Sperry (King Calder). 30 minutes. B/W.

1961 *The Robert Herridge Theater*

"The Chrysanthemums." #18. Anthology. SYN. Host: Robert Herridge. Director: Karl Genus. Written by: Robert Herridge. Music: Tom Scott. 30 minutes. Limited broadcast in the United States. No further information available.

1/7/61 & 1/14/61 *Have Gun Will Travel*

"A Quiet Night in Town." Part I & II. Western series. Network: CBS. Filmaster Productions, Inc. Created by: Herb Meadow and Sam Rolfe. Producer: Frank R. Pierson. Director: Buzz Kulik. Written by: Harry Julian Fink. Editor: Samuel Gold. Photography: Frank Phillips. Music: Fred Steiner. Ballad of Paladin sung by Johnny Western. Written by: Johnny Western, Richard Boone and Sam Rolfe. **Regulars:** Richard Boone (Paladin), James Best, Robert Emhardt, Phyllis Love. **Guests:** Sydney Pollack (Joe Culp), Robert Carricart, Kevin Hagen, Fredd Wayne, William Challee, Cece Whitney, Lisa Lu. 30 minutes.

4/29/61 *The Deputy*

"Spoken in Silence." Western series. Network: NBC. Produced by: Top Gun Productions. Executive Producer: William Frye. Producer: Michael Kraike. Created by: Roland Kibbee and Norman Lear. Director of Photography: Ellsworth Fredericks. Art Director: Martin Obzina. Music: Jack Marshall. **Regulars:** Henry Fonda (Chief Marshal Simon Fry), Allen Case (Clay McCord), Betty Lou Keim (Fran McCord), Read Morgan (Sgt. Hapgood Tasker), Wallace Ford (Herk Lamson). **Guests:** Robert Burton, Frances Helm, Sydney Pollack (Chuck Johnson). 30 minutes. B/W.

10/31/61 *The New Breed*

"Compulsion to Confess." Police series. Network: ABC. A Quinn Martin production. **Regulars:** Leslie Nielsen (Lieut. Price Adams), John Beradino (Sgt. Vince Cavelli), John Clarke (Patrolman Joe Huddleston), Greg Roman (Patrolman Peter Garcia), Byron Morrow (Cpt. Keith Gregory). **Guests:** Telly Savalas, Sydney Pollack. 60 minutes.

1/11/86 *Putting It Together: The Making of the Broadway Album*

Special. Network: HBO. Produced by: Barbra Streisand. Directed by: William Friedkin. **Appearances:** William Friedkin, David Geffen, Stephen Sondheim, Sydney Pollack. 40 minutes. Taped 7/25/85.

1986   *West 57th*

News magazine format. Network: CBS. Produced by: Kenneth Fink. **Guest:** Sydney Pollack. 52 minutes.

10/9/87   *Crazy About the Movies*

"Starring Natalie Wood." Network: Cinemax. Producer: Ellen M. Krass Productions. **Appearance:** Sydney Pollack, among others. 50 minutes. 10:00 P.M.

1987   *Hello Actors Studio*

Documentary. Interview by Annie Tresgot.

6/14/89   *Later in LA*

Interview format. Network: NBC. Executive Producer: Dick Ebersol. Host: Bob Costas. **Guest:** Sydney Pollack.

12/9/90   *Robert Redford & Sydney Pollack: The Men and Their Movies*

(AKA *Robert Redford: The Man, the Movies and the Myth*). Special. Interview format. Network: NBC. Host: Dick Cavett. The Berkeley Group. **Guests:** Sydney Pollack and Robert Redford. 60 minutes. 8:00 P.M.

3/17/91   *Crazy About the Movies*

"Robert Mitchum: The Reluctant Star." Network: Cinemax. Producers: Gene Feldman and Suzette Winter. 50 minutes. 8:00 P.M.

8/13/91   *Crazy About the Movies*

"Jessica Lange: It's Only Make-Believe." Network: Cinemax. Producers: Gene Feldman and Suzette Winter. 9:00 P.M.

8/25/91 & 8/31/91   *Naked Hollywood*

"One Foot In; One Foot Out." Documentary. Network: Arts and Entertainment. Producer: BBC Productions in association with BBC Lionheart Television. Directors: Margy Kinmonth, Alan Lewen. Interview format. 60 minutes. 8:00 P.M.

6/9/92   *Street Scenes: New York on Film*

Documentary special. SYN. Network: AMC. Executive Producers: Sandy Shapiro, Brad Siegel. Produced, directed and written by: Lewis A. Bogach. **Appearances:** Sydney Pollack, Danny Aiello, Joe Pesci, among others. 60 minutes. 9:00 P.M.

3/29/93   *Great Performances*

"John Barry's Moviola." PBS. Film music performed by Royal Philharmonic Orchestra. 8:00 P.M.

5/22/93 *Willie Nelson The Big Six-O: An All-Star Birthday Celebration.*

Musical Special. Network: CBS. **Guests:** Paul Simon, Bonnie Raitt, Bob Dylan, Ray Charles, Waylon Jennings, Kris Kristofferson, Lyle Lovett, Travis Tritt, Emmylou Harris, B.B. King. Birthday greetings from others including Sydney Pollack. 9:00 P.M. 2 hrs.

3/18/94 *South Bank Show*

"Sydney Pollack." Interview format. Network: BRAVO. Host: Melvyn Bragg. Producer: London Weekend TV; Frances Dickinson. **Guest:** Sydney Pollack. 60 minutes.

5/10/94 *Life and Times*

Host: Hugh Hewitt. Interview format. PBS. Funded by The James Irvine Foundation. Senior Producer: Martin Burns. Producer: Saul Gonzalez. Director: Steve Miller. Art Director: John Ritsek. Coordinating Producers: Dan Leighton, Trace Percy. **Guest:** Sydney Pollack. 30 minutes. 12:00 A.M.

11/8/94 *Frasier*

"The Candidate." Sitcom. Network: NBC. Created by: David Angell, Peter Casey and David Lee. Executive Producers: Christopher Lloyd, David Angell, Peter Casey, David Lee. Co-Executive Producers: Linda Morris Vic Rauseo. Producers: Elias Davis, David Pollock, Maggie Randell. Co-Producers: Chuck Ranberg, Anne Flett-Giordano. Associate Producer: Mary Fukuto. Creative Consultants: Ken Levine, David Isaacs. Executive Story Editor: Joe Keenan. **Cast:** Kelsey Grammer (Frasier Crane), Jame Leeves (Daphne Moon), David Hyde Pierce (Niles Crane), Peri Gilpin (Roz Doyle), John Mahoney (Martin Crane), Moose (Eddie the Dog), Dan Butler (Bulldog), Boyd Gaines (Phil Patterson), Luck Hari (Waitress), Jack Tate (Director), Christopher Walberg (Boy), Sydney Pollack (Holden Thorpe).

1/23/95 *American Cinema*

"The Hollywood Style." Interview format. PBS. Host: John Lithgow. Narrator: Joe Morton. A co-production of the New York Center for Visual History, KCET Los Angeles and the BBC. Executive Producer: Lawrence Pitkethly. Senior Producers: Greg Martinelli, Rita Mate, and Molly Ornati. Producer: Molly Ornati. Director: Lawrence Pitkethly. Editor: Corey Shaff. **Featured Interviews:** Dede Allen, David Bordwell, Allen Daviau, Howard Hawks, Lawrence Kasdan, Jack Lemmon, Joseph Mankiewicz, Roman Polanski, Sydney Pollack, Martin Scorsese, Richard Sylbert, Bertrand Tavernier, Robert Towne. 60 minute premiere episode, 9:00 P.M.

7/9/95 *Salute to the Top 10 Comedy Movies*

Special. Interview format. Network: Fox. **Interviewees:** Paul Hogan, Tom Selleck, Leonard Nimoy, Sydney Pollack. 30 minutes. 8:30 P.M.

11/95   *Inside the Actor's Studio: The Craft of Theater and Film*

Interview format. Network: BRAVO. Hosted by James Lipton. Filmed at: The New School. The John L. Tishman Theatre, New York. **Guest**: Sydney Pollack.

2/24/95   *Mad About You*

"Cheating on Sheila." Episode 127. Sitcom. Network: NBC. Infront Productions, Inc., and Nuance Productions in association with TriStar Television, Inc. Written by: Sheila R. Lawrence. Directed by: Helen Hunt. Executive Producers: Paul Reiser, Victor Levin. Creators: Paul Reiser, Danny Jacobson. Producers: Helen Hunt, Maria Semple, Jenji Kohan, Bob Heath, Craig Knizek. Director of Photography: Bobby Byrne. **Cast**: Paul Reiser, Helen Hunt, Leila Kenzle, John Pankow, Cynthia Harris, Louis Zorich, Maui. **Guest**: Sydney Pollack. 30 minutes. 8:00 P.M.

Directing Credits

10/20/59   *The Turn of the Screw* (Dialogue Director)

Television Special. Network: NBC. Producer: John Frankenheimer. Director: John Frankenheimer. Music: David Amrom. Writer: James Costigan. Executive Producer: Hubbell Robinson. Dialogue Director: Sydney Pollack. **Cast**: Ingrid Bergman (Miss Giddens), Alexandra Wagner (Flora), Hayward Morse (Miles), Isabel Elsom (Mrs. Grose), Paul Stevens (Peter Quint), Laurinda Barrett (Miss Jessel).

6/4/61   *Shotgun Slade*

"Something to Die For." Western series. Syndicated. Executive Producer: Nat Holt. Producer: Frank Gruber. Produced by: Shotgun Production Company. Written by: Lawrence Kimble. Directed by: Sydney Pollack. **Regulars**: Scott Brady (Slade), Monica Lewis (Monica). **Guests**: Otto Waldis, Phyllis Hill, Brian Hutton, John Crawford, John Lasell. 30 minutes. B/W.

10/12/61   *Frontier Circus*

"The Smallest Target." Western series. Network: CBS. Produced by: Calliope Productions, Inc., Revue Productions, Inc. Executive Producer: Richard Irving. Producer: Samuel A. Peeples. Directed by: Sydney Pollack. Created by: Samuel A. Peeples. Story Editor: Samuel A. Peeples. Associate Producer: Frank Price. Director of Photography: Benjamin H. Kline. Film Editor: Lee Huntington. Original Music: David Buttolph, Jeff Alexander. Music Supervision: Stanley Wilson. **Regulars**: Chill Wills (Colonel Casey Thompson), John Derek (Ben Travis), Richard Jaeckel (Tony Gentry). **Guests**: Barbara Rush, Brian Keith. 52 minutes. B/W.

10/24/61 *Cain's Hundred*

"King of the Mountain." Dramatic series. Network: NBC. MGM-TV. Vanadas Productions. Executive Producer: Paul Monash. Directed by: Sydney Pollack. Music: Jerry Goldsmith, Morton Stevens. **Regulars:** Mark Richman (Nicholas Cain). **Guests:** Edward Andrews (Herman Coombs), Barbara Baxley (Clara), Robert Duvall (Tom Nugent), Milton Selzer (Lou Metzger), Jan Shepherd (Karen), Paul Birth (Sheriff), John Cliff (Sgt. Burdick). 60 minutes. B/W.

11/9/61 *Frontier Circus*

"Karina." Western series. Network: CBS. Directed by: Sydney Pollack. **Guest:** Elizabeth Montgomery. 52 minutes. B/W.

12/12/61 *Cain's Hundred*

"The Fixer." Dramatic series. Network: NBC. MGM-TV. Vanadas Productions. Executive Producer: Paul Monash. Directed by: Sydney Pollack. **Regulars:** Mark Richman (Nicholas Cain). **Guests:** Pat Hingle (Sam Cortner), Cloris Leachman (Katie Cortner), Henry Silva (Riley), DeForest Kelley (Riley), Don Hammer (George Dedmon).

1/29/62 *Ben Casey*

"The Big Trouble with Charlie." Network: ABC. Medical drama series. Bing Crosby Productions. Producers: Wilton Schiller, Jack Laird, Irving Elman. Executive Producers: James E. Moser, John E. Pommer, Matthew Rapf. Created by: James E. Moser. Directed by: Sydney Pollack. Written by: Norman Katkov. **Regulars:** Vincent Edwards (Dr. Ben Casey); Sam Jaffe (Dr. David Zorba); Bettye Ackerman (Dr. Maggie Graham); Nick Dennis (Nick Kanavaras); Jeanne Bates (Nurse Wills); Harry Landers (Dr. Hoffman). **Guests:** Jack Warden, Myron McCormick, Norma Crane. 49 minutes. B/W.

2/10/62 *The Tall Man*

"Rio Doloroso." Western series. Network: NBC. Produced by: MCA TV. Directed by: Sydney Pollack. **Regulars:** Barry Sullivan (Sheriff Pat Garrett), Clu Gulager (Billie the Kid). **Guests:** Dennis Patrick (Curtis), Alex Montoya (Domingo), Julia Montoya (Maria), Jose Gonzalez Gonzalez (Umberto). 30 minutes. B/W.

3/2/62 *Target: The Corruptors*

"The Wrecker." Crime Drama. Network: ABC. Four Star Productions. Producers: Leonard Ackerman, John Burrows. Associate Producer: Lester Velie. Directed by: Sydney Pollack. Music: Rudy Schrager, Hans Salter, Jerry Fielding, Pete Rugolo. Based on the articles of investigative reporter Lester Velie. **Regulars:** Paul Morino (Stephen McNally), Jack Flood (Robert Harland). **Guests:** Luther Adler, Cloris Leachman, Linden Chiles. 52 minutes. B/W.

3/5/62   *Ben Casey*

"For the Ladybird, One Dozen Roses" (Previously titled: "Fly Away Home"). Medical drama series. Network: ABC. Directed by: Sydney Pollack. Written by: Jack Curtis. **Guests:** Cliff Robertson, Michael Davis. 49 minutes. B/W.

3/15/62   *Frontier Circus*

"The Inheritance." Western series. Network: CBS. Directed by: Sydney Pollack. **Guests:** Marc Marno (Yuki Yamoto), Allan Hale (Lait), J. Pat O'Malley (Duffy), Tsuruka Kobayashi (Hideko). 60 minutes. B/W.

3/19/62   *Ben Casey*

"Monument to an Aged Hunter." Medical drama series. Network: ABC. Directed by: Sydney Pollack. Teleplay: Gilbert Ralston from a story by Oliver Crawford. **Guests:** Wilfred Hyde-White, Robert F. Simon, Chris Robinson, Sydney Pollack (as the Young Man). 49 minutes. B/W.

5/24/62   *Frontier Circus*

"Incident at Pawnee Gun." Western series. Network: CBS. Directed by: Sydney Pollack. **Guests:** Joe Maross (Al Buchanan), Robert Lowery (Tigard), Kathie Browne (Mauvereen), John Pickard (Murdoch), Dick Haynes (Phillips). 60 minutes. B/W.

5/26/62   *The Tall Man*

"Phoebe." Western series. Network: NBC. Produced by: MCA TV. Directed by: Sydney Pollack. **Cast:** George Macredy (Cyrus Canfield), Floy Dean Smith (Phoebe Canfield), Cyril Delevanti (Summers), John Lormer (Medford), Eve McVeagh (Lily Varnell). 30 minutes. B/W.

5/28/62   *Ben Casey*

"When You See an Evil Man." Medical drama series. Network: ABC. Directed by: Sydney Pollack. Written by: Gilbert Ralston. **Guests:** Tuesday Weld, Simon Oakland, Jeanette Nolan. 49 minutes. B/W.

8/1/62   *Ben Casey*

"Mrs. McBroom and the Cloud-Watchers." Medical drama series. Network: ABC. Directed by: Sydney Pollack. Written by: Harry Brown and James E. Moser. From a story by Harry Brown. (Previously titled "A Cave Full of Pretty Things"). **Guests:** Patty Duke, Joanne Linville. 49 minutes. B/W.

8/8/62   *Ben Casey*

"The Night That Nothing Happened." Network: ABC. Directed by: Sydney Pollack. Written by: Oliver Crawford. **Guests:** Michael Constantine, Divi Janiss, Jerry Parris. 49 minutes. B/W.

8/29/62   *Ben Casey*

"Go Not Gently into the Night." Medical drama series. Network: ABC. Directed by: Sydney Pollack. Written by: Arthur L. Murphy. **Guests**: Ann Barton, John McLiam, Pat Rosson. 49 minutes. B/W.

11/15/62   *The Alfred Hitchcock Hour*

"Black Curtain." Mystery/suspense anthology. Network: CBS. Hosted by: Alfred Hitchcock. Shamley Productions, Inc. and Revue Productions, Inc. Executive Producer: Alfred Hitchcock. Associate Producer: Gordon Hessler. Producers: Joan Harrison, Norman Lloyd. Directed by: Sydney Pollack. Music: Lyn Murray. Film Editor: Edward Williams, Douglas Stewart. Music Supervisor: Stanley Wilson. Teleplay: Joel Murcott. Based on the story by Cornell Woolrich. **Cast**: Richard Basehart, Lola Albright, Harold J. Stone, Gail Kobe, James Farentino, Neil Nephew, Celia Lovsky, George Mitchell, Andy Romano, William Sharon, Joe Trapaso, Frank Sully, Lee Philips. 50 minutes. B/W.

1/5/63   *The Defenders*

"Kill Or Be Killed." Legal dramatic series. Network: CBS. Plautus Productions; Defenders Productions in association with CBS-Television. Producers: Herbert Brodkin, Robert Maxwell, Kenneth Utt. Created by: Reginald Rose. Written by: Larry Cohen. Directed by: Sydney Pollack. Music: Leonard Rosenman. Announcer: Bob Bryce, Herbert Duncan. **Regulars**: E.G. Marshall (Lawrence Preston), Robert Reed (Ken Preston), Polly Rowles (Helen Donaldson), Joan Hackett (Joan Miller). **Guests**: Simon Oakland, Joanne Linville, Gerald O'Laughlin, Dan Morgan, Frank Marth, Bill Lazarus, Wendell Phillips, Joanna Roos. 52 minutes. B/W.

1/7/63   *Ben Casey*

"I'll Be Alright in the Morning." Medical drama series. Network: ABC. Directed by: Sydney Pollack. Written by: Wilton Schiller. From a story by Theodore Apstein and Wilton Schiller. **Guests**: Steven Hill and Bethel Leslie. 49 minutes. B/W.

1/14/63 & 1/21/63   *Ben Casey*

"A Cardinal Act of Mercy," Part I and Part II. Medical drama series. Network: ABC. Directed by: Sydney Pollack. Written by: Norman Katkov. **Guests**: Glenda Farrell, Kim Stanley, Timmy Everett, Gary Crosby. Emmy Nomination for Kim Stanley. 49 minutes. B/W.

2/6/63   *Wagon Train*

"The Hollister John Garrison Story." Western series. Network: ABC. Directed by: Sydney Pollack. **Regulars**: Frank McGrath, John McIntire, Denny "Scott" Miller, Terry Wilson. **Guests**: Charles Drake, Gary Cockrell, Evans Evans. 60 minutes. B/W.

2/25/63   *Ben Casey*

"Suffer the Little Children." Medical drama series. Network: ABC. Directed by: Sydney Pollack. Written by: James E. Moser. **Guests**: Elizabeth Allen, Jacqueline Scott, Leslye Hunter. 49 minutes. B/W.

3/1/63   *The Alfred Hitchcock Hour*

"Diagnosis: Danger." Drama. Pilot. Network: CBS. Aired as a segment of *The Alfred Hitchcock Hour*. Producer: Roland Kibbee. Associate Producer: Gordon Hessler. Directed by: Sydney Pollack. Written by: Roland Kibbee. **Cast**: Michael Parks, Charles McGraw, Rupert Crosse, Allen Joseph, Berkeley Harris, Dee J. Thompson, Douglas Henderson, Helen Westcott, Marc Cavell, Gus Trikonis, Marc Rambeau, Clarke Gordon, Al Ruscio, Celia Lovsky, Irene A. Martin, Howard Wendell, Audrey Swanson, Stefan Gierasch. 50 minutes. B/W.

3/21/63   *Alcoa Premiere*

"The Dark Labyrinth." Dramatic anthology. Network: ABC. Produced by: Revue Studios. Hosted by: Fred Astaire. Adapted by Mark Rodgers from a novel by Lawrence Durrell. Directed by: Sydney Pollack. **Cast**: Patrick O'Neal (Frederic Warren), Salome Jens (Madelyn Warren), Carroll O'Connor (Charles Campion), Arthur Malet (Peter Fearmax), Barbara Barrie (Virginia Stanley). 60 minutes. B/W.

9/9/63   *Ben Casey*

"Solo for B-Flat Clarinet-Part 1." (AKA "For This Relief, Much Thanks") Medical drama series. Network: ABC. Directed by: Sydney Pollack. Written by: Steven Carabatsos. Story by: Steven Carabatsos and John T. Dugan. **Guests**: Paul Richards, Eduard Franz, Oscar Homolka, Scott Marlowe, Millie Perkins. 49 minutes. B/W.

9/16/63   *The Breaking Point*

"Solo for B-Flat Clarinet-Part 2. Pilot. Network: ABC. Directed by: Sydney Pollack. Teleplay: George Lefferts. Story by John T. Dugan. **Cast**: Scott Marlowe, Millie Perkins, Oscar Homolka, Sheree North. 52 minutes. B/W.

10/11/63   *Bob Hope Chrysler Theatre*

"Something About Lee Wiley." Dramatic anthology. Network: NBC. Hosted by: Bob Hope. Executive in charge of production: Gordon Oliver. Executive Producers: Dick Berg, Alan J. Miller. Producer: Dick Berg. Written by: David Rayfiel. Directed by: Sydney Pollack. Associate Producer: Ron Roth. Executive Story Consultant: Robert Kirsch. Theme Music by: Alex North. Color by: Pathe. Produced by: Hovue Productions, Hope Productions, Morpics, Revue Productions, Inc., Universal Television. **Cast**: Piper Laurie, Steven Hill, Claude Rains, Dabney Coleman. 52 minutes. Color. Syndicated as Universal Star Time and Theatre of Stars.

11/17/63   *Arrest and Trial*

"The Quality of Justice." Police/courtroom drama. Network: ABC. Executive Producer: Frank Rosenberg. Produced by: Revue Productions, Inc. Directed by: Sydney Pollack. Written by: Howard Rodman. Film Editors: Danny Landres, Milton Shifman, Richard G. Wray. **Regulars:** Ben Gazzara (Nick Anderson), Chuck Connors (John Egan), John Larch (Jerry Miller), John Kerr (Barry Pine), Roger Perry (Dan Kirby), Noah Keen (Lt. Bone), Don Galloway (Mitchell Harris), Joe Higgins (Jake Shakespeare), Jo Anne Miya (Janet Okada). **Guests:** Robert Duvall (Morton Ware), Jack Klugman (Celina), Carol Rossen (Mrs. Celina). 90 minutes. B/W.

12/26/63   *Kraft Suspense Theater*

"The Name of the Game." Dramatic anthology. Network: NBC. Roncon Productions, Inc. and Revue Productions, Inc. Executive in Charge of Production: Roy Huggins. Executive Producer: Frank P. Rosenberg. Directed by: Sydney Pollack. Theme Music: Johnny Williams. Music Score: Lyn Murray. Art Director: John J. Lloyd. Film Editor: Robert B. Warwick. Sound: William Lynch. Assistant Director: John Clarke Bowman. Set Decorators: John McCarthy, Robert C. Bradfield. Costume Supervisor: Vincent Dee. Makeup: Jack Barron. Hair Stylist: Florence Bush. Music Supervision: Stanley Wilson. **Cast:** Jack Kelly, Pat Hingle, Nancy Kovack, Barry Atwater, Steve Ihnat. 52 minutes. B/W.

1/3/64   *Bob Hope Chrysler Theatre*

"War of Nerves." Dramatic anthology. Network: NBC. Directed by: Sydney Pollack. Written by: Mark Rodgers from Paul Brickhill's novel. **Cast:** Louis Jourdan, Stephen Boyd, Emile Genest, Monique Le Marie. 52 minutes. Color.

1/31/64   *Bob Hope Chrysler Theatre*

"Two Is the Number." Dramatic anthology. Network: NBC. Produced by: Dick Berg. Directed by: Sydney Pollack. Teleplay by: Franklin Barton. Editor: Howard Epstein. Music: Johnny Williams. **Cast:** Shelley Winters, Martin Balsam, David Opatishu, George Voskovex, Mike Kellen, Joseph Mell. 52 minutes.

2/25/64   *Mr. Novak*

"Fear Is a Handful of Dust." Dramatic series. Network: NBC. Producers: William Froug, John T. Dugan, Jack E. Neuman. Directed by: Sydney Pollack. Written by: Carol O'Brien. Music: Lyn Murray. **Regulars:** James Franciscus (Novak), Dean Jagger (Vane), Burgess Meredith (Woodridge), Phyllis Avery (Miss Wilkinson), David Sheiner (Webb). **Guests:** Brenda Scott, Tony Dow, Jeanne Bal. 52 minutes.

5/14/64   *Kraft Suspense Theatre*

"Second Look." Drama. Pilot. Network: NBC. Aired as "The Watchman." Producer: Jack Laird. Directed by: Sydney Pollack. Written by: David Rayfiel. Music: Lalo Schifrin. **Cast**: Telly Savalas, Victoria Shaw, Jack Warden, Lawrence Dobkin, Tol Avery, Carlos Rivas, Peter Mamakos, Arthur Batanides, Sam Gilman, Eddy Williams, Frank DeKova. 52 minutes. B/W.

9/24/64   *The Fugitive*

"Man on a String." Dramatic series. Network: NBC. A Quinn Martin Production in Association with United Artists Television. Produced by: Alan A. Armer and Wilton Schiller. Created by: Roy Huggins. Executive Producer: Quinn Martin. Directed by: Sydney Pollack. Written by: Barbara and Milton Merlin and Harry Kronman. Music: Peter Rugolo. **Regulars**: David Janssen (The Fugitive), Barry Morse (Lt. Gerard), William Conrad (Narrator). **Guests:** Lois Nettleton (Lucey Russell), John Larch (George Duncan), Patricia Smith (Amy Adams), Malcolm Atterbury (Sheriff Mead), Cyril Delevanti (Old Timer), Russell Collins (Doc Phillips). 50 minutes. B/W.

10/9/64   *Bob Hope Chrysler Theatre*

"Murder in the First." Dramatic anthology. Network: NBC. Written by: Stirling Silliphant from Barrett Prettyman, Jr. "Death and the Supreme Court." Directed by: Sydney Pollack. **Cast**: Janet Leigh, Bobby Darin, Lloyd Bochner, Eduard Franz, Ivan Dixon, Steve Ihnat. 52 minutes.

10/26/64   *Slattery's People*

"Question: What Became of the White Tortilla?" Dramatic series. Network: CBS. Produced by Bing Crosby Productions. Producer: Matthew Rapf. Directed by: Sydney Pollack. Written by: William McGivern, Jack Raphael Guss. **Regulars**: Richard Crenna (James Slattery), Edward Asner (Radcliffe), Maxine Stuart (B.J. Clawson), Tol Avery (Bert Metcalf), Paul Geary (Johnny Ramos). **Guests:** Ricardo Montalban, Miriam Colon, Milton Selzer, Lane Bradford, Robert Corso, Don Diamond, Robert Jacquin, Alex Montoya, David Munez, Art Peterson, Francine York. 50 minutes. B/W.

11/5/64   *Dr. Kildare*

"A Candle in the Window." Medical drama series. Network: NBC. Producers: David Victor, Calain Clements, Norman Felton, Herbert Hirschmann. Directed by: Sydney Pollack. Script by: Rita Lakin. Music: Herry Goldsmith, Pete Gugolo, Harry Sukman. **Regulars**: Richard Chamberlain (Dr. James Kildare), Raymond Massey (Dr. Leonard Gillespie), Jud Taylor (Dr. Thomas Gerson), Eddie Ryder (Dr. Simon Agurski), Jean Inness (Nurse Fain). **Guests:** Ron Howard, Ruth Roman, Walter Burke, Isobel Elsom, Edward Firestone, J.J. Helton, Jesse Jacobs, Paula Prentiss, Patricia Priest, D. Starling, N. Welch, W. Blough, Sydney Pollack. 52 minutes. B/W.

2/6/65   *Bob Hope Chrysler Theatre*

"The Fliers." Pilot. Network: NBC. Produced by: Dick Berg. Directed by: Sydney Pollack. Written by: David Rayfiel and Lorenzo Semple, Jr. Music: Cyril Mockridge. **Cast:** John Cassavetes, Chester Morris, Carol Lynley, Alfred Ryder, Tom Simcox. 52 minutes.

3/11/65   *Kraft Suspense Theatre*

"The Last Clear Chance." Dramatic anthology. Network: NBC. Produced by: Mort Abrams. Directed by: Sydney Pollack. Written by: Abraham Polonsky. **Cast:** Glenn Corbett, Bruce Bennett, Barry Sullivan, Suzanne Cramer, Ben Wright. 52 minutes. B/W.

9/15/65   *Bob Hope Chrysler Theatre*

"The Game." Dramatic anthology. Network: NBC. Executive Producer: Dick Berg. Directed by: Sydney Pollack. Original teleplay: S. Lee Pogostin. **Cast:** Cliff Robertson, Maurice Evans, Dina Merrill, Nehemiah Persoff, Cyril Delivanti, Renzo Cesana, Ivan Triesault, Alita Rotell. 52 minutes.

Producing Credits

1990   *The American Masters*

"Sanford Meisner: The Theatre's Best Kept Secret." Documentary. Playhouse Repertory Company. Network: PBS. Executive Producer: Sydney Pollack. Photographed, edited and directed by: Nick Doob. Associate Producer: Robert Owens Scott. Meisner Interviewer: Sydney Pollack. Creative Advisor: Stephen Harvey. Video Production: Telequest Inc. and the Video Team, Inc. Supervised by: Richard Blofson. Music Consultant: Ellen Haag. Available for broadcast: 8/27/90. 60 minutes.

6/20/92   *A Private Matter*

Special. Network: HBO. Produced by: Lindsay Doran. Directed by: Joan Micklin Silver. Written by: William Nicolson. **Cast:** Sissy Spacek, Aiden Quinn, Estelle Parsons, Sheila McCarthy, Leon Russom, W.H. Macy. 120 minutes.

1993   *Fallen Angels*

Anthology. Network: SHOWTIME. A Mirage production in association with Propaganda Films. Producers: William Horberg, Lindsay Doran, Steve Golin. Executive Producer: Sydney Pollack. Created by: William Horberg. Editor: Stan Salfas. Photography: Emmanuel Lubezki. Theme Music: Elmer and Peter Bernstein. Teddy Edwards on tenor sax. Hosted by: Lynette Walden. 6 episodes.

8/1/93   "Dead End for Delia." Directed by: Phil Joanou. Teleplay by: Scott Frank. Based on a short story by William Campbell Gault. **Cast:**

Gabrielle Anwar, Gary Oldman, Meg Tilly. Dan Hedaya (Calender). Paul Guilfoyle (Prokowski). Wayne Knight (Landlord). 35 minutes.

8/15/93   "I'll Be Waiting." Directed by: Tom Hanks. Teleplay by: C. Gaby Mitchell. Based on a short story by Raymond Chandler. Cast: Mark Helgenberger, Bruno Kirby. Dan Hedaya (Ralls). 35 minutes.

8/29/93   "Quiet Room." Directed by: Steve Soderbergh. Teleplay by: Howard A. Rodman. Based on a story by Jonathan Craig. Cast: Joe Mantegna, Bonnie Bedelia, Vinessa Shaw, Patrick Breen, J.E. Freeman, Peter Gallagher, Wayne Grace, Kathy Kinney, Genia Michaela, Hank Stone, Norman Large. 35 minutes. Emmy Award Nominee.

9/5/93   "The Frightening Frammis." Directed by: Tom Cruise. Teleplay by: John Robin Baitz and Howard A. Rodman. Based on the short story by Jim Thompson. Cast: Peter Gallagher, Isabella Rosselini, Nancy Travis. 35 minutes.

9/19/93   "Murder, Obliquely." Directed by: Alfonso Cuaron. Teleplay by: Amanda Silver. Based on a short story by Cornell Woolrich. Cast: Laura Dern, Alan Rickman, Diane Lane, Robin Bartlett, Patrick Massett, John A. Zee, Michael Vartan. 35 minutes. Emmy Award Nominee.

9/26/93   "Since I Don't Have You." Directed by: Jonathan Kaplan. Teleplay by: Steven Katz. Based on a short story by James Ellroy. Cast: Gary Busey, Tim Matheson, James Woods. 35 minutes.

1998   *Grand Concorse*

Television Pilot. Network: CBS. Executive Producers: Sydney Pollack, John Sacret Young. Directed by: Thomas Carter. Written by: Barry Schindler.

Poodle Springs

Feature. Network: HBO. Executive Producers: Sydney Pollack, Jim Avnet, Jordan Kerner. Directed by: Bob Rafelson. Written by: Tom Stoppard. Cast: James Caan.

Stage Credits

Acting Credits

Summer 1954   *Stalag 17*

Written by: Donald Bevan and Edmund Trzcinski. Directed by: Edward Binns. **Cast:** Sydney Pollack (Sergeant Sefton), Milton Selzer, Johnny Fiedler, Tige Andrews. Summer stock production.

1954   *A Stone for Danny Fisher*

Opened October 21, 1954 at the Downtown National Theatre, New York City. Off-Broadway. Produced by: Henrietta Jacobson and Julius Adler. Based on the novel by Harold Robbins. Adapted by Leonard Cantor for the stage. Directed by: Francis Kane (pseudonym for Luther Adler). Scenery and Lighting: William Riva. Musical Director: Manny Fleischman. Incidental music: Earl Wild. **Cast:** Susan Cabot (Nellie), Zero Mostel (Maxie Fleiss), Joe De Santis (Sam Gordon), Sylvia Miles (Arlene), Joseph D. Sargent (Steve), Phillip Pine (Danny Fisher), Jeanette Roony (Mrs. Fisher), Barbara Joyce (Mimi), Wolfe Barzell (Mr. Fisher), Sydney Pollack (Pete), Maurice Gosfield (Spit), Gloria McGehee (Ronnie), Joe Bernard (Abe), Alfred Stone (Jack), Robert Gibbons (Mr. Wiser).

1955   *The Dark Is Light Enough*

Opened February 23, 1955 at ANTA — American National Theatre and Academy Theatre, New York City. Closed April 23, 1955. Written by: Christopher Fry. Produced by: Katharine Cornell and Roger L. Stevens. Directed by: Guthrie McClintic. Decor by: Oliver Messel. **Cast:** Katharine Cornell (Countess Rosmarin Ostenberg), Tyrone Power (Richard Gettner), Arnold Moss (Colonel Janik), John Williams (Belmann), Marian Winters (Gelda), Eva Condon (Bella), William Podmore (Dr. Kassel), Christopher Plummer (Count Peter Zichy), Donald Harron (Jakob), Charles McCauley (Willi), Paul Roebling (Stefan), Ted Gunther (Beppy), Sydney Pollack (Rusti), Jerome Gardino (3rd Soldier), Dario Barri (4th Soldier). 69 performances.

Directing Credits

1964   *P.S. 193*

April 3–May 10, 1964. The Theatre Group, UCLA Extension.
Directed by: Sydney Pollack. Written by: David Rayfiel. **Cast**: Donnelly Rhodes (Mario Saconne — a student), James Whitmore (Jonathan Kobitz — a professor), Cloris Leachman (Irene Kobitz — his wife); Doug Lambert, Dabney Coleman, Dennis Helfend, Anne Marie Bailey, John Piazza (students).

Film Awards

1962 *War Hunt*
NATIONAL BOARD OF REVIEW—#10 of the 10 Best Films of 1962

1965 *The Slender Thread*
ACADEMY AWARD NOMINATIONS/WINNERS*[1]—Art Direction: Hal Pereira, Jack Poplin; Set Direction: Robert Benton, Joseph Kish; Costume Design: Edith Head
ARGENTINE AWARDS—International Film Festival at Mar Del Plata, Argentina; Nacionale De Cinematograpia De Argentina: Best Picture; Office Catholique International du cinéma; Award to Sydney Pollack as Best Director
INTERSTATE THEATER CHAIN AWARD—New Director of the Year: Sydney Pollack

1969 *They Shoot Horses, Don't They?*
ACADEMY AWARD NOMINATIONS/WINNERS*—Actress: Jane Fonda; Supporting Actor: Gig Young*; Supporting Actress: Susannah York; Director: Sydney Pollack; Best Screenplay—Material from Another Medium: James Poe, Robert Thompson; Art Direction: Harry Horner; Set Direction: Frank McKelvy; Score of a Musical: John Green and Albert Woodbury; Costume Design: Donfeld; Editing: Fredric Steinkamp.
D.W. GRIFFITH, NATIONAL BOARD OF REVIEW—One of ten best pictures in English
NEW YORK CRITICS—Best Actress: Jane Fonda
GOLDEN GLOBE AWARDS—Best Supporting Actor: Gig Young
UNITED KINGDOM BAFTA AWARDS—Best Supporting Actress: Suzanna York
JAPAN KINEMA JUMPO (Best Ten)—One of ten best foreign films, 1970
FRANCE ETOILEDE CRISTAL—Best Foreign Actress: Jane Fonda
DIRECTOR'S GUILD OF AMERICA nomination
Awards from Cannes, Belgium, Yugoslavia, and Moscow film festivals
SCHOLASTIC MAGAZINE—Senior Scholastic Merit Award

*Winners are denoted by asterisk.

215

1972   *Jeremiah Johnson*

American Heritage Award for Best Western; Yugoslavian Film Festival Award; Parents Magazine Award

1973   *The Way We Were*

ACADEMY AWARD NOMINATIONS/WINNERS*
Actress: Barbra Streisand; Cinematography: Harry Stradling, Jr.; Best Song: Marvin Hamlisch, Alan Bergman, Marilyn Bergman*; Best Original Dramatic Score: Marvin Hamlisch*; Costume Design: Dorothy Jeakins, Moss Mabry; Art Direction: Stephen Grimes; Set Design: William Kieman
NATIONAL BOARD OF REVIEW—#10 in 10 Best Films in English
GOLDEN GLOBE AWARDS—Song "The Way We Were." Marvin Hamlisch, Alan Bergman and Marilyn Bergman
ITALY DAVID DI DONATELLO PRIZES—Best Foreign Actor: Robert Redford; Best Foreign Actress: Barbra Streisand

1976   *Three Days of the Condor*

ACADEMY AWARD NOMINATIONS/WINNERS*—Film Editing: Fredric Steinkamp and Don Guidice
ITALY DAVID DI DONATELLO PRIZES—Best Director
SOVIET UNION SOVYETSKI EKRAN POLL—Foreign Film from a Western Nation; Prize from the Yugoslavian Film Festival
EDGAR ALLEN POE MYSTERY WRITERS AWARD

1979   *The Electric Horseman*

ACADEMY AWARD NOMINATIONS/WINNERS*—Sound: Arthur Piantadosi, Les Fresholtz, Michael Minkler, Al Overton, Jr.
SCHOLASTIC MAGAZINE—Bell Ringer Award

1980   *Honeysuckle Rose*

ACADEMY AWARD NOMINATIONS/WINNERS*—Best Song: "On the Road Again" by Willie Nelson

1981   *Absence of Malice*

ACADEMY AWARD NOMINATIONS/WINNERS*—Best Actor: Paul Newman; Best Supporting Actress: Melinda Dillon; Screenplay for the Screen: Kurt Luedtke
SCHOLASTIC MAGAZINE—Bell Ringer Award

1982   *Tootsie*

ACADEMY AWARD NOMINATIONS/WINNERS*—Best Picture: Sydney Pollack, Producer; Best Actor: Dustin Hoffman; Best Supporting Actress: Teri Garr; Best Supporting Actress: Jessica Lange*; Best Director: Sydney Pollack;

Cinematography: Owen Roizman; Sound: Les Lazarowitz, Arthur Piantadosi, Les Fresholtz, Dick Alexander; Music (Song): "It Might Be You"— Dave Grusin, Alan Bergman, Marilyn Bergman; Film Editing: Fredric Steinkamp; Screenplay: Larry Gelbart, Don McGuire, Murray Schisgal

NEW YORK FILM CRITICS— Best Director: Sydney Pollack; Supporting Actress: Jessica Lange; Screenplay: Larry Gelbart, Don McGuire, Murray Schisgal.

GOLDEN GLOBE AWARDS— Best Musical/Comedy: Sydney Pollack; Actor in Musical/Comedy: Dustin Hoffman; Supporting Actress: Jessica Lange

NATIONAL SOCIETY OF FILM CRITICS AWARD— Best Film: Sydney Pollack; Actor: Dustin Hoffman; Supporting Actress: Jessica Lange; Screenplay: Larry Gelbart, Don McGuire, Murray Schisgal

NATO DIRECTOR OF THE YEAR AWARD— Sydney Pollack

L.A. CRITICS— Screenplay: Larry Gelbart, Don McGuire, Murray Schisgal

NATIONAL BOARD OF REVIEW— One of the 10 best English Speaking Films

UK-BAFTA— Nomination for Best Film; Best Actor: Dustin Hoffman; Makeup: Dorothy Pearl, George Masters, C. Romania Ford, Allen Weisinger.

DENMARK BODIL— Best Non-European Film

GERMAN DEMOCRATIC REPUBLIC CRITICS PRIZE—#3 out of the 3 Best Films. Awarded in 1984

JAPAN KJ—#8 out of the 10 best Foreign Films

SOVIET UNION SOVYETSKI EKRAN POLL— Best Film from a Western Nation; Actor: Dustin Hoffman; Actress: Jessica Lange

Prizes at the Moscow, Taormina, Brussels, Belgrade, and San Sebastian Film Festivals

1984 *Songwriter*

ACADEMY AWARD NOMINATIONS/WINNERS*— Best Original Song Score: Kris Kristofferson

1985 *Out of Africa*

ACADEMY AWARD NOMINATIONS/WINNERS*— Best Picture: Sydney Pollack*; Best Actress: Meryl Streep; Best Supporting Actor: Klaus Maria Brandauer; Best Director: Sydney Pollack*; Best Screenplay— Adapted from Another Medium: Kurt Luedtke*; Sound: Peter Handford, Gary Alexander, Larry Stensvold, Chris Jenkins*; Cinematography: David Watkin*; Art Direction/Set Direction: Stephen Grimes— Art; Josie MacAvin, Set*; Original Score: John Barry*; Costume Design: Milena Canonero; Editing: Fredric Steinkamp, William Steinkamp, Pembroke Herring, Sheldon Kahn

D.W. GRIFFITH AWARDS, NATIONAL BOARD OF REVIEW— One of ten best films in English, 1985; Best Supporting Actor: Klaus Maria Brandauer

NEW YORK CRITICS— Best Supporting Actor: Klaus Maria Brandauer; Cinematography: David Watkin

LOS ANGELES CRITICS— Best Actress: Meryl Streep; Cinematography: David Watkin

GOLDEN GLOBE AWARDS—Best Picture-Drama: Sydney Pollack; Supporting Actor: Klaus Maria Brandauer; Music: John Barry

ITALY SILVER RIBBON AWARDS—Best Foreign Director: Sydney Pollack

ITALY DAVID DI DONATELLO PRIZES—Best Foreign Film: Sydney Pollack; Best Foreign Actress: Meryl Streep

UNITED KINGDOM BAFTA AWARDS, 1986—Best Adapted Screenplay: Kurt Luedtke; Cinematography: David Watkin; Sound: Peter Handford

UNITED KINGDOM CRITICS, 1986—Music: John Barry

1986 FRENCH MINISTER OF CULTURE AWARD TO SYDNEY POLLACK—Commander of Arts and Letters

1988   *Scrooged*

ACADEMY AWARD NOMINATIONS/WINNERS*—Makeup: Tom Burman and Bari Drieband-Burman

1989   *The Fabulous Baker Boys*

ACADEMY AWARD NOMINATIONS/WINNERS*—Actress: Michelle Pfeiffer; Cinematography: Michael Ballhous; Editing: William Steinkamp; Original Score: David Grusin

UK SUTHERLAND TROPHY, 1990

NATIONAL BOARD OF REVIEW—#4 of 10 Best Films in English. Best Actress: Michelle Pfeiffer

NEW YORK CRITICS—Actress: Michelle Pfeiffer

NATIONAL SOCIETY OF FILM CRITICS—Actress: Michelle Pfeiffer; Supporting Actor: Beau Bridges; Cinematography: Michael Ballhous

LA CRITICS—Actress: Michelle Pfeiffer; Cinematography: Michael Ballhous.

GOLDEN GLOBE AWARDS—Actress in a Drama: Michelle Pfeiffer

1990   *Havana*

ACADEMY AWARD NOMINATIONS/WINNERS*—Original Score: David Grusin

1992   *The Player*

ACADEMY AWARD NOMINATIONS/WINNERS*—Director: Robert Altman;Screenplay: Michael Tolkin; Editing: Geraldine Peroni

1992   *Death Becomes Her*

ACADEMY AWARD NOMINATIONS/WINNERS*—Winner of Best Achievement in Visual Effects—Ken Ralston, Doug Chiang, Doug Smythe, Tom Woodruff*

1993   *The Firm*

ACADEMY AWARD NOMINATIONS/WINNERS*—Best Supporting Actress: Holly Hunter; Original Score: Dave Grusin

BAFTA—Best Supporting Actress: Holly Hunter
THE PEOPLES CHOICE AWARD—Favorite Dramatic Motion Picture

1993 *Searching for Bobby Fisher*

ACADEMY AWARD NOMINATIONS/WINNERS*—Cinematography: Conrad L. Hall

1995 *Sabrina*

ACADEMY AWARD NOMINATIONS/WINNERS*—Original Score: John Williams; Best Song: "Moonlight" by John Williams; Lyrics by Alan and Marilyn Bergman

GOLDEN GLOBE AWARDS—Nominated for Best Motion Picture—Musical or Comedy; Best Performance by an Actor in a Motion Picture—Musical or Comedy (Harrison Ford); Best Original Song ("Moonlight"—John Williams; Alan and Marilyn Bergman)

CHICAGO FILM CRITICS ASSOCIATION—Winner of Most Promising Actor (Greg Kinnear)

1995 *Husbands and Wives*

ACADEMY AWARD NOMINATIONS/WINNERS*—Supporting Actress: Judy Davis; Screenplay for the Screen: Woody Allen

1995 *Sense and Sensibility*

ACADEMY AWARD NOMINATIONS/WINNERS*—Best Screenplay: Emma Thompson*; Best Picture: Sydney Pollack; Best Actress: Emma Thompson; Cinematography: Michael Coulter; Supporting Actress: Kate Winslet; Original Score: Patrick Doyle; Costume Design: Jenny Bevan and John Bright

BAFTA (United Kingdom)—Won for Best Film, Best Actress (Emma Thompson), Best Supporting Actress (Kate Winslet). Also nominated for Best Director, Adapted Screenplay, Best Supporting Actress (Elizabeth Spriggs), Best Supporting Actor (Alan Rickman), Best Film Music, Best Cinematography, Best Production Design, Best Costume Design, Best Makeup/Hair

WRITERS GUILD OF AMERICA—Best Screenplay: Emma Thompson, based on material previously produced or published

DIRECTORS GUILD OF AMERICA—Ang Lee nominated for Best Director

PRODUCERS GUILD OF AMERICA—Lindsay Doran nominated for Golden Laurel Award

BERLIN INTERNATIONAL FILM FESTIVAL—Winner of Golden Bear for Best Picture

GOLDEN GLOBE AWARDS—Winner of Best Motion Picture/Drama and Best Screenplay. Nominated for Best Director, Performance by an Actress (Emma Thompson), Best Supporting Actress (Kate Winslet), Best Original Score

SCREEN ACTORS GUILD—Winner of Best Supporting Female Actor (Kate Winslet). Also nominated for Best Lead Female Actor (Emma Thompson) and

Outstanding Motion Picture Cast (Hugh Grant, Emma Thompson, Alan Rickman, Kate Winslet)

EIGHTH ANNUAL SCRIPTER AWARD—Friends of the University of Southern California Libraries for the best film adaptation of a book

NATIONAL BOARD OF REVIEW—Winner of Best Picture and Best Director. Emma Thompson also won Best Leading Actress in *Sense and Sensibility* and *Carrington*

NEW YORK FILM CRITICS—Winner of Best Director and Best Screenplay

L.A. FILM CRITICS—Best Screenplay

BOSTON SOCIETY OF FILM CRITICS—Winner of Best Picture, Best Director and Best Screenplay

BROADCAST FILM CRITICS ASSOCIATION—Winner of Best Picture and Best Screenplay

SOCIETY OF TEXAS FILM CRITICS—Winner of Best Actress (Emma Thompson)

Notes

Preface

1. Tim Bywater and Thomas Sobchack, *Introduction to Film Criticism: Major Critical Approaches to Narrative Film* (New York: Longman, Inc., 1989), 27.

Introduction

1. Peter Bart, "Can Our New Directors Steal the Show Away from Europe's?" *New York Times Encyclopedia of Film*, 25 December 1966.

2. Bart, *New York Times Encyclopedia of Film*.

3. David Ansen, "Paradise Remembered," *Newsweek*, 23 December 1985: 74.

4. Sydney Pollack, "Dialogue on Film: Sydney Pollack," *American Film*, April 1978: 33.

5. Sydney Pollack, interview, *South Bank Show*, BRAVO Cable Network, April 1994.

6. Susan Dworkin, *Making Tootsie* (New York: Newmarket Press, 1983), 12.

7. Sydney Pollack, interview, *Life and Times*, KCET Television, 5 October 1994.

8. *Life and Times.*

9. T.S. Eliot, *The Four Quartets* (San Diego: Harcourt Brace and Company, 1943), 59.

10. Dworkin 49.

11. Dworkin 52.

Chapter 1

1. William Taylor, *Sydney Pollack* (Boston: Twayne Publishers, 1981), 19.

2. Sanford Meisner, *Sanford Meisner on Acting* (New York: Vintage Books, 1987), Introduction by Sydney Pollack, xv.

3. Taylor, 22.

4. Taylor, 22.

Chapter 2

1. *South Bank Show.*
2. *Frasier*, Program Guide by Dean Adams (see www.avimall.com/entertain/Frasier.txt).

Chapter 3

1. Paramount Pictures, production notes from *The Slender Thread*, 1 January 1965.
2. Paramount Pictures production notes.
3. Brendon Gill, "Current Cinema: Desperate Moments," *The New Yorker*, 15 January 1966: 21.

Chapter 4

1. Paramount production notes, *This Property Is Condemned.*
2. "This Property Is Condemned," *Variety Film Reviews*, 14 June 1966.
3. Sydney Pollack, dir. *This Property Is Condemned.* 1966.

Chapter 5

1. *The Scalphunters*, dir. Sydney Pollack, with Burt Lancaster, Telly Savalas, Shelley Winters; United Artists, 1968.

Chapter 6

1. Production file, Fact Sheet, Academy of Motion Picture Arts and Sciences Library, on *Castle Keep.*
2. Sydney Pollack interview; "Sydney Pollack: The Way We Are," *Film Comment*, September/October 1975: 29.
3. *Film Comment* 29.
4. *Film Comment* 29.
5. Alex Keneas, "Burt-Watching," *Newsweek*, 11 August 1969: 74.
6. Richard Schickel, "Fine Defense of Fantasy Fortress," *Life*, 1 August 1969: 12.
7. Arthur Knight, "Little Lulus," SR Goes to the Movies, *Saturday Review*, 9 August 1969: 22.
8. Knight, 22.
9. Schickel, 12.

Chapter 7

1. *Film Comment*, 26.
2. Aljean Harmetz, "Sydney Didn't Want to Shoot *Horses*," *New York Times Encyclopedia of Film*, 8 March 1970.
3. Harmetz, *New York Times Encyclopedia of Film*.
4. Patricia Erens, "Sydney Pollack," *International Dictionary of Films and Filmmakers*: 25.
5. Erens, 25.
6. *They Shoot Horses, Don't They?*, dir. Sydney Pollack, with Jane Fonda, Gig Young, Michael Sarrazin, 1969.
7. Erens, 26.

Chapter 8

1. Jay Robert Nash and Stanley Ralph Ross, *The Motion Picture Guide*, Volume IV: 1454.
2. Sydney Pollack and Robert Redford interview, "Robert Redford and Sydney Pollack: The Men and Their Movies," TV Special with Dick Cavett, 1990.
3. Sydney Pollack interview, "Dialogue on Film." *American Film*, April 1978: 47.
4. Erens, 2.
5. *American Film*, 48.
6. *American Film*, 47.

Chapter 9

1. Patricia Erens, "Robert Redford on Sydney Pollack," *Film Comment*, September/October 1975: 28.
2. Laserdisc jacket, *The Way We Were*.
3. Sydney Pollack interview, *Later in LA*, NBC, 14 June 1989.
4. Sydney Pollack interview, "Inside the Actor's Studio: The Craft of Theatre and Film," BRAVO Cable Network, premiered 11/95 with James Lipton.
5. Sydney Pollack, dir., *The Way We Were*, with Barbra Streisand and Robert Redford, Columbia Pictures, 1973.
6. *American Film* 41.
7. Erens, 28.
8. Erens, 28.

Chapter 10

1. Louis Black, *The Daily Texan*, 8 June 1979: 11.
2. "The Yakuza," *Variety Film Reviews*, 8 March 1975.
3. Rex Reed, "Rex Reed Byline: *Yakuza*: Fresh, Exciting; *Brannigan*: Routine, Boring," *The Daily News*, 21 March 1975.

4. Donald Richie, "Slice-Out," *Newsweek*, 27 January 1975: 46.
5. Richie, 46.
6. Richie, 46.
7. *The Yakuza.*
8. Erens, 29.
9. Erens, 29.
10. Erens, 29.
11. Pauline Kael, *The New Yorker*, 24 March 1975: 101.
12. Louis Black, "Yakuza represents genre at best," *The Daily Texan*, 8 June 1979.

Chapter 11

1. Erens, 25.
2. Erens, 25.
3. Erens, 25.
4. Rob Edelman, "Three Days of the Condor," *Magill's Cinema Annual*, 1982 ed.: 2495.
5. Erens, 25.
6. *American Film*, 35.

Chapter 12

1. *American Film*, 35.
2. *American Film*, 35.
3. *American Film*, 35.
4. *American Film*, 35.
5. *American Film*, 36.
6. Janet Maslin, "Valentino and *Bobby Deerfield*—Where Did They Go Wrong?", *Encyclopedia of Film.*
7. Maslin.
8. Maslin.

Chapter 13

1. Laserdisc jacket, *The Electric Horseman.*

Chapter 14

1. Production brochure, *Absence of Malice*, Columbia Pictures, 1981.
2. Deac Rossell, Esquire Film Quarterly, July 1981: 68.
3. Rossell, 69.

4. Rossell, 69.

5. Vincent Canby, "Free Spirits Versus Generalizers," *New York Times*, 22 November 1981: 154.

6. Sydney Pollack, dir., *Absence of Malice*, 1981.

7. Edelman, 58.

Chapter 15

1. Susan Dworkin, *Making Tootsie*, (New York: Newmarket Press, 1983), 14.

2. Dworkin, 83–84.

3. Dworkin, 8–10.

4. Pauline Kael, "Tootsie, Gandhi and Sophie," *For Keeps* (New York: Dutton, 1994), 964.

5. Dworkin, 22.

6. Dworkin, 1.

7. *South Bank Show.*

8. Dworkin, 357.

Chapter 16

1. "Karen Blixen," *Contemporary Authors*, Vol. 2: 63–64.

2. David Ansen with Peter McAlevey, "Paradise Remembered," *Newsweek*, 23 December 1985: 74.

3. Ansen, 73.

4. M. Scott Peck, M.D., *The Road Less Traveled* (New York: Simon and Schuster, 1978), 168.

5. *South Bank Show.*

6. *Out of Africa.*

7. Kurt Luedtke, *Out of Africa*, screenplay, 1985.

Chapter 18

1. *Baseline* database on film, *The Firm.*

2. Sydney Pollack, dir., *The Firm*, with Tom Cruise, Paramount Pictures, 1993.

3. *South Bank Show.*

4. *South Bank Show.*

Chapter 19

1. *Book of Facts* 1995.

2. Cyndi Stivers, "Scions of the Times," *Premiere*, November 1995: 72.

3. Stivers, 72.

4. Marcrelu Sajbel, *L.A. Times,* 5 October 1995: E3.
5. Kenneth Turan, *L.A. Times,* 15 December 1995: F1.
6. Stivers, 72.
7. Stivers, 72.
8. Stivers, 72.
9. Roger Ebert. *Roger Ebert on Movies*, 12/15/95, Internet.

Bibliography

Personal Interviews with Sydney Pollack

By Janet Meyer. May 21, 1991, and July and August 1996.

Published Interviews with Sydney Pollack

1970. "Sydney Didn't Want to Shoot *Horses*." By Aljean Harmetz. *New York Times Encyclopedia of Film*, 8 March.

1972. By G. Langlois in *Cinéma* (Paris), July/August.

1972. "Entretiens avec Sydney Pollack et Robert Redford." By N. Arnoldi and Michel Ciment. *Positif* (Paris), October: 51–62.

1974. "Nos Plus Belles Années." By Max Tessier. *Écran* (Paris), April.

1975. By L. Salvato. *Millimeter* (NY), June.

1975. "Sydney Pollack: The Way We Are." By Patricia Erens. *Film Comment*, September–October: 24–29.

1975. "Les 3 Jours du condor." By Max Tessier. *Écran*, December.

1977. "On acheve bien les chevaux de Sydney Pollack." By J.M. Lardinois. *Revue belge du cinéma* (Brussels), October.

1977/1978. "De Propriété interdite a Bobby Deerfield." *Positif*, December/January: 129–137.

1978. "Dialogue on Film: Sydney Pollack." *American Film*, April: 33–48.

1979. "Sydney Pollack: An Actor's Director." By P. Childs. *Millimeter*, December.

1981. By P. Carcassonne and J. Fieschi. *Cinématographe* (Paris), March/April.

1983. By T. Ryan and S. Murray. *Cinema Papers* (Melbourne), May-June.

1983. "Sydney Pollack: An Interview." *Post Script* (Jacksonville, FL), Fall: 2–18.

1985. "Paradise Remembered." By David Ansen with Peter McAlvey. *Newsweek*, 23 December: 72–74.

1986. "Le mal d'Afrique comme litote sur 'Out of Africa.'" *Positif* (Paris), April: 2–8.

1986. "Dialogue on Film: Sydney Pollack." *American Film* (Washington, D.C.), December: 13–15.

1988. "Architectural Digest Visits: Claire and Sydney Pollack." By Judith Thurman. *Architectural Digest* 45, March 1988: 108–115.

Television Interview Videocassettes

1986. *West 57th Street*. Prod. Kenneth Fink. Guest: Sydney Pollack.

1989. *Later in L.A.* With Bob Costas. Prod. Dick Ebersol. Guest: Sydney Pollack. NBC.

1990. *Robert Redford and Sydney Pollack: The Men and Their Movies*. With Dick Cavett. The Berkeley Group. Guests: Robert Redford and Sydney Pollack. KCET.

1990. "Sanford Meisner: The Theater's Best Kept Secret." Dir. Nick Doob; Exec. Prod. Sydney Pollack. Guests: Sydney Pollack and others. *American Masters.* PBS.

1994. *Life and Times.* With Hugh Hewitt. Prod. Martin Burns and Saul Gonzales. Guest: Sydney Pollack.

1994. *South Bank Show.* Guest: Sydney Pollack. BRAVO.

1995. *Inside the Actor's Studio: The Craft of Theater and Film.* With James Lipton. Guest: Sydney Pollack. BRAVO.

Books, Articles and Manuscripts

Ansen, David. "Havana." *Newsweek*, 17 December 1990: 68.

_____. "Paradise Remembered." *Newsweek*, 23 December 1985.

_____. "Wayward Press." *Newsweek*, 23 November 1981: 125. 72–74.

Baker, Rick. "John Seale, ACS lends firm hand to law thriller." *American Cinematographer* 74, July 1993: 36–40.

Bart, Peter. "Can Our New Directors Steal the Show Away from Europe's?" *New York Times Encyclopedia of Film*, 25 December 1966.

Bywater, Tim, and Sobchack, Thomas. "The Humanist Approach: Traditional Aesthetic Responses to the Movies." *Introduction to Film Criticism: Major Critical Approaches to Narrative Film.* New York: Longman, 1989.

Camy, G. "Sydney Pollack: Souvenirs d'Amerique." *Jeune Cinéma* (Paris), May/June 1986: 3–9.

Canby, Vincent. "Free Spirits Versus Generalizers." *New York Times*, 22 November 1981: 154.

_____. "Screen. *Out of Africa.* Starring Meryl Streep." *New York Times*, 18 December 1985: 25.

"Le Cavalier électrique" *Avant-Scène du Cinéma* (Paris), Special Issue, 15 June 1980.

Cohn, Bernard. "Sur 'Jeremiah Johnson.'" *Positif* (Paris), October 1972: 48–49.

Corliss, Richard. "Out of Affluence." *Film Comment* 22, March/April 1986: 7–12.

Dworkin, Susan. *Making "Tootsie": A Film Study with Dustin Hoffman and Sydney Pollack.* New York: New Market, 1983.

Edelman, Rob. "Absence of Malice." *Magill's Cinema Annual.* 1982.

Eliot, T.S. "The Four Quartets." *Selected Poems.* San Diego, New York, London: Harcourt Brace, 1930.

Erens, Patricia. "Sydney Pollack." *International Dictionary of Films and Filmmakers.* 1984.

Gianakos, Larry J. *Television Drama Series Programming: A Comprehensive Chronicle 1959–1975.* Metuchen, N.J.: Scarecrow, 1978.

_____. *Syndicated Programming.* Metuchen, N.J.: Scarecrow, 1978.

Gili, Jean A. *Sydney Pollack.* Nice: U.E.R. Lettres et Sciences Humaines Sous-Section d'Historie du Cinéma: 1971.

Gili, C., et al. "Jeremiah Johnson." *Cahiers de la Cinémathèque* (Paris), Winter 1974.

Hachem, Samir. "Lights, Camera, Emulsions for *Out of Africa.*" *American Cinematographer* 67, February 1986: 66–72.

Henry, M. "Je est un autre." Special Section. *Positf* (Paris), April 1980.

Hindes, Andrew, and Busch, Anita. "Pollack Packs Full Bag." *Variety* 361, 11 December 1995: 17–18.

Inman, David. "Sydney Pollack." In *The Television Encyclopedia.* New York: Perigee, 1991. p. 646.

James, Nick. "The Firm." *Sight and Sound* n.s. 3, 5 October 1993: 44–5.

"Jeremiah Johnson." *Variety Film Reviews*, 10 May 1972.

Kael, Pauline. *For Keeps.* New York: Dutton, 1994.

_____. *The New Yorker*, 24 March 1975: 98–101.

Knight, Arthur. "SR Goes to the Movies." *Saturday Review* 9, August 1969: 22.

La Polla, Franco. *Sydney Pollack*. Firenze: La Nuova Italia, 1978.

Leon, Michelle. *Sydney Pollack*. Paris: Pygmalion, 1991.

Lorenz, Janet E. "Tootsie." *Magill's Cinema Annual*. 1983.

Luedtke, Kurt. *Out of Africa: The Shooting Script*. Introduction and annotations by Sydney Pollack. New York: New Market, 1985.

Madson, Axel. "Pollack's Hollywood History." *Sight and Sound*, Summer 1973.

Malpezzi, Frances, and Clements, William. "Jeremiah Johnson." *Magill's Cinema Annual*. 1973.

Maslin, Janet. "Absence of Malice." *New York Times*, 19 November 1981: 21.

Massuyeau, M. "Dossier: Hollywood 79: Sydney Pollack." *Cinématographe* (Paris), March 1979.

Matthews, Peter. "Sabrina." *Sight and Sound* n.s. 6, February 1996: 53.

McCarty, John, and Kelleher, Brian. *Alfred Hitchcock Presents*. New York: St. Martin's, 1985.

McNeil, Alex. *Total Television*. New York: Penguin, 1984.

Meyer, Janet L. *A Humanistic Analysis of the Films of Sydney Pollack*. Unpublished thesis, 1992. Copies: Academy of Motion Picture Arts and Sciences Library, Los Angeles; California State University, Dominguez Hills.

Nash, J. Robert, and Ross, Stanley Ralph. *The Motion Picture Guide*. All volumes. Chicago: Cinebooks, 1986.

Nathan, Paul S. "On Pollack's Plate." *Publishers Weekly* 231, 15 May 1987: 248.

New York Times Company. *New York Times Theatre Reviews*. New York: Arno, 1971.

New York Times Company. *New York Times Film Reviews*. New York: Arno, 1971.

O'Neil, Thomas. *The Emmys*. New York: Penguin, 1992.

Peck, M. Scott. *The Road Less Traveled*. New York: Simon and Schuster, 1978.

Perry, Jeb. *Universal Television: The Studio and Its Programs, 1950–1980*. Metuchen, N.J., and London: Scarecrow, 1983.

Phillips, Mark, and Garcia, Frank. "The Twilight Zone: 1959–1964." In *Science Fiction Television Series*. Jefferson, N.C., and London: McFarland, 1996.

Pollack, Sydney. Introduction. *Sanford Meisner on Acting*. By Sanford Meisner and Dennis Longwell. New York: Vintage, 1987. pp. xiii–xix.

Pollack, Sydney. "The Way We Are." *The American Enterprise* 3, May/June 1992: 92–9.

Proctor, Mel. *The Official Fan's Guide to "The Fugitive."* Stamford, Conn: Longmeadow, 1995.

Robertson, Ed. *The Fugitive Recaptured: 30th Anniversary Companion to a Television Classic*. Los Angeles: Pomegranate, 1993.

Schickel, Richard. "Havana." *Time* 136, 17 December 1990: 91.

Schneider, Wolf. "Film Preservation: Whose Responsibility Should It Be?" *American Film*, August 1991.

Stivers, Cyndi. "Scions of the Times." *Premiere*, November 1995: 72.

"Sydney Pollack." *Contemporary Theatre, Film and Television*. vol. 7. Eds: Linda S. Hubbard, Owen O'Donnell. Detroit: Gale Research, 1989. p. 314.

Taylor, William. *Sydney Pollack*. Boston: Twayne, 1981.

Television Programming Source Books (BIB Television Programming Source Books). Vols. 1–4. New York: BIB/Channels, 1995–96.

Terrace, Vincent. *Complete Encyclopedia of Television Programming: 1947–1979*. Vols. 1 and 2. South Brunswick, N.J., and New York: A.S. Barnes, 1979.

_____. *The Encyclopedia of Television Series, Pilots and Specials 1937–1973*. Volume I. New York: New York Zoetrope, 1986.
"They Shoot Horses, Don't They?" *Variety*, 18 November 1969.
"This Property Is Condemned." *Variety Film Reviews*, 14 June 1966.
The Video Source Book. 19th ed. Vols. I and II. Detroit: Gale Research, 1997.
Webster, Andy. "Filmographies." Premiere, 9 November 1995: 116.
Willoughby, Bob. Nur Pferden gibt man den Gnadenschuss. Kiel: Nieswand Verlag, 1990.
"The Yakuza." *Variety Film Reviews*, 8 March 1975.
Zicree, Mark Scott. *The Twilight Zone Companion*. Los Angeles: Silman James, 1992.

Films

Allen, Woody, dir. *Husbands and Wives*. Prod. Robert Greenhut. With Judy Davis, Woody Allen, Mia Farrow and Sydney Pollack. TriStar, 1992.
Altman, Robert, dir. *The Player*. Prod. David Brown, Michael Tolkin, Nick Wechsler. With Tim Robbins and Greta Scacchi. Avenue Pictures in association with Spelling Entertainment, 1992.
Branagh, Kenneth, dir. *Dead Again*. Prod. Lindsay Doran and Charles H. Maguire. With Kenneth Branagh and Emma Thompson. Paramount, 1991.
Bridges, James, dir. *Bright Lights, Big City*. Prod. Sydney Pollack and Mark Rosenberg. With Michael J. Fox and Keifer Sutherland. MGM/UA, 1988.
Donner, Richard, dir. *Scrooged*. Prod. Richard Donner and Art Linson. In association with Mirage Productions. With Bill Murray and Karen Allen. Paramount, 1988.
Frankenheimer, John, dir. *The Young Savages*. Prod. Pat Duggan. With Burt Lancaster and Dina Merrill. United Artists, 1961.
Kloves, Steve, dir. *The Fabulous Baker Boys*. Prod. Paula Weinstein and Mark Rosenberg. With Jeff Bridges, Michelle Pfeiffer, and Beau Bridges. 20th Century–Fox, 1989.
_____. *Flesh and Bone*. Prod. Mark Rosenberg, Paula Weinstein. With Dennis Quaid and Meg Ryan. Paramount, 1993.
Lee, Ang, dir. *Sense and Sensibility*. Prod. Lindsay Doran. With Emma Thompson, Kate Winslet, Alan Rickman, Hugh Grant. Columbia, 1995.
Mandoki, Luis, dir. *White Palace*. Prod. Mark Rosenberg, Amy Robinson, Griffin Dunne. With Susan Sarandon and James Spader. Universal, 1990.
Pakula, Alan, dir. *Presumed Innocent*. Prod. Sydney Pollack and Mark Rosenberg. With Harrison Ford and Greta Scacchi. Warner Bros., 1990.
Perry, Frank, dir. *The Swimmer*. Prod. Frank Perry and Roger Lewis. With Burt Lancaster. Columbia Pictures, 1968.
Pollack, Sydney, dir. *Absence of Malice*. Prod. Sydney Pollack. With Paul Newman and Sally Field. Columbia, 1981.
_____. *Bobby Deerfield*. Prod. Sydney Pollack. With Al Pacino. Columbia at Warner Bros., 1977.
_____. *Castle Keep*. Prod. Martin Ransohoff and John Calley. With Burt Lancaster. Columbia, 1969.
_____. *The Electric Horseman*. Prod. Ray Stark. With Robert Redford and Jane Fonda. Columbia and Universal, 1979.
_____. *The Firm*. Prod. Sydney Pollack, Scott Rudin. With Tom Cruise and Gene Hackman. Paramount, 1993.
_____. *Havana*. Prod. Sydney Pollack. With Robert Redford and Lena Olin. Universal, 1990.
_____. *Jeremiah Johnson*. Co-Prod. Joe Wizan and Sydney Pollack. With Robert Redford. Warner-Columbia, 1972.

———. *Out of Africa.* Prod. Sydney Pollack. With Meryl Streep and Robert Redford. CIC, 1985.

———. *Sabrina.* Prod. Sydney Pollack. With Harrison Ford and Julia Ormond. Paramount, 1995.

———. *The Scalphunters.* Prod. Jules Levy, Arthur Gardner, Arnold Laven. With Burt Lancaster, Telly Savalas, Shelley Winters. United Artists, 1968.

———. *The Slender Thread.* Prod. Stirling Silliphant and Stephen Alexander. With Anne Bancroft and Sidney Poitier. Paramount, 1965.

———. *They Shoot Horses, Don't They?.* Prod. Sydney Pollack. With Jane Fonda and Michael Sarrazin. 20th Century–Fox, 1969.

———. *This Property Is Condemned.* Prod. John Houseman and Ray Stark. With Natalie Wood and Robert Redford. Paramount, 1966.

———. *Three Days of the Condor.* Prod. Stanley Schneider. With Robert Redford and Faye Dunaway. Paramount, 1975.

———. *Tootsie.* Co-Prod. Sydney Pollack and Dick Richards. With Dustin Hoffman. Columbia, 1982.

———. *The Way We Were.* Prod. Ray Stark and Sydney Pollack. With Barbra Streisand and Robert Redford. Columbia, 1973.

———. *The Yakuza.* Prod. Sydney Pollack. With Robert Mitchum. Warner Bros., 1975.

Rudolph, Alan, dir. *Songwriter.* Prod. Sydney Pollack. With Willie Nelson and Kris Kristofferson. TriStar, 1984.

Shatzberg, Jerry, dir. *Honeysuckle Rose.* Prod. Sydney Pollack. With Willie Nelson and Dyan Cannon. Warner Bros., 1980.

Ward, David, dir. *Major League.* Prod. Mark Rosenberg, Chris Chesser, Irby Smith. With Tom Berenger and Charlie Sheen. Paramount, 1989.

———. *King Ralph.* Prod. Jack Brodsky. With John Goodman. Universal, 1990.

Zaillian, Steve, dir. *Searching for Bobby Fisher.* Prod. Scott Rudin, William Horberg. With Joe Mantegna, Marc Pomeranc, Ben Kingsley. Paramount, 1993.

Zemeckis, Robert, dir. *Death Becomes Her.* Prod. Robert Zemeckis and Steve Starkey. With Goldie Hawn, Meryl Streep, Bruce Willis. Universal, 1992.

Zwick, Edward, dir. *Leaving Normal.* Prod. Lindsay Doran. With Christine Lahti and Meg Tilly. Universal, 1992.

Television Episode Videocassettes

Pollack, Sydney, dir. "Something About Lee Wiley." *Bob Hope Chrysler Theatre.* NBC. With Piper Laurie, Steven Hill, and Claude Rains. 1963.

Online Sources

Baseline databases. Baseline II, Inc.
Los Angeles Times website: www.latimes.com.
Museum of Television and Radio, New York and Los Angeles.
Orion Database. UCLA Archives for Television and Film.

CD ROM

Cinemania '95. Microsoft Corporation. 1992.

Miscellaneous Sources

Studio Cast and Bits Lists/Production Notes.

Biographical Files/Production Files, program brochure for *The Yakuza*, bound shooting scripts, photographs, property of Sydney Pollack.

The Library of the Academy of Motion Picture Arts and Sciences. Film files and Sydney Pollack Biographical Files: press releases, clippings, newspaper and magazine articles, 1965–present.

Mirage Enterprises, Sony Pictures Entertainment, 10202 West Washington Blvd., Culver City, CA 90232-3195. (310) 244-2044. (Sydney Pollack, CEO; William Horberg, Producer; Geoff Stier, Vice President of Creative Development/Producer; David Rubin, Producer; and Donna Ostroff, Assistant to the CEO.)

Index

233